Praise for Jennifer W...

'These are powerful stories delivered with sweet charm and controlled outrage' *Times Literary Supplement*

'Worth is a vivid writer with a talent for the sting in the tail . . . a highly readable book – and a must for social planners
Evening Standard

'Jennifer Worth has a gift for storytelling and a keen eye for the evocative' BBC: *Who Do You Think You Are?*

'Worth is indeed a natural storyteller – in the best sense of the term, with apparent artlessness in fact concealing high art – and her detailed account of being a midwife in London's East End is gripping, moving and convincing from beginning to end . . . *Call the Midwife* is also a powerful evocation of a long-gone world . . . and in Worth it has surely found one of its best chroniclers' David Kynaston, *Literary Review*

'A chilling insight into life for the average mother [in the 1950s]' *Sunday Express*

'This delightful memoir brings to vivid life London's East End . . . full of humour . . . Worth's talent shines from every page'
Sainsbury's Magazine

'Worth's book made me cry in a railway carriage'
Matthew Parris, *Spectator*

'A candid, poignant memoir . . . this gripping narrative includes breech babies, adulterous relationships, urban pig-breeding and a surreal strip show in a brothel' *Townswoman*

'In her marvellous new book . . . [t]here are desperately sad stories here, but tales of great hope too. Or ordinary people living, giving birth and building their families despite enormous hardship and poor sanitation. And of midwives delivering superb care in the toughest conditions' *East End Life*

'Nobody who reads *Call the Midwife* will ever forget it'
The Woman Writer

Jennifer Worth was a nurse, midwife, ward sister and night sister from 1952 until 1973, working mainly in London. Her first passion was – and still is – music, and she is a Fellow of the London College of Music. She taught piano and singing for about 25 years but retired from teaching in order to concentrate on writing. She still sings in choirs all over England and Europe. She plays her piano (a 1904 Bluthner) daily, and is a present studying all the piano works of J. S. Bach – a long-term project. She has been married for forty-five years and has two daughters and three grandchildren.

By Jennifer Worth

Eczema and Food Allergy
Shadows of the Workhouse
Call the Midwife
Farewell to the East End

Shadows of the Workhouse

JENNIFER WORTH

PHOENIX

This edition published for
Index Books Ltd

A PHOENIX PAPERBACK

First published in Great Britain in 2005
by Merton Books
This paperback edition published in 2009
by Phoenix,
an imprint of Orion Books Ltd,
Orion House, 5 Upper St Martin's Lane,
London WC2H 9EA

An Hachette UK company

Typeset by Input Data Services Ltd, Bridgwater, Somerset

Printed and bound in Great Britain by Clays Ltd, Elcograf S.p.A.

The Orion Publishing Group's policy is to use papers that
are natural, renewable and recyclable products and
made from wood grown in sustainable forests. The logging
and manufacturing processes are expected to conform to
the environmental regulations of the country of origin.

www.orionbooks.co.uk

Dedicated with respect and gratitude to
Patricia Holt Schooling of Merton Books
whose vision, enterprise and courage led
to the first publication of these books.

ACKNOWLEDGEMENTS

Maysel Brar, for legal advice; Douglas May, Peggy Sayer, Betty Hawney, Jennie Whitefield, Joan Hands and Helen Whitehorn for advice, proof-reading, typing and checking; Philip and Suzannah, for everything; all the kind people who have written to me about the workhouse system, particularly Kathleen Daley and Dennis Strange; Chris Lloyd, Bancroft Library, Mile End, London; Jonathan Evans, Royal London Hospital Archives, London; Eve Hostettler, Island History Trust, the Isle of Dogs, London E14; Jean Todd, Allan Young and Jeff Wright for help with archive pictures; London Metropolitan Archives, London EC1; Hackney Archives, London N1; Camden Local Studies and Archives Centre; The Local History Collection of Gravesend Library, Kent; Peter Higginbotham for his help in checking the material on the history of the workhouse.

CONTENTS

PART III: THE OLD SOLDIER

Part I

WORKHOUSE CHILDREN

NONNATUS HOUSE

Nonnatus House was both a convent and the working base for the nursing and midwifery services of the Sisters of St Raymund Nonnatus.* The house was situated in the heart of the London Docklands and the practice covered Poplar, the Isle of Dogs, Stepney, Limehouse, Millwall, Bow, Mile End and parts of Whitechapel. I worked with the Sisters in the 1950s. It was a time, shortly after the Second World War, when the scars of the devastated city could be seen everywhere – bomb sites, blown-out shops, closed streets and roofless houses (often inhabited). It was a time when the docks were fully operational, and millions of tons of cargo poured in and out every day. Huge merchant vessels sailed up the Thames, to be piloted into the wharves through a complex system of canals, locks and basins. It was not unusual to pass along a road within a few feet of the towering hulk of a merchant ship. Even in the 1950s about sixty per cent of all cargo was unloaded manually, and the ports teemed with labourers. Most of them lived with their families in the little houses and tenements around the docks.

Families were large, sometimes huge, and living conditions cramped. In fact, by today's standards, the living conditions would be considered Dickensian. Most dwellings had running cold water, but no hot water. About half had an indoor lavatory, but for the other half the lavatory was outside, usually shared with other families. Very few homes had a bathroom. A bath was taken

---

* The Midwives of St Raymund Nonnatus is a pseudonym. I have taken the name from St Raymund Nonnatus, the patron saint of midwives, obstetricians, pregnant women, childbirth and newborn babies. He was delivered by Caesarean section ('*non natus*' is the Latin for "not born") in Catalonia, Spain, in 1204. His mother, not surprisingly, died at his birth. He became a priest and died in 1240.

in a tin bath placed on the floor of the kitchen or living room, though public bath houses were also frequently used. Most houses had electric light, but gaslight was still common, and I have delivered many a baby by this flickering light, as well as by torchlight or hurricane lamp.

It was a time just before the social revolution of 'the Pill', and women tended to have many children. A colleague of mine delivered an eighteenth baby to one woman and I delivered a twenty-fourth! Admittedly these were extreme cases, but ten babies was quite common. Although the fashion for hospitalisation for a birth was fast gaining ground, this "fashion" had not affected the Poplar women, who were slow to change, and a home birth was still preferred. Earlier in the century, even as little as twenty or thirty years previously, women were still delivering each other's babies as they had done in earlier centuries, but by the 1950s, with the advent of the National Health Service, all pregnancies and births were attended by trained midwives.

I worked with the Sisters of St Raymund Nonnatus, a religious order of Anglican nuns with a history dating back to the 1840s. This was also a nursing order pioneered at a time when nurses were commonly regarded as the dregs of female society. The Sisters, bound for life by the monastic vows of poverty, chastity and obedience, had been in Poplar since the 1870s. They started their work at a time when there was virtually no medical help for the poorest of the poor, and a woman and her baby survived or died unattended. The Sisters lived a life of ceaseless dedication to their religion and to the people whom they felt were in their care. At the time when I worked at Nonnatus House, Sister Julienne was Sister-in-Charge.

Convents tend to attract within their portals ladies of middle years who are unable to cope with life in one way or another. These ladies are always single, widowed or divorced, and lonely. They are nearly always gentle, timid and shy, with an immense yearning for the goodness which they see in the convent but

4

cannot find in the harsh world outside. Usually they are very devout in points of religious observance and have an unrealistic or romanticised idea of monastic life and long to be part of it. However, they often do not have a true vocation that would enable them to take the life vows of poverty, chastity and obedience. Nor, I suspect would they possess the strength of character necessary to live within these vows. So they hover on the fringe, neither fully within the world, nor withdrawn from it.

Such a lady was Jane. She was probably around forty-five when I met her, but she looked much older. She was, tall, thin, aristocratic in appearance, with delicate bone structure, beautifully sculpted features, and refined manners. In another context she would have been an outstanding beauty, but her excessive dowdiness made her look plain and nondescript. It was almost as if she did it on purpose. Her soft grey hair could have curled prettily around her face, but she cut it herself, so that it was jagged and shapeless. Her height, which should have rendered her distinguished, she reduced by bending her shoulders, so that her carriage and walk were stooped and cringing. Her large, expressive eyes were filled with nameless anxiety and surrounded by worry lines. Her speech was so soft that it sounded like a far-off twitter, and her laugh a nervous giggle.

In fact, nervousness was her chief characteristic. She seemed frightened of everything. I noticed that, even at meals, she did not dare to pick up her knife and fork until everyone else had done so, and when she did, her hands frequently shook so much that she would drop something. Then she had to apologise profusely to everyone, especially to Sister Julienne, who was always at the head of the table.

Jane had lived at Nonnatus House for many years and fulfilled a role that was neither nurse, nor domestic servant, but a mixture of the two. I had the impression she was a highly intelligent woman who could easily have trained as a nurse, and been very good at it, but something must have prevented her. No doubt it was her chronic nervousness, for she could never have taken the responsibility that is a daily part of any nurse's life. So Sister Julienne sent her out to do simple jobs, like blanket baths, or enemas, or delivering various things to patients. In doing these little jobs, Jane was all of a twitter with anxiety, going over and over her bag obsessively, muttering to herself such things as, "Soap, towels. Have I got everything? Is it all there?" Consequently it took her two or three hours to do a job that any competent nurse could have achieved in twenty minutes. When she had finished, she was pathetically eager for recognition, her eyes almost pleading for someone to say that she had done well. Sister Julienne always praised her small achievements, but I could see that it was a strain for her to be so constantly alert to Jane's craving for praise.

Jane also helped the nurses and midwives in the clinical room in small ways, such as cleaning instruments, packing bags and so on, and again she was irritatingly eager to please. Asked for a syringe, she would rush off and get three. Asked for some cotton-wool swabs for one baby, she would bring enough for twenty and then almost grovel as she handed over the item with a nervous giggle. This craven urge to please brought her no rest, no comfort.

It was all very disconcerting, especially as she was old enough to be my mother, and as it generally took her about three times as long as it took me to do a job, I refrained from asking. But she intrigued me, and I watched her.

Jane spent most of her time in the house, so one of her jobs was to take telephone messages, which she did with meticulous, and needless, over-attention to detail. She also helped Mrs B in the kitchen. This led to many a rumpus, because Mrs B was a quick and efficient cook, and Jane's dithering nearly drove her to distraction. She shouted at Jane to "put a move on", and then poor Jane would be paralysed with terror, faltering, "Oh dear, yes, of course, yes, quickly, of course." But her limbs wouldn't move, and she just stood stock-still, whimpering.

Once I heard Mrs B tell Jane to peel the potatoes and cut them in half for roasting. Later, when she wanted to put the potatoes in the oven, she found that Jane had cut every potato into about twenty pieces. She had been so desperately anxious to please by cutting them into exact halves that she couldn't stop and every half had been cut in half again, and so on until all that was left was a mound of tiny pieces. When Mrs B exploded, Jane fell back against the wall, pleading for forgiveness, shaking all over and white with terror. Fortunately, Sister Julienne came into the kitchen at that moment, saw the situation, and rescued Jane. "Never mind, Mrs B, we'll have mash today. They are just the right size for steaming. Jane, come with me, will you, please? The laundry has just come back and needs checking."

Poor Jane's eyes said it all – her fears, her grief, her gratitude and her love. I watched her go, and wondered what had happened to make her so fragile. Despite the kindness always shown to her by the Sisters, she seemed to live in a world of unfathomable loneliness.

She was very devout and attended Mass every day. She also attended most of the five monastic offices of the nuns. I had seen her in chapel, her fingers counting her rosary, her eyes earnestly fixed on the altar, half-intoning the words "Jesus loves me, Jesus loves me," over and over again, a hundred times or more. It is easy to scoff at such devotion. Women like Jane can be seen everywhere and they are always fair game for a cheap laugh.

I was with Jane on one occasion in Chrisp Street Market. It was just before Christmas and the stalls were laden with knick-knacks and curios – obvious Christmas presents. We approached one of these stalls. Lying in the centre was a small wooden object, about five or six inches long. It was nearly, but not quite, round and smooth, with a slight ridge running up the under side towards a pronounced rim. The tip was rounded, smooth and polished, with a small hole in the centre.

Jane picked up the object and held it between thumb and forefinger for everyone to see.

"Oh, what's this?" she said enquiringly.

Everyone fell silent and stared at Jane and the object. No one laughed.

The stall-holder was a fast-talking, street-wise coster of about fifty, who had been selling bric-a-brac most of his life. With a theatrical gesture he pushed his cap to the back of his head, took the fag out of his mouth and stubbed it out slowly on the edge of his stall. He glanced at his audience and opened his eyes wide with surprised innocence before answering: "Wha' is it, lady? Wha' is it? Why, lady, haven' chew seen one o' these fings afore?"

Jane shook her head.

"Why, it's a honey-stirrer. Vat's what it is, lady. An 'oney-stirrer, for stirrin' 'oney."

"Really? How interesting!" murmured Jane.

"Well, yes, very interestin', it is. They're old, you know, lady. Been around a long time, they 'ave. I'm surprised you ain't come across one 'afore now."

"No, never. You learn something new every day, don't you? How do you use it?"

"How do you use it? Ah, well now, allow me to show you, lady, if you don' mind."

He leaned forward and took the object from Jane's outstretched hand. The crowd, which had grown considerably, pressed forward, eager not to miss a word.

"Let me show you, lady. You sticks vis 'ere 'oney-stirrer in yer 'oney pot, and you stirs yer 'oney like vis" – he made a slight movement of the wrist – "an the 'oney, it catches on vis 'ere rim – you see vis 'rim 'ere, lady?" (He rubbed his fingers around it appreciatively.) "Well, ve honey, it catches on the rim, an' drips off, like."

"Really?" said Jane, "how fascinating. I would never have thought of it. I suppose it must be used a lot by country people who keep bees."

"Oh, yes, country people, vey use it all the time, wha' wiv all 'em birds an' bees an' all.'

"Well, I'm sure it must be very useful. Sister Julienne likes honey. I think I will buy this for her as a Christmas present. I am sure she would appreciate it."

"Oh yes. Sister Julienne will appreciate it all right, not 'arf she won't. If you asks my opinion, lady, you couldn't get Sister Julienne a Christmas present as wha' she'd appreciate more. Now, I was askin' four shillins for vis 'ere remarkable honey-stirrer, but seein' as how it's you, lady, wot's buyin' it for Sister Julienne for Christmas, I'll let you 'ave it for two shillin' and sixpence, an' you got a real bargain, I can tell you."

The coster beamed benignly.

"That's very good of you," exclaimed Jane as she handed over the money. "I must say I'm delighted, and I'm sure Sister will be delighted when she sees it."

"No doubt abaht it. No doubt at all. It's bin a pleasure doin' business wiv you, madam, an' I must say you've made my day, you 'ave."

"Have I really?" said Jane with a sweet, sad smile. "I can't think how, but I'm so glad. It's always nice to give pleasure to someone, isn't it?"

Christmas Day arrived. We returned from morning church and prepared the dining room for Christmas lunch. A tableau of angels adorned the table centre. Our presents were exchanged at lunch time and were placed on the dining table beside each person's plate. I found it hard to take my eyes off a small box, wrapped in silver paper, decorated with a red ribbon, resting beside Sister Julienne's plate. What was going to happen?

We were fourteen to lunch that Christmas Day, including two visiting nuns from North Africa, beautiful in their white habits. Grace was said, with a special remembrance for the gifts of the Magi, then we all sat down to open our presents. A chorus of "oohs" and "ahs" and little squeaks and giggles arose from the table, as kisses were exchanged between the ladies. Sister Julienne picked up the silver box, saying, "Now what can this be?" and my heart stood still. She removed the paper and opened the box. Just the flicker of an eyebrow, instantaneous and then gone, was all that betrayed her. She carefully put the lid back on the box and turned to Jane with a radiant smile, her eyes alight with pleasure.

"How very kind. A most charming thought, Jane. It is just what I have always wanted, and I am truly grateful. I will treasure it always."

Jane leaned forward eagerly. "It's a honey-stirrer. They are very old."

"Oh yes, I know. I saw that at once. A delightful gift and so like you, Jane, to be so thoughtful."

Sister Julienne kissed her gently and quietly tucked the box away beneath her scapular.

To all appearances Jane was a bit of a dimwit. It was her reading that gave me the clue that she was, in fact, exactly the opposite. She was a voracious, almost obsessive reader. Books were her only self-indulgence, and she handled them with loving care. I took to spying on her authors: Flaubert, Dostoevsky, Russell, Kierkegaard. I was astonished. Predictably, she had a daily discipline of Bible-reading, but beyond the Old and New Testaments her devotional reading was formidable: St Thomas Aquinas, Augustine, St John of the Cross. I looked at her with new eyes. Aquinas for recreation! This was no dimwit.

Yet if anyone came into the room whilst she was reading she would jump up, all of a dither, and throw down her book guiltily, saying something like: "Do you want anything? Can I get you anything?" or, on one occasion: "I was just about to lay the table for breakfast. I haven't been idle, really I haven't." This did not seem like the behaviour of an intelligent woman.

Later I discovered that Jane had spent twenty years in domestic service. She had been put into service at the age of fourteen, when life for a humble servant girl was very hard indeed. She had to be up at about 4 a.m. to fetch the wood and coal, clear the grates and light the fires. Then it would be a day of constant heavy work, at the beck and call of the mistress of the house, until ten or eleven at night, when she would finally be allowed to go to bed.

Jane had been hopeless at the job. However hard she tried she could never master the skills of simple housework. Consequently the mistress was always cross with her. She became increasingly nervous, breaking things, bungling things. She lived in a state of sheer terror that she would do something wrong, which she always did, so she was continually getting the sack and having to find another position – where the cycle started all over again.

Few domestic servants can have been less suited to the job than Jane. Her incompetence was monumental, although it is not uncommon for highly intellectual people to be baffled by the practicalities of everyday life.

Poor Jane! I once saw her trying to light a gas mantle. It took her forty minutes. First she spilled the matches all over the floor, and by the end she had broken the mantle, broken the glass shade, cut herself, set fire to a tea towel and scorched the wallpaper. No wonder she was always getting the sack.

I remember another occasion at Nonnatus House when Jane spilled a drop of milk on the floor. She trembled and whimpered, "I'll clean it up. I'll clean it up. I'll do it."

She then proceeded to wash the entire kitchen floor, including moving all the tables and chairs. No one could stop her. She insisted on doing the whole kitchen. I asked Sister Julienne why she behaved in this way.

"Jane was utterly crushed as a child," explained Sister; "she will never get over it."

Jane very seldom went out, and never left Nonnatus House for a night. The only person she was ever known to visit was Peggy, who lived on the Isle of Dogs with her brother Frank.

No one could describe Peggy as plump. Voluptuous would be a better description. Her softly rounded curves spoke eloquently of ease and comfort. Her large grey eyes, fringed with dark curling lashes, had a sensuous quality in their dreamy depths. Her smooth, clear skin glowed with radiance and every time she smiled, which was often, dimples enhanced her beauty, making you want to look upon her all the more. "Allure" might well have been her middle name.

Yet Peggy was not an idle lady of leisure, preserving her beauty with creams and lotions, or toying with men for her own amusement. Peggy was a charwoman. What with office cleaning in the early hours of the morning, her "ladies" in Bloomsbury and Knightsbridge, and restaurants and banks each afternoon, she was always busy.

Peggy cleaned at Nonnatus House three mornings a week and the house always smelled sweetly of wax polish and carbolic soap when she left. Everyone liked her. Her beauty was refreshing, and her smile raised the spirits. Furthermore, she sang quietly to herself as she polished and scrubbed. She had a pretty voice, and sang in tune. Her repertoire consisted of old-fashioned folk songs and hymns, the sort that children used to learn in schools and Sunday schools; it was a delight to listen to her. Her speaking voice was equally charming.

She was kind to everyone, and never seemed to get ruffled. I recall once when I had been out half the night (in my memory, babies always seem to have been born in the middle of the night, especially when it was raining!) and came in wet and muddy. I had been obliged to wait in Manchester Road for forty minutes, whilst the swing bridge was opened for cargo boats, and consequently was tired and ill-tempered. I crossed the hallway leading to the Clinical Room, not even conscious that I was leaving wet, muddy footmarks all over the fine Victorian tiles that Peggy had just buffed up to a glow. Something made me turn at the top of the stairs and I saw the mess I had made of her hard work.

"Oh, gosh – sorry!" I said, feebly.

Her eyes sparkled with laughter, and she was down on her knees in a trice. "Don't give it another thought," she said, affably.

Peggy was a good deal older than she looked. Her beautiful skin, in which the only wrinkles were laughter lines around her eyes, made her look about thirty, but in fact she too was approaching forty-five. Her supple body was as agile as that of a young girl and she was graceful in all her movements. Many women of forty-five would wish to look as youthful, so what was her secret, I wondered? Was it a sort of inner glow, a secret joy that irradiated her features?

Although they were around the same age, Peggy looked at least twenty years younger than Jane. Her softly rounded curves contrasted with Jane's stiff, angular bones; her clear, youthful skin with the other's dried-out wrinkles; her pretty blonde hair with Jane's ill-cut greyness. Her easy-going laughter was infectious, whilst Jane's nervous giggle was irritating. Yet Peggy treated the tall, angular woman with great tenderness, making allowances for her nervous twitter and general silliness, and often making her laugh in a way that no one else could. Jane seemed more relaxed when Peggy was in the house; she smiled more readily and seemed, if possible, less apprehensive.

Peggy's brother Frank was a fishmonger, known to all as "Frank the Fish". By common consent he kept the best wet-fish stall in Chrisp Street Market. Whether his ability to sell his fish was due to the excellence of the fish, the ebullience of his personality, or his commitment to hard work was not known. Probably his success was due to a combination of all three.

He slept little, and rose about three o'clock each morning to go to Billingsgate Fish Market. He had to push his barrow along the quiet streets, as very few working men had a van in those days. At Billingsgate he personally selected all his fish, having an encyclopedic knowledge of his customers' likes and dislikes, and he was back at Chrisp Street by 8 a.m. to set up his stall.

He was an effervescent bundle of energy and he loved his work. He brought fun and laughter to hundreds of people, and many dockers were served kippers for tea, simply because their good wives couldn't resist the bantering flirtation that fell from his lips as he slid the slippery fish into their outstretched hands, always with a wink and a squeeze.

He shut up the stall at 2 p.m. every day, and started on his delivery round. He kept no books, but carried in his head a detailed knowledge of his customers' daily requirements. He never made a mistake. He called at Nonnatus House twice every week and he and Mrs B, who was not a great admirer of men, were best of friends.

Frank was a bachelor and, because he was comparatively well off and always good-natured, half the ladies of Poplar were after him – but he just wasn't interested. "'E's wedded to 'is fish," they grumbled.

Frank seemed an unlikely friend for Jane, who was pathologically shy of men. If the plumber or the baker called at the house and Jane opened the door, she would go to pieces. She would chirrup and twitter around them, trying to be pleasant, but merely succeeding in being ridiculous. But with Frank she was different somehow. His ready banter and Cockney wit were tempered by gentleness and consideration, to which Jane responded with a shy, sweet smile and eyes filled with gratitude. Or was it love, my colleagues Cynthia and Trixie wondered. Did repressed, dried-up Jane also harbour a secret passion for the extrovert fishmonger?

"Could be," reflected Cynthia. "How romantic! And how tragic for poor Jane! He's wedded to his fish."

"Not a chance," said Trixie, the pragmatist. "If it were a case of unrequited love, she would go to pieces with him even more than she does with other men."

Once, after Jane had been to visit Peggy and Frank, she said wistfully, "If only I had a brother. I would be happy if I had a brother." Later, Trixie said, acerbically, "It's a lover she needs, not a brother." We all had a good laugh at Jane's expense.

It was only later that I learned the sad stories that brought these three people together. Jane, Peggy, and Frank had been brought up in the workhouse. The two girls were nearly the same age, Frank was four years older. Jane and Peggy had become best friends and shared everything. They had slept in adjacent beds in a dormitory of seventy girls. They had sat next to each other in the refectory, where meals for three hundred girls were taken. They had gone to the same school. They had shared the same household chores. Above all, they had shared each other's thoughts and feelings and sufferings, as well as their small joys. Today, workhouses may seem like a distant memory, but for children such as Jane, Peggy, and Frank the impact of having spent their formative years in such an institution was almost unimaginable.

THE RISE OF THE WORKHOUSE

My own generation grew up in the shadow of the workhouse. Our parents and grandparents lived in constant fear that something unpredictable would happen and that they would end up in one of those terrible buildings. An accident or illness or unemployment could mean loss of wages, then eviction and homelessness; an illegitimate pregnancy or the death of parents or old age could lead to destitution. For many the dreaded workhouse became a reality.

Workhouses have now disappeared, and in the twenty-first century the memory of them has all but faded. Indeed, many young people have not even heard of them, or of the people who lived in them. But social history is preserved in the accounts of those who lived at the time. Very few personal records written by workhouse inmates exist, so the little we do know makes the stories of people such as Jane, Frank and Peggy all the more compelling.

In medieval times, convents and monasteries gave succour to the poor and needy as part of their Christian duty. But in England Henry VIII's Dissolution of the Monasteries put a stop to that in the 1530s. Queen Elizabeth I passed the Act for the Relief of the Poor in 1601, the aim being to make provision for those who could not support themselves because of age or disability. Each parish in England was encouraged to set aside a small dwelling for the shelter of the destitute. These were known as poorhouses. It was a remarkable act of an enlightened queen, and crystallised the assumption that the state was responsible for the poorest of the poor.

The 1601 Act continued in force for over two hundred years

and was adequate for a rural population of around five to ten million souls. But the Industrial Revolution, which gathered pace in the latter part of the eighteenth century, changed society for ever.

One of the most remarkable features of the nineteenth century was the population explosion. In 1801, the population of England, Wales and Scotland was around 10.5 million. By 1851 it had doubled to 20 million and by 1901 it had doubled again to 45 million. Farms could neither feed such numbers nor provide them with employment. The government of the day could not cope with the problem, which was accentuated by land enclosure and the Corn Laws. Industrialisation and the lure of employment drew people from the villages into the cities in huge numbers. Overcrowding, poverty, hunger and destitution increased exponentially and the Poor Law Act of 1601 was inadequate to deal with the number of emerging poor. There can be no understanding of the poverty of the masses in the nineteenth century without taking into consideration the fact of a fourfold increase of population in one hundred years.

Victorian England was not the period of complacency and self-satisfaction that is so often portrayed in the media. It was also a time of growing awareness of the divide between the rich and the poor, and of a social conscience. Thousands of good and wealthy men and women, usually inspired by Christian ideals, were appalled by the social divide, saw that it was not acceptable, and devoted their lives to tackling the problems head on. They may not always have been successful, but they brought many evils to light and sought to remedy them.

Parliament and reformers constantly debated schemes to change and improve the old Poor Law Act. A Royal Commission was set up, and in 1834 the Poor Law Amendment Act was passed. Responsibility for relief of destitution was removed from individual parishes and handed over to unions of parishes. The small parish poorhouses were closed and the unions were required to provide large houses, each designed to accommodate several hundred people. The aim was that "the poor shall be set to work, and they shall dwell in working houses".

And so, the union workhouses were born. Each was to be run by a master and his wife, who were responsible for day-to-day administration, together with a number of paid officers, who assisted them. Overall responsibility for each workhouse was in the hands of a local Board of Guardians and they were financed partly by the local Poor Law rates and partly through government loans that had to be repaid. Running costs were to be met by local rates, but income could also be generated through the work of the inmates.

It can be argued that the workhouse system was the first attempt at social welfare in this country. Certainly it was intended as a safety net to house and feed the very poorest of society, and it laid the foundations of our modern welfare state. In this respect it was nearly one hundred years ahead of its time, yet the implementation of the high ideals of the reformers and legislators went tragically wrong, and the workhouses came to be dreaded as places of shame, suffering and despair. People would often rather have died than go there – and some did. My grandfather knew a man who hanged himself when the guardians informed him that he must go into the workhouse. Most of the labouring poor lived on a perpetual knife-edge between subsistence and destitution. For them, the workhouse represented not a safety net, but a dark and fearsome abyss from which, should they fall, there would be no escape.

The authors of the 1834 Act proposed separate workhouses for different categories of paupers, but within a year or two, economy and ease of management dictated that mixed workhouses became the norm. These were built to house *all* groups of paupers – the old, the sick, the chronically infirm, children, the mentally disabled – as well as able-bodied men and women who were unemployed and therefore destitute. However, such a great diversity of people under one roof and one administration was doomed to failure.

The original policy was that the workhouse should be a "place of last resort", therefore that conditions inside a workhouse should be less comfortable than a state of homeless destitution outside. Strict rules for admission were introduced and enforced nation-wide, and these rules were intended to deter the idle and shiftless from seeking admission. But the result, in a mixed workhouse, was that all classes of paupers suffered. Nobody could come up with an answer to the question of how to deter the idle without penalising the defenceless.

In order that the workhouse really should be a "place of last resort" a rigid, inflexible system of discipline and punishment was introduced. Families were separated, not only men from women, but husbands from wives and brothers from sisters. Children over seven were taken away from their mothers. The official policy was that babies and children under seven could stay with their mothers in the women's quarters. But policy and practice often diverge and mothers and toddlers were frequently separated. The construction of the buildings was such that there was no access from one group of paupers to another. Heating was minimal, even in the depths of winter. People had to sleep in dormitories in which anything up to seventy paupers could be accommodated. For each, an iron bedstead, a straw palliasse and a blanket were provided; inadequate protection against the cold winters. Paupers were locked into the dormitory each night and the sanitary arrangements were disgusting. A coarse rough uniform, often made of hemp, which was very harsh on the skin and offered no real warmth in the winter, was provided. Paupers' heads were sometimes, though not always, shaved. Regulations permitted the hair of children to be forcibly shaved. This was intended for the control of lice or fleas, but was sometimes done as a punishment, especially on little girls, for whom it was a humiliation.

Food was minimal and meals frequently had to be eaten in

silence, the paupers sitting in serried rows. The quantity of food for a workhouse pauper in the middle of the nineteenth century was less than that provided for a prisoner in jail, although this improved towards the end of the century.

Paupers were only allowed to go outside the workhouse walls with the permission of the master, to look for work, or for special reasons such as attending a baptism, funeral or wedding. In theory a pauper could discharge him- or herself from the workhouse, but in practice this seldom happened because of their abject poverty and the limitations of available work.

All these rules, and many more, had to be obeyed on pain of harsh punishments, which included flogging, birching, with-holding food, and solitary confinement. Complaints about the daily living conditions were usually dealt with by punishment. Deference to the master, his wife and the officers was required at all times.

It is easy at this distance of time to be critical, and to sneer at what we call "Victorian hypocrisy". But we should remember that this *was* the first attempt at a form of social welfare, and mistakes will always be made in any pioneering venture. Numerous reports were commissioned and published during the century of workhouse existence and many attempts at reform and improvement were made.

These evils had been designed to deter the indolent from entering the workhouse. The tragedy was that in a mixed work-house with one administration, one central building and one staff, the rules, regulations, and punishments applied universally, with the result that old people, the sick, the crippled, the mentally disabled, and children, suffered dreadfully. The atmosphere inside a workhouse was not only stifling to the human soul, but destroyed the last shreds of human dignity.

Another great problem that led to the ill repute of workhouses was the staff. In the early years none of them had any training or qualifications. This could not be expected, because there was no precedent, but the unfortunate result was that it opened the floodgates to all sorts of petty dictators who enjoyed wielding power. The masters had unlimited authority, and their character determined the lives of the paupers, for good or ill. Rules had to be obeyed, and the Master could be a good and humane man, or he could be harsh and tyrannical. The "deterrent rules" ensured that the only qualification required of applicants for the posts of Workhouse Master and officers was the ability to enforce discipline. Many came from the armed forces, reflecting the controlling and disciplinary role that was expected of them.

The "work" aspect of the system rapidly became an acute and intractable problem. The sale of goods was not the primary purpose of the Poor Law Act, but to generate some income for the day-to-day running of the workhouse items and produce made by the paupers were sometimes sold in the open market. This led to protests from employers in the private sector, on two counts: firstly, that goods produced in the workhouses by cheap labour and sold in the marketplace would seriously undercut them; secondly, that the resulting loss of business would affect their employees, who would either have to accept reduced wages or even lose their jobs. This would be a dire outcome when, in most cases, and unlike their workhouse counterparts, they had families to support. On top of these difficulties there was, of course, the problem (still alive and well in the twenty-first century) that in a free-market system work cannot be created out of thin air. Although the British industrial economy was booming throughout the nineteenth century, it was subject to periodic recessions that threw unskilled labourers out of work in their thousands, thus swelling the workhouse population. So pointless, profitless work was introduced to keep the paupers busy. For example, stone-breaking was required of the men. Industrial England could break stones using machinery, but the paupers had to break granite with a mallet. Animal bones could be ground into powder for fertiliser by machine, but paupers had to grind bones by hand. In one workhouse there was a corn mill for men to push round and round for hours on end, but it had no function; it was grinding nothing.

The women did all the cooking and laundry for their fellow inmates. "Scrubbing" is a word I have encountered frequently in this context. Hours of scrubbing vast lengths of stone floors, corridors and stairs was a daily requirement. Sewing sails for sailing boats, by hand, and picking oakum for caulking ships were further tasks that fell to the women and children. Oakum was old rope, frequently impregnated with tar or sea salt, which had to be unpicked by hand and tore the skin and nails. The fibres were then used for filling in the cracks between the wooden planks of ships.

The 1834 Poor Law Act required elementary education (basic numeracy and literacy) for children three hours per day, and a schoolmaster was employed by each Board of Guardians. When the Education Act of 1870 was passed, children were removed from the mixed workhouses and placed in separate establishments and had to attend the local Board School.

Under the 1834 Act a qualified medical officer was required to attend the sick, but nursing was carried out by untrained female inmates. In large groups of enclosed people who were not allowed out, infectious diseases spread like wildfire. For example, in the 1880s in a workhouse in Kent, it was found that in a child population of one hundred and fifty-four, only three children did *not* have tuberculosis.

One hears about "the insane" crowded into workhouses. I think workhouse life bred and fostered its own insanity. I once heard, in the 1950s, what used to be called "the workhouse howl" emitted from the throat of a woman who had been a workhouse inmate for about twenty years in the early twentieth century. It was a noise to make your blood run cold.

Medical infirmaries were also available for the hospital treatment of the poor who could not afford to pay a doctor or to go to hospital. But the infirmaries came to be feared almost as much as the workhouses themselves, and were regarded as places of disease, insanity, neglect and death. Medical and nursing staff were of the lowest order, and were frequently brutal and ignorant – it was work which no doctor who valued his career would undertake. The attitudes of medical and nursing staff, who were careless of the lives of paupers, reflected the mores of the time.

The stigma of illegitimacy has destroyed the lives of millions of unfortunate young women and blighted those of their children. If a girl's lover deserted her, and her parents could not, or would not, support her and the child, the workhouse was often the only form of relief available. The baby would be born in the infirmary. After weaning, the girl would be encouraged to leave the workhouse with her baby to seek employment. But this was usually impossible to find because of the limited labour market for women, further restricted because of the presence of a baby. The girl would also be encouraged to give her baby up for adoption. Many girls were medically certified as "hysterical" or "of unsound mind" or even "morally degenerate", and the baby would be forcibly removed and brought up in the workhouse. The young mother would be expected to leave, find work outside and contribute to the poor rates to offset the cost of keeping and educating the child. If she could not find work, she would have to return to the women's section of the workhouse. The system was heartless and stupid, but those were the rules, and they reflected the social attitude that a "fallen woman" should be punished.

It was one such story that brought Jane to the workhouse when her mother was dismissed for an illicit liaison with her employer.

JANE

"We'll have to watch that one, saucy little madam. Did you hear the way she spoke out of turn at breakfast?"

"Don't you worry, my dear. I'll break her before she leaves here."

The Master and Mistress were talking about Jane, who had been in the workhouse since birth. It was rumoured that her father was a high-class gentleman, distinguished in Parliament and at the Bar. When his wife found him in bed with a servant girl, the girl was immediately dismissed and went to the work-house, where Jane was born.

The baby stayed with her mother to be breast-fed, but was removed when weaning commenced and was then taken to the infants' nursery. The mother returned to the women's section of the workhouse and never saw her baby again. Thus Jane was entirely reared by the institution and knew no other life.

It was a harsh, repressive existence, but no amount of smacks or punishments could subdue Jane's bubbling laughter and *joie de vivre*. In the playground, she chased the other children, or hid and jumped out on them with a delighted "boo". In the dormitory she crept under the beds and poked the mattresses of sleeping children with a stick. Her behaviour caused uproar and an officer would run in with smacks and orders to be quiet. Jane always got smacked, being the cause of all the trouble. But she cried herself to sleep, then giggled and did it again.

As she grew, her high spirits got her into endless trouble. Docility and obedience were expected from the children at all times, and if there was any deviation from this, naughty little Jane could generally be found at the centre of it. Who was it that tied Officer Sharp's shoelaces together as she sat darning socks, so that she fell over when she stood up and took a step? No one knew for certain, but as Jane had been seen in the vicinity, the little girl got a good smacking for it. Who was it that climbed the drainpipe in the playground? Why, Jane, of course. And who mixed up all the boots in the dormitory so that everyone had the wrong sizes? If it wasn't Jane, it might as well have been, so she got the punishment.

Jane's great misfortune was that she stood out. In a group of children she could not be overlooked. She was a good deal taller than average, and also prettier, with her dark curls and clear blue eyes. Worse than this, which was bad enough, she was a great deal more intelligent than most of the other children, and the Master and Mistress feared an intelligent child. They told the officers to keep an eye on her.

"Keep in line, don't straggle. Heads up, now. Don't slouch."

Officer Hawkins would show them how to do it!

The girls were marching to church one Sunday morning. It was a very long crocodile, consisting of nearly one hundred girls. Jane, halfway along on the outside, watched fat old Officer Hawkins strutting along like a penguin and with an instinctive gift for mimicry she copied the walk, head thrown back, arms flapping, feet splayed. The girls behind started to giggle. A hand shot out and hit Jane on the head with such force that she fell through the column of girls on to the road on the other side. She was hauled up and hit again and then pushed back into line. Her ears were ringing and lights were darting before her eyes, but she had to keep marching. She was six years old.

"Where did it come from?" demanded the Master, his eyes bulging, his face turning red. "Who is guilty of this piece of insolence?"

He was looking at a sketch of himself, on a page torn from an exercise book. It was a remarkable drawing for a child, but the Master couldn't see it that way. All he could see was himself with an exaggerated moustache, a square head, small eyes, and an exceedingly large stomach. The picture had been circulating among the girls for three days, causing endless amusement, which only added to the Master's fury.

He assembled all the girls in the hall and addressed them from the pulpit. He reminded them that they were paupers who must respect and obey their betters. No act of disobedience, disrespect or insubordination would be tolerated. He held up the pencil drawing.

"Who did this?" he demanded, menacingly.

No one moved.

"Very well. Every single girl in this room will be beaten, starting now, with the first row."

Jane stood up. "I did it, sir," she whispered.

She was taken to the discipline room – a small, square room with no windows and no furniture except for one stool. Several canes were hanging on the wall. Jane was beaten severely on her bare bottom. She could not sit down for several days. She was only seven years old.

That should be enough to break her spirit, thought the Master to himself with satisfaction. But it wasn't. He couldn't understand it. Why the very next morning, he had seen her, with his own eyes, dancing across the playground, as though she hadn't a care in the world.

The reason why Jane's spirit was not broken was that she had a secret. It was her own special secret and she had told no one else except Peggy. She locked it in her heart and hugged it to herself. It was this glorious secret that filled her with such irrepressible joy and exhilaration. But it was also to be the cause of her greatest disaster, and her life-long grief.

The rumour that her father was a high-born gentleman in Parliament must have reached Jane's ears when she was a little girl. Perhaps she had heard the officers talking about it, or perhaps another child had heard the adults talking and told her. Perhaps Jane's mother had told another workhouse inmate, who had passed it on. One can never tell how rumours start.

To Jane, it was not a rumour. It was an absolute fact. Her daddy was a high-born gentleman, who one day would come and take her away. She fantasised endlessly about her daddy. She talked to him, and he talked to her. She brushed her hair, and cast a flirtatious eye at him, as he looked over her shoulder, admiring her curls. She ran down the playground as fast as she could, because he was standing at the other end, admiring her strength and speed. He was always with her. He was everywhere.

She had a very clear picture of him in her mind. He was not like any other man she had seen at the workhouse, not like the coal man, nor the baker, nor the boiler man. They were ugly and short, and wore rough working men's clothing and cloth caps. He was not like the Master or any of the officers. Jane's little nose wrinkled with disgust at the thought. Her daddy was quite different. He was tall and slim with fine features and pale skin. He had long fingers; she looked at her own slender hands and knew that she had inherited her daddy's fingers. He had lots of hair – she didn't like bald men – and it was a soft, grey colour, always clean and nicely brushed. His clothes were nothing like the awful stuff worn by the workmen she saw, and her daddy didn't smell of sweat the way they did. He always wore beautiful suits smelling of lavender, and he wore a top hat and carried a walking-cane with a gold crest on top.

She knew just what his voice sounded like also – after all, he was constantly talking to her – it was not rough and grating like other men's voices; it was musical and deep, full of laughter. She knew this because he was always laughing with her and making fun of the Master and the officers. His eyes had twinkled with amusement, and he had called her 'his clever girl' when she had drawn a funny picture of the Master.

So how could Jane be unhappy? The more they beat her, the closer she drew to her daddy. He comforted her when she cried at night. He dried her tears and told her to be a brave girl. She swallowed her tears quickly, because she knew that he liked to see her smiling and happy, and she made up a funny story to amuse him, because she knew that he liked her funny stories.

She had also invented his house. It was a beautiful house with a long drive and fine trees in the grounds. There were steps up to the front door and, inside, the rooms smelled of beeswax and lavender. There were pictures on the walls and fine rugs on the floors. Her daddy took her by the hand and led her through the rooms, one by one. He told her that one day he would come and take her away from the workhouse, and they would live together in the beautiful home with the long drive and fine trees.

Jane was seven years old when she began to attend the local council school. She was very proud – it was a big, proper school for big girls and Jane loved it. It brought her into contact with a life outside the workhouse which she had not known existed. It also introduced her to learning, which she loved, and her young mind began to expand. She realised that there were thousands of things that she could learn and she absorbed and retained her lessons quickly. Excellent reports of her progress were sent back to the workhouse. The Master was not impressed. A request from the school's headmistress for Jane to be allowed to take piano lessons, as she showed an unusually good ear for music, was refused, the Master saying that no workhouse pauper should be singled out for special treatment. A request that Jane should be allowed to take the role of Mary in the school's nativity play was refused for the same reason.

Jane was bitterly disappointed at this, chiefly because her daddy would have been so proud to see her playing Mary, and she cried herself to sleep for several nights, until he whispered to her that the silly old school nativity play was not worth crying over. She would have the chance to perform in many more, much nicer plays when she came to live with him in the beautiful house with the long drive.

The workhouse girls were kept apart, as much as possible, from the other girls at the school. This was because several local mothers had complained that they did not want their daughters mixing with 'them workhouse bastards'. This segregation was a source of great pain to many of her friends, but not to Jane. She laughed at the rule that workhouse girls should not play in the same playground as the other children, and tossed her dark curls scornfully. Just let them wait. She would show them. All those dreary girls whose fathers were dustmen and street-sweepers and costermongers. They would be sorry one day, when they saw her daddy, a high-born gentleman, drive up to the school in a carriage. She would run up to him, and all those dreary girls would see her. He would pick her up, kiss her, and take her to the waiting carriage, and all the girls would see and be jealous. The teachers would say to each other: "We always knew that Jane was different."

Jane was fortunate in her class teacher. Miss Sutton was young, well educated and eager. In fact, to say that she possessed a missionary zeal for teaching the poorest of the poor would not be overstating her dedication and enthusiasm. She saw in the vivacious Jane unusual qualities that she was determined to promote. The child learned to read and write in about a quarter the length of time that it took the other children, so whilst Miss Sutton was engaged with the rest of the class, who were learning the alphabet and painstakingly spelling out words, she asked Jane to write stories for her. Jane did so with great joy and fluency, picking up any subject Miss Sutton suggested and weaving a delightful child's story around it. Several of these stories were shown to the Headmistress, who commented: "There is an unusual mind at work here," and she obtained a copy of *A Child's Garden of Verse*, which she handed to Miss Sutton for Jane's use. The child was enraptured by the rhythm of the words and quickly learned many of the poems by heart, which she recited to her daddy when they were alone together.

Miss Sutton also introduced Jane to history and geography, using a children's encyclopedia as her textbook. These lessons had to be surreptitious, because Miss Sutton was employed to teach reading, writing, and arithmetic. Furthermore, she was canny enough to suspect that if she requested extra lessons for Jane, the request would be refused and that would be the end of history and geography for Jane.

Miss Sutton took the wise step of introducing one volume at a time, with the words, "I think you will enjoy reading this. When you have done so, write me a story about it, and we will talk about it at lunch time."

Jane adored Miss Sutton, and their lunch-time conversations about kings and queens and faraway places were the high point of her day.

The children's encyclopedia was her treasure. There were ten large volumes, each beautifully bound in dark blue with gold lettering, and she pored over each one with a hungry mind. She loved the books, their feel and touch and smell, and wanted to keep them, but she knew she couldn't; they were kept in the classroom cupboard, but she knew that Miss Sutton would let her see them any time she wanted. To Jane these books were sacred. Every word she read was – must be – gospel truth, because it was written in the "'cyclopedia".

One day she came across a long word she had not met before. She traced it with her finger and tried to say it to herself: "Par" – that was easy; "lia" – what did that mean? "ment" – that was easy, too; but what was it all put together? Suddenly, like a lightning stroke, it came to her: *Parliament*. People had said her daddy was in Parliament. She devoured the relevant pages as though her life depended on it. In the background the other children were reciting C-A-T, D-O-G. Jane heard nothing. She was busy poring over information on Parliament and the British Constitution. She didn't understand it all, but that didn't matter, it was about her daddy. Like one possessed she read on. She turned a few pages; and then she saw him. The picture leaped towards her. It was her daddy, as she had always known he would look: tall and slim, with slightly grey hair, a thoughtful face, but kindly. He was wearing a beautiful frock coat with tails, just as she had always known he would, with slender trousers and elegant shoes. He was carrying a top hat and a walking-cane with a gold crest. He had long, slender fingers just like she had. She kissed the page.

The lunch bell sounded. Miss Sutton roused her.

"Come on, Jane, time for lunch."

"What is Parliament?" demanded the child.

"The Houses of Parliament are where His Majesty's Government sits. Now come along to lunch."

"Where are these Houses? Can I go? Will you take me?"

Miss Sutton laughed. An eager pupil is the breath of life to a dedicated teacher.

"I will tell you as much as I know about Parliament. But you must have your lunch first. You want to grow to be a big strong girl, don't you? Come back to the classroom after lunch."

After lunch Miss Sutton did her best to explain to the understanding of a seven-year-old that the Members of Parliament made the rules that govern the country.

"Are they very important people, and very important rules?" the child enquired.

"Very; there are none higher in the land."

"More important than the workhouse Master?"

"Oh, much. Members of Parliament are the most important people in the land, after the King."

Jane's breath was coming fast. She seemed unable to contain her excitement. Miss Sutton was watching her closely with astonishment. Jane looked up at her teacher, her blue eyes flashing through dark lashes (extraordinary, the vivid combination of blue eyes and dark hair, thought Miss Sutton). Jane's white teeth showed as she bit her lower lip. One of her milk teeth had come out and she drew air in through the gap with a sucking sound, then poked her tongue through it and wiggled it around. A smile spread across her face, as she whispered, confidentially: "My daddy is in Parliament."

Miss Sutton was, to say the least, taken aback. She was too

fond of the child to reply, "Don't be silly," but she felt it necessary to say something to dispel this illusion.

"Oh, come now, Jane, that cannot possibly be."

"But he is, he is, he's here in the book. I've seen him."

She turned a few pages on and pointed the artist's impression of a Member of Parliament.

"That's my daddy. I know it is. I've seen him lots and lots of times."

"But Jane, that is not a real man. That's just a drawing to show the clothes that a Member of Parliament might wear. That's not your daddy, dear."

"It is, it is, I know it is!" Jane began to cry, and jumped up. "You don't know anything. You don't know my daddy. I do, and I know it's him." Jane ran from the classroom in tears.

Poor Miss Sutton was troubled by this scene, and discussed it with the Headmistress. They agreed that Jane's reaction was just the longing of a highly imaginative child for a father she had never known. The Headmistress advised channelling Jane's thoughts in other directions and said it would be best not to mention Parliament again. That way Jane would forget about it.

Alone, Jane had also decided upon a similar course. She would never again mention her father to anyone, except Peggy. No one, not even Miss Sutton, was worthy of being let into her secret. She pretended she had forgotten all about the lunch-time conversation and carried on as though it had never occurred. But now she knew the book and the page where her daddy was to be found, and whenever she could, she went to the cupboard and opened the page, to gaze upon him with rapture in her heart. If anyone came near, she turned the page quickly, pretending she was looking at something else.

SIR IAN ASTOR-SMALEIGH

Sir Ian Astor-Smaleigh was a true philanthropist. He was an Oxford man who had devoted most of his life, and a considerable part of his fortune, to improvement of living conditions and life expectancy among children in the poorest areas of London. He was a founder member of the Oxford Philanthropic Society for the Improvement of Poor Children, having formed a charity dedicated to the provision of holidays for workhouse children. This work was also close to the heart of his wife, Lady Lavinia. They had made a systematic study of the workhouse system, and though they acknowledged that conditions had improved a great deal since the 1850s, they had seen with their own eyes hundreds of grey, unsmiling children crowded into workhouses and orphanages and were determined to do something about it. The idea of an annual holiday was Lady Lavinia's. Surely, she argued, two weeks by the sea for unwanted children, with healthy air and sunshine, was not too much to ask of society?

The opposition was loud in its scorn. "Holidays! For pauper children! What next? Let them learn to be grateful that they are given food and shelter."

Sir Ian and his lady battled on. When it was proved that one of the causes of rickets was lack of sunlight, they knew that this information could be used to further their cause. Were not many workhouse children afflicted with rickets? And were they not advocating a holiday in the sunshine?

Eventually they won the debate and, to their overwhelming relief, the committee passed, by a narrow majority, the resolution that money should be set aside for holidays for the children of one London workhouse. Additional funds were approved for a further five, if the experiment proved successful.

Suitable premises were found in Kent. These consisted of a series of large barns and sheds that could be adapted as dormitories for the children, who would sleep on straw mattresses on the floor. One of the sheds could be converted into a kitchen. The sheds were situated in fields that ran down to the sea. Sir Ian and members of the committee travelled to Kent to inspect the site and the accommodation. It all seemed perfect.

Sir Ian's next visit was to the workhouse selected for the experiment, in order to address the children himself and tell them of their good fortune. He wasn't going to hand over that pleasant task to anyone else, he told his wife. Was it not he who had haggled with the committee, hour after hour? Now he was going to have the reward of seeing the children's faces when they were told.

Accordingly Sir Ian had taken the train from Oxford, and was in a cab bound for his destination in the East End. He told the cabman to halt about a mile from the workhouse, because he wanted to walk the rest of the way in order to absorb the atmosphere. He attracted much attention in the London streets. He was tall and slim and well dressed. He was also clean. "Vere's a toff, nah, do-goodin'," was one of many whispers as he passed. Sir Ian was unaware of the sideways glances. His mind was fixed on his mission and he was determined that, in years ahead, the holiday project would be expanded to all workhouse children, nationwide.

The crocodile of little girls was returning from school. Jane was about halfway along the line, humming to herself as she marched along. She was looking at the pigtails of the little girl in front of her, watching them bounce up and down and wondering why they bounced more times than each step. "There must be some reason," she was thinking. She looked up, and her heart stopped beating. Pigtails, marching, the street, the buildings, the very sky itself vanished from her universe. Her daddy was on the other side of the street, walking straight towards the workhouse. She stood stock-still. The girls behind piled into her, causing commotion in the line.

"Get along there," shouted Officer Hawkins and hit her on the head. She neither heard nor felt a thing. Her daddy had turned into the workhouse gate and was walking straight towards the main door. She knew that it was him. Not a shadow of doubt. He was exactly as she had always known he would look, and exactly like the picture in the book – tall, slim, grey trousers, a frock coat, a top hat and a walking-cane. He had come to take her away, as he had always said he would.

Joy, unspeakable joy, flooded through Jane, with a rush of love impossible for a mere adult to describe. The intensity of a child's feelings is quite beyond our understanding, though we have all been children. Jane was almost suffocating with the power of her emotions. She felt that something huge and unknown was inside her and she was going to burst wide open.

"Get on there, I told you."

Another clout round the head, and Jane ran a few steps to catch up with the others. The door had closed behind her daddy, and the girls marched round the back to their usual entrance and stood in line for inspection before being told that they were to go to the hall.

Jane didn't stand in line with the others. She rushed straight upstairs to the dormitory, colliding with an officer on the stairway. She was flushed and breathless, but she grabbed the officer's hand, almost shouting.

"Quick, quick! I must have a clean dress and a clean apron!"

The officer was not used to being spoken to by a child in that manner. She shook Jane off.

"Don't be stupid. You'll have a clean dress on Sunday. Not before."

The child stamped. "But I must, I must! My daddy's downstairs, and I want a clean dress and apron before I see him."

"Your what?"

"My daddy. He's downstairs. He's in the Master's office. I saw him go in."

There was something so intense, so urgent and compelling about the child, that the officer gave in, and Jane was supplied with a clean dress and apron, against all the rules. She rushed to the washroom and washed her face and hands, brushed her hair until her curls shone, then flew downstairs to join the other children.

The officer plodded downstairs and told her colleagues of the extraordinary scene. They agreed that the child was mad, but one, with a snigger, said, "She may be right. Everyone says Jane's father was a high-born gentleman. Well, there's a fancy-lookin' gent gone in Master's office. We don't know what for." And she rubbed the side of her nose suggestively.

The girls filed into the hall and sat in rows, the youngest at the front, and the oldest at the back. Jane sat in the fifth row, her eyes fixed on the door where she knew her daddy would enter. She was burning with expectation.

The door opened and Sir Ian walked in, followed by the Master. Her heart stopped beating again. Yes, it was him, the same grave yet kindly face, the same smooth grey hair, and the same deep-set eyes with a smile at the corners. She sat up straight and tall. She was taller than the other girls anyway, but she increased her height by her posture. Her eyes were aflame with love, her mouth was slightly open, her teeth gleamed white as she smiled.

Sir Ian spoke to the children from the pulpit. He could see right down the long hall, with the massed young faces staring up at him. Most of the faces looked glum and unresponsive, and it is always difficult to address an audience from whom the speaker feels no wave of sympathy. He had a joyful message to impart; he had hoped for a joyful response. But most of the girls looked straight ahead, no emotion registering on their features. However, there was one little girl, sitting in the middle near the front, who looked really animated. Sir Ian therefore did what many public speakers do; he fixed his attention on one face in the audience and spoke to that person alone. He spoke of the coming summer and how hot London became at that time of year. He said: "I am going to take you away in the summer."

The little girl stifled a gasp, her eyes alight.

He spoke of the countryside and the seaside, and said: "I am going to take you to a beautiful place by the sea." The little girl could scarcely contain her emotion as he continued: "You will be able to paddle and swim, and build sandcastles and collect shells."

The little girl in the fifth row was now breathing fast, alternately clenching and stretching her fingers.

Sir Ian said, "We will do all this when the summer comes."

The little girl gave a sigh of delight as he stepped down from the pulpit. He felt pleased with himself. Overall, it had been a good address, and a good response.

The Master had also seen Jane's reaction and made a silent note to reprimand her about exhibitionism. He had not yet heard from his subordinate officers about the clean dress and apron.

The girls stood up to leave the hall. One by one they filed past the Master and Sir Ian. It was at this point that Jane lost all control of herself. As she passed, she rushed out of line and flung her arms around Sir Ian's waist, crying, "Thank you, Daddy, thank you, thank you," then she burst into tears, sobbing into his waistcoat.

He was surprised by this, and not a little touched. He ruffled her pretty hair and murmured, "There, there, my child. Don't take on so. You'll go to the seaside, and have a lovely time."

The Master tried to apologise and pull Jane away, but Sir Ian restrained him, saying that it was to the child's credit that she showed so much gratitude. He patted her hair and shoulders and took out a fine lawn handkerchief to wipe her eyes.

"There, now, dry your eyes. You can't go spoiling your pretty little face with tears. Let's see you smile. That's better."

The girls continued to file past, but Jane still clung to him.

The Master was standing beside them, seething with fury. After all the girls had left the hall, Sir Ian finally disentangled Jane's arms from around him. "There now, little one," he said, "off you run. Join your playmates. And I promise you will go to the seaside in the summer time."

Jane reached up and touched his face, and breathed the words: "Oh Daddy, I love you, Daddy, I love you so much."

She whispered it very softly, for him alone, but the Master heard every word. He said, out of the side of his mouth, to an officer: "Take her to the punishment room." He then escorted his guest to the boys' section, where Sir Ian gave his second address.

Jane ran to join the rest of the girls. They were agog with excitement and she was the centre of attention. She entered, proud and confident, her eyes dancing.

"That's my daddy. He's going to take me away."

They crowded around, chattering. Most of the girls believed her, although some of the older ones didn't. "Don't be silly. We're all going on holiday, not just you."

Jane replied haughtily. "Oh well, perhaps he will take some of you as well. He's very rich. But he's my daddy and he's taking me specially. After that we will live together in his big house."

An officer was standing right behind her. Jane was not aware of it while she spoke, but when she saw the girls looking over her shoulder, she turned round. The officer grabbed her.

"You come along with me, my girl. The Master wants to see you."

Jane's heart leaped. Her bright eyes looked over to the other girls. "There, you see! My daddy's going to take me away now. That's why the Master wants to see me."

The officer looked grim and most of the girls looked nervous. Only Jane was happy as she walked confidently away with the officer.

She was taken to the punishment room. The door was opened, she was pushed in, then the door was locked from the outside.

Jane was surprised, even startled, to find herself in a small room, about eight feet square, with no windows except the slit of a fanlight high up on one wall. There was no furniture, except for a three-legged stool sitting alone on the stone floor. Around the wall hung several canes of different lengths and a leather-thonged whip which had three tails, with a small lead pellet attached to the end of each tail.

She couldn't understand it. Why should they want her to wait here? Still, what did it matter, she thought to herself. She could still feel her daddy's kind, warm hands as he caressed her hair, and the sound of his voice as he called her "my child". What did it matter? What did anything in the world matter but that she had told him she loved him and he had called her his child and promised to take her away?

Jane sat down on the stool to wait.

Sir Ian Astor-Smaleigh returned to Oxford that evening full of philanthropic satisfaction. It had been a wonderful day. All the arrangements had been agreed with the workhouse master, the dates settled, the travelling arranged, catering organised, even the clothing supplier had been contracted. No wonder he was pleased. Over three hundred desperately poor children would benefit. He would be able to give a full and satisfactory report to his committee.

Lady Lavinia read his face as he entered the house. She shared her husband's happiness. The maid brought in a late meal and they sat down to discuss the day's work. He told her how he had addressed the children twice, first the girls and then the boys. They were poor, grey little things, he said, with very little life or vitality about them, not like their own children, who tumbled all over the place, and couldn't be contained. She protested that their children were not all that bad – "but do go on, dear."

"However," he said, "there was one little girl who seemed different. She was full of life. She was hanging on to every word as I spoke. She didn't take her eyes off me and she was obviously overcome with joy at the news. In fact she ran up to me afterwards to thank me."

Sir Ian had been on the point of saying that the little girl had called him 'Daddy', but then he thought better of it. After all, women were funny creatures and you never knew what they might think once they got an idea into their heads.

Lady Lavinia asked what the child was like.

"Oh, I don't know. Those damnation workhouse uniforms make all children look alike. I know she had dark hair. That's all I can say. But one thing I do know for certain: she was the only one to come up and say 'thank you' personally."

Lady Lavinia smiled fondly at her husband. "It does her much credit," she said, "and you can be sure of another thing: there is one little girl for whom this will be a day to remember."

A DAY TO REMEMBER

Jane waited for nearly two hours in the punishment room. This was because the Master had to accompany Sir Ian to the boys' section, after which many practical arrangements had to be sorted out. Then the Master wanted his supper, and a chance to discuss Jane's wickedness with his wife.

Two hours is a long time for a small child to wait alone in a closed room (Jane was eight years old). She grew hungry and fidgety. She was not particularly worried or frightened, in fact her mind was still buoyant. Her daddy had cuddled her and called her "my child".

She heard a key in the lock, and jumped up expectantly, smoothing out her apron and running her fingers through her curls, her face eager. The Master and a male officer entered. Her face fell.

"Where's my daddy?" she asked in a little voice.

The Master was bent on vengeance, and her question only added fuel to his fury. He took two steps across the room and hit her full in the face. She fell against the wall.

"You wicked girl. I'll knock that nonsense out of you."

But Jane was a girl of spirit, and now that she had her protector, she wasn't afraid of anyone. Her eyes gleaming, she faced the Master.

"I'll tell my daddy on you," she shouted.

The Master hit her again, harder this time. "Sir Ian Astor-Smaleigh is *not* your father. Do you understand? Now say it after me: 'Sir Ian Astor-Smaleigh is *not* my father.' Say it."

Now at this point a very curious thing happened. Curious to an adult, that is, but logical to the mind of a child. Children frequently hear something quite different from what has actually been said, particularly if it is something new and unrelated to anything else in their experience. (For example, throughout her childhood, my daughter thought our telephone number was "fried potato". She had heard us say "53280".)

Jane thought the Master had said: "See a nasty smelly is not my father." It didn't make sense. She stared at him in sullen amazement.

"Say it, say it," shouted the Master.

She didn't say a word, but just looked at him.

The Master repeated the whole sentence, and demanded she say it, his hand raised threateningly.

The child continued to stare at him in amazement. "A nasty smelly?" she exclaimed, her tone raised enquiringly.

"You insolent little bastard," the man roared. "First you insult Sir Ian, and now you insult me."

To the officer: "Undress her."

The officer grabbed her and started to undo the buttons of her dress. At this Jane really became alarmed and tried to pull away.

"Stop it, let me go. I'll tell my daddy on you, I will."

"Oh, the wickedness! Has she no shame?" muttered the officer, and continued to undress Jane until she stood naked before them. She was crying and frightened now, but still she resisted as much as her puny strength would allow.

"Hold her hands tight and turn her around," ordered the Master, selecting the leather-thonged whip from the wall. Jane saw him take it down, and screamed.

"No! No! Don't! Let me go! Da—"

The first lash fell across her back, knocking all the breath out of her. Pain like fire shot through her body, and the second stroke fell before she had time to breathe. When the third fell, with excruciating pain, Jane realised what was happening. She gathered all her strength and pulled hard at the hands holding her screaming, "No, stop it. Daddy, Da—"

The fourth lash fell with added force. The three lead pellets at the end of the thongs cut into her back.

The pain was like nothing we can imagine. A flogging across the back and shoulders causes indescribable agony because the bones, which are a mass of sensitive nerve endings, are only just beneath the skin surface, and there is very little soft tissue to protect them. The leather thongs were hard and cut the skin, exposing the bones to further pain and injury. The lead pellets struck in random places, tearing the flesh.

By the fifth lash, Jane began to lose consciousness. All her weight fell on to the arms of the officer who held her, and she vomited down his trousers.

"Dirty little thing," he exclaimed, and jerked his knee upwards, catching her in the mouth. Her teeth clamped together over her tongue, which was lolling forward, and blood trickled out of her mouth.

Still the Master continued his self-appointed task. He had intended twenty lashes of the whip, but his wife had cautioned him, saying, "You don't want to kill her. Questions might be asked. Ten lashes will be enough to teach the girl the lesson she deserves."

Jane felt no more pain. She was only conscious of a terrible jolt to her body each time the lash fell. She could hear and see nothing beyond a red mist that swam all around her.

Eight . . . nine . . . ten. The Master brought down the last stroke with satisfaction. The officer let go of Jane's hands, and she fell to the floor. She had wet herself, and she slid into the urine that was mixed with vomit and blood.

"Get a couple of the women to take her to the dormitory. She is to come to my office at eight o'clock tomorrow morning, before she goes to school."

The Master issued the orders, hung the whip on the hook, and left the punishment room.

A nurse and a female officer came to collect Jane and take her up to the dormitory. The nurse was shocked with what she saw but the officer, who had seen it all before, was very blasé.

"She'll get over it. A good beating never did a child any harm. 'Spare the lash and spoil the child.' Come on. Get up on your feet, you lazy girl, and put your dress on."

The nurse was horrified. "You can't put a dress on with her back like that. She needs lint and gauze and ointments."

"Well she won't get them," said the female officer, with finality in her voice. "The Master would never stand for favouritism."

The nurse took off her apron and wrapped the child in it. Jane could barely stand, let alone walk, so the nurse carried her upstairs to the dormitory. She laid her on the bed, face down, and fetched a bowl of cold water. She sat beside the bed for hours, bathing the girl's back with cold water to reduce the blood flow and restrict the terminal capillaries, so reducing the inflammation.

In spite of the pain Jane fell asleep. The nurse continued to bathe her back and all the girls crept into the dormitory, subdued and silent. They slipped into bed, and only a few whispers were heard. One of their number, the brightest and liveliest, had been terribly flogged, and a wave of shock and horror united them in silence.

A little girl with blonde hair crept up to the nurse. She was crying piteously. She said her name was Peggy and she laid her fair hair against Jane's dark curls, whispering to her, kissing her, and sobbing. She asked the nurse if she could help, and so she took a cold sponge and bathed Jane's back just as the nurse showed her. Together, the stunned and silent nurse and the weeping little girl ministered to the stricken Jane, until Peggy was so tired that she too fell asleep.

It was probably this action on the part of the nurse and her child helper that saved Jane's life. All night she drifted in and out of consciousness, and the nurse sat up with her through the long hours whilst the other girls slept. Sometimes Jane moaned in pain, and moved her limbs. Sometimes she let out a weak cry of "Daddy". Sometimes she took the nurse's hand, and held it fast. The blood on her back was clotting, the nurse noted with satisfaction, and the child could obviously move her legs, so at least her spine had not been broken. The hours slipped past.

The Master had ordered that Jane should report to his office at 8 a.m. before school. But Jane could not be roused. The Mistress was called and she, although secretly shocked by the child's appearance, declared that she was shamming, and pulled the mattress so hard that Jane fell out of bed onto the floor, where she lay, immobile. The Mistress then looked coldly at her, turned her with her foot and declared that she could have the day in bed, but must be ready for school the following morning.

Thinking to be helpful, the nurse (who knew nothing of the background), said to the Mistress as she was leaving. "The child has been calling for her daddy all night long, madam. Do you think it would be helpful if we were to fetch him?"

To her surprise the Mistress exploded. "Her daddy! Oh, the iniquity, the sinfulness! Will there be no end to this child's wickedness?" and she stormed off to tell the Master this latest revelation. Something else must be done to purge Jane of her lies.

Jane was not able to go to school the next day, nor for many days after that. Gradually the pain eased, and her mind began to clear. She was able to stand, and to take a little food. She barely spoke, and scarcely raised her eyes from the ground.

The Mistress came to the dormitory to tell her that all this shamming would not be tolerated a moment longer and she must go to school, but first the Master wished to see her. Jane went deathly white and started to shake all over. She attempted to follow the Mistress out of the dormitory, but her legs gave way, and she sank to the floor. An officer hauled her to her feet and dragged her downstairs. As she approached the door of the Master's office Jane vomited the contents of her stomach all down her apron. The Mistress was furious.

"We'll soon have that off you," she shouted, and tore off the apron.

The Master sat at his desk and eyed Jane up and down. The officer kept hold of her, or she would probably have fallen.

"You wicked child. You monstrous liar. It seems there is no end to your depravity. In spite of just chastisement you persist in calling Sir Ian Astor-Smaleigh your father. If you ever do so again, I will flog you again. But, at my wife's request, I will not do so now. You see how good and kind the Mistress is to you, and how little you deserve it. For the time being, as a reminder to you of your wickedness and as an example to the others, you will be deprived of your dress and apron, and you will wear a sack. Now go. And remember, if you say that Sir Ian Astor-Smaleigh is your father one more time I will flog you. And the next time I will show no mercy."

Jane was taken away to the laundry room and her dress removed. A sack with three holes, for head and arms, was put on her with string tied around the waist. Her hair was shorn as close as possible, so that she looked nearly bald. She was sent to school like that.

If Miss Sutton was horrified at her appearance, she was even more horrified at the change in the child's behaviour. The little girl sat shivering and cringing. Each time Miss Sutton went up to her, she reacted with terror. In fact she seemed terrified of everyone, even the other children who spoke to her. She did not read, and she barely joined in any of the lessons. If she held a pencil, her hand shook so much that she was unable to write. The most alarming feature was her total silence. For two whole weeks she said absolutely nothing.

The Headmistress wrote to the Master of the workhouse, asking what had happened. He replied to the effect that he had absolute authority over the workhouse children and was answerable to no one. He reminded the Headmistress that he was a member of the Board of Governors of the school. If there was any interference, he was in a strong position to complain to the Chairman about the conduct and competence of the Headmistress. No further action was taken.

Humiliations were heaped upon Jane. She started bedwetting.

The workhouse punishment for this was that the offending child would be stood on the detention platform, which was at the front of the dining hall, visible to everyone, holding her wet sheet. The child had no breakfast that day. Morning after morning, throughout the winter and spring, Jane, shorn of her hair and wearing a sack tied with string, stood miserably, conspicuously on that platform, clutching a wet sheet. Day after day she went to school with no breakfast. This morning penance continued with monotonous regularity.

The scars on Jane's back healed more quickly than the scars on her mind. In fact, her mind and personality never did fully recover. She was never seen to smile, nor heard to laugh. Her buoyant, bouncing step changed to a cringing shuffle. Her flashing blue eyes were scarcely seen, because she would look up briefly, fearfully, and then look down again quickly. Her voice changed to a whisper. Her precocious level of schoolwork changed to average or below average in the class. Miss Sutton was heartbroken, but however much she tried to encourage Jane to write stories for her, as she had in the old days, she had no success. Jane would put her hands up to her mouth, cast fearful sideways glances at her teacher, and whisper: "Yes, Miss Sutton." But after half an hour the page would still be blank.

Jane's mind was largely blank as well. She had very little memory of the events that led up to her flogging, and she hadn't the faintest idea why it had occurred. She went through it all in her mind, over and again, round and round, an endless repetition of thought that got her nowhere. Everything was confused. Nothing made sense.

She was clear in her mind that it had something to do with the day her daddy had come to the workhouse and told her that he would take her away in the summer. But why had the Master been so cross with her? Her daddy wasn't cross, so why should the Master be cross? Why had he flogged her, and made her wear the sack? She tried and tried to think what she had done wrong, but could think of nothing. And why had the Master shouted several times: "See a nasty smelly is not your father?" This was the biggest puzzle of all. "A nasty smelly?" What did it mean? Her daddy wasn't a "smelly". Her daddy smelled of lavender, as she had always known he would. She had cuddled him and smelled the lavender. She had never called the Master or Mistress nasty smellies, so why had he flogged her? Like a swarm of wasps these thoughts buzzed in her mind all the time, day and night, until she felt she would go mad with the buzzing.

But not for one moment did Jane, in her thoughts, impute any blame to her daddy or cease to love him. In fact her love grew stronger and more real because she had seen him and touched him, and he had stroked her hair, called her "my child" and said he would take her away in the summer time. The spring came, and Jane knew that the summer would follow. It would not be long now. She only had to endure and be good, and not get into any more trouble. Her daddy would come, as sure as the summer sunshine, and take her away from the workhouse for ever. This fragile dream she clung to. It was her one solace in her misery and bewilderment.

May, June, July. The summer days were drawing out. There was a buzz of excitement amongst the workhouse girls – they were going on holiday. It had never happened before. Jane's crushed spirits rose a little, and occasionally she allowed herself to lift her eyes from the floor.

August arrived, and preparations were made. Summer dresses and sandals were provided. The girls could talk of nothing else. There was a fever pitch of excitement. The day for departure arrived.

The girls were standing in the dining hall after breakfast and everything was ready.

The Mistress entered. "Right, now. Form a line and march out quietly. We will proceed to the station."

The girls stepped forward.

"Not you. Stay where you are."

The Mistress pointed at Jane. The other girls marched out.

Sick disappointment took possession of Jane. She saw the last girl leave, as she stood in her place. She heard footsteps echo down the corridors and doors banging. Then silence.

Now it was that Jane's heart finally broke. Hitherto her suffering had been physical. Now the torture was mental, emotional, and spiritual. The utter desolation of rejection was hers to savour. Her daddy was not going to take her away. Her daddy did not love her, or want her. That was why she was there in the workhouse. He had put her there because he did not want her and she would never see him again. She knew it in her heart.

Throughout the long weeks, alone but for the porter's wife who brought her food twice a day, Jane lived with this bitter knowledge. She had nothing to do, day after day; no books, no toys, no pencils and paper. She cried herself to sleep alone in the dormitory; ate alone in the huge refectory; went out alone in the yard (euphemistically called a playground) and walked around the walls. She spoke to no one except the porter's wife, twice a day.

The other girls returned, sun-browned and happy. Jane heard stories of the seaside and paddling and catching crabs and building sandcastles. She didn't say a word.

The knowledge of rejection, of being unwanted, is more terrible to live with than anything else, and a rejected child will usually never get over it. A physical pain entered Jane's body, somewhere in the region of the solar plexus, which ached all the time and from which she would never be free.

Unknown to Jane, Sir Ian and Lady Lavinia had visited the children's holiday camp. They had played with the children by the sea, organised races for them across the sands, hired a man with a donkey to give them rides and read stories to them in the evening. They were very happy with their work.

At the end of the day, Sir Ian asked the Master: "I have not seen that pretty child who came up to thank me when I first met you. Where is she?"

The Master was nonplussed, but his resourceful wife stepped forward with a curtsey. "The child has an aunt, sir, who always takes her on holiday each year. I assure you, sir, that at this very moment the child is playing happily on a beach somewhere in Devon." She curtsied again.

"I am glad to hear it," said Lady Lavinia, "but for my part, I am sorry not to see the child. My husband spoke most highly of her."

After they had left, the Master said. "What a blessing we did not bring that wretched child. If she had gone running up to that man in front of his wife, and clung to him and called him Daddy, heaven knows what trouble it would have stirred up."

And on this occasion – who can tell? – the Master may have been right.

FRANK

*Give me a boy for the first five years
of his life, and I will make the man.*
Rousseau

Frank had but a dim recollection of his father. He remembered a
tall, strong man, whom he held in awe. He remembered his big
voice and huge, rough hands. He could remember once tracing
the veins on the back of this vast hand with his little fingers, and
looking at his own smooth white skin and wondering if he would
ever have hands like that. To be like his father was his only
ambition and he worshipped him. In the later, sadder years of his
childhood he tried desperately to remember what his father had
been like, but a phantom that comes and goes could not have
been more elusive and only the dimmest memory remained.

He remembered his mother much more clearly; his sweet,
gentle mother who was never strong because she was always
coughing. He remembered the sound of her voice as she sang
songs to him and played with him. Above all, he remembered
her cuddles as she put him to bed and lay down beside him.

In the winter his mother hardly went out of doors because of
her weak chest and his father would say, as he went off to work,
"Now you look after your mother while I'm away, Frank lad.
I'm relying on you to take care of her for me." And Frank would
look up at his god with big solemn eyes and accept the task as a
sacred duty.

When a tiny baby was born – so tiny that everyone said she
would not live – Frank was four years old. He had been an only
child all his life and could not conceive of any other child entering
his world. Many boys of that age become very jealous of a new-
born baby, but not Frank. He was mesmerised by this tiny
creature, hardly bigger than a teacup, who could move and cry,

and who needed so much care. Not for a moment did he resent the hours of attention given to the baby. In fact, he liked to help. The most fascinating thing of all was to watch his mother breast-feeding the baby, and he tried never to be far away when this mysterious and beautiful ritual was going on. He kept very quiet, crept close to his mother and watched, spellbound, as the baby sucked and the milk oozed from the nipple.

The baby was premature and sickly, and for a long time her life hung in the balance. His father said to him, many times: "You've got a special job to do, young man. You've got to look after your little sister. That's your job now, lad."

So Frank watched over her, and hardly went out to play with the other boys in the court, because he was so busy looking after his little sister.

The baby didn't die. She gained strength and became quite robust, although she always remained small. She was christened Margaret but was called Peggy, because Margaret seemed too long a name for such a small baby. After the christening Frank's father said, "You done a good job there, son; and I'm proud of yer."

Then catastrophe struck. In those years typhoid was raging through East London. His huge, strong father, who had never known a day of illness in his life, was hit by the disease and died within a few days. His mother, who had never been strong, was spared and so was the baby. His mother went out to work, cleaning offices. She left home in the early hours each morning, and again each evening, leaving Frank to look after Peggy, who was by now a toddler.

One day Frank ran home from school (he didn't think much of school, regarding it as a waste of time) to take over the domestic responsibilities from his mother, so that she could go out to her job. It was cold and she was coughing badly, but she went nonetheless. Money had to be earned, or they would be homeless. Frank did as he had so often done before: he put some wood that he had found on his way home from school onto the fire, made some tea for himself and Peggy, played with her and, as the fire was dying, he undressed her and put her to bed, creeping in beside her for warmth.

In the middle of the night he woke up, aware that something was wrong. It was pitch-black, and the quiet was terrifying. He could hear Peggy breathing, but that was all. Something was missing. Nausea seized him as he realised that his mother was not there. In a panic he felt all over the bed, but the side where his mother usually slept was empty. He called out in a small voice so as not to wake Peggy, but there was no reply. He crept out of bed and found the matches. He struck one and the flame leaped up, lighting the whole room momentarily. His mother was not there. Blinded by tears, he crept back into bed and held Peggy in his arms.

The cold had badly affected his mother as soon as she stepped outside. She was asthmatic and bronchitic, and had been fighting off a chest infection for several weeks. She had a mile to walk to the bus, and the freezing mist rising off the river had got into her lungs. She was thankful for the brief respite of sitting in the bus, but by the time she got to the building where she was employed, she felt more dead than alive. She went to the cleaning cupboard to get out her things, but the bucket felt so heavy that she could hardly move it. She asked permission to make herself a cup of tea, saying she would feel better with something warm inside her. The tea was indeed comforting, but the building was cold and she sat shivering in the basement, pulling her shawl around her shoulders and coughing. One by one the office workers left and she found herself alone.

Normally, this office took her about three hours, but after one hour, she had scarcely cleaned one tenth of it. She felt so weak she could scarcely drag herself around, and there was still the scrubbing to do. She returned to the basement to get the bucket – the one that had felt impossibly heavy when empty – and filled it with water. She pushed it along the floor with her feet and then lifted it up the stairs one by one, resting it on each stair as she did so. She reached the second storey this way, and then her failing strength must have given out. She fell down the stairs that she had climbed so laboriously, knocking the bucket over as she fell. She was drenched with water and lay on the stone floor all night. In the morning they found her dead at the bottom of the stairs.

Frank had never spent a night away from his mother. There was only one bed so they had all slept together even when his father was alive. He had never even contemplated a time without the comforting warmth of her body beside him. Now, in the dark and cold of the room, the bed felt like a hostile and alien territory, and he wanted to run away from it, run to the next-door neighbours, screaming. But there was Peggy to think of. She was quietly sleeping, unaware that anything was wrong. So he bit his lips, rubbed his fists into his eyes and cuddled up close to her.

He was six years old.

He must have slept, because it was daylight when he was awoken by Peggy crying. There was some milk and water left from the night before but it was cold and she pushed it away. He did not know what to do. He took a wet nappy off her, as he had seen his mother do, but then he didn't know what to do with it, so hid it under the bed. There was no more wood for the fire. He drank the cold milk himself and crept back into bed. They fell asleep again.

He awoke as a crowd of neighbouring women entered the room.

"Oh, it's a shame, oie tells ya."

"Poor li'l kids. Vey didn' ask 'a be born."

"Both dead in six months."

"It makes yer wanna cry, don' it?"

Frank looked around him in bewilderment and held Peggy defensively, pulling the blanket up higher.

A man entered the room. "Are these the children of the deceased?" he enquired.

A chorus of voices answered.

"Yeah, more's the pity."

"Poor li'l lambs."

"Vey don' know wha's 'appened."

"And is there no relative to look after them?"

"No' as 'ow I knows on, do you, Lil?"

"Nah, no one."

"They will have to come with me, and the effects sold to contribute to the Guardians' expenses."

He looked around the room at the meagre furniture – one bed, one table, and two chairs, a small cupboard, a washing bowl, a chamber pot, a candlestick, some tin plates and cups – all back-breakingly acquired by the father, to provide for his family.

"Will someone get them ready while I take an inventory?"

Two women stepped forward, and Frank grabbed the back of the bed, clutching Peggy. "Where's Mummy?" he asked plaintively.

"Yer mum's dead, luvvy, more's the pity."

"No, my dad's dead," he insisted.

"An so's yer mum, dearie. Found dead vis mornin' in ye office."

"Blue, she was," chorused the women to each other.

"Froze stiff, vey say, an' soakin' wet."

"Wet froo, an' all, and 'er wiv her weak chest."

"No' surprisin', is it?"

Frank looked from one to another, and horror struck his heart. Was his mother dead? He had promised his father that he would look after her! What had gone wrong? Peggy was beginning to whimper again. Kind hands were placed on him. He clung to the bars of the bedstead with all his strength and turned his back on the women, holding Peggy, who was beginning to scream now, between his body and the head of the bed.

"You will have to get him free," said the man. "They cannot stay here alone."

It took four women to loosen his fingers from the bars. A child's fingers can be incredibly strong if they are curled around something. Eventually two women were holding him and Peggy in their arms. He was biting and scratching and kicking in a hysteria of fear and rage. He shouted at the woman holding Peggy, "Give her to me. She's my sister. Don't take her away." Tears were streaming down his face.

"We will have to go. Does anyone know where the key is kept?" said the man.

The door of the room was locked, and they made their way downstairs. The woman holding Frank was badly bruised. They walked through the streets, collecting a crowd of onlookers as they went.

Frank and Peggy were admitted to the infants' section of the workhouse, where boys and girls under seven years of age were housed. They were undressed and bathed and treated not unkindly. In fact, Peggy's tiny stature and wispy blonde hair evoked a stream of sympathy from the women who received them. Frank had exhausted his fury, and sullenly allowed himself to be washed and his hair examined for fleas.

"We'll have to cut it off. You know the rules."

He submitted to having his head shaved, but when he saw a large woman doing the same to Peggy, he rushed at her and butted her in the stomach with his head. She collapsed onto a chair winded, then grabbed the boy and thrashed him soundly, whilst another officer shaved Peggy.

"It's a shame, cutting this pretty hair. But it will soon grow again."

Poor little Peggy looked like a tiny Martian when they had finished, and Frank sobbed with impotent rage.

The children were dressed in workhouse clothes and taken to the playroom to meet the other children. We would not call it a playroom today, because there was nothing to play with. It was just a large, bare room, about forty feet long by twenty feet wide, with high, uncurtained windows and rough floorboards.

"Now you play quietly with the others until tea time." The door was shut, and the officer left.

They stood shyly in the doorway, looking at about forty other children, all wearing the same clothes. Frank, acutely self-conscious that he and Peggy had no hair, tried to hide her under his jacket. A boy of about his age ran up to them, shouting: "You're new. You're new. Where've you come from? What's your name, baldy? An' who's this little squirt, then?" He pulled at Peggy's arm and tickled her scalp.

Frank flung himself at the boy, fighting with savage fury. All the rage that had been building up during the day was concentrated in his attack. The rest of the children stood back to watch the fun. The other boy was no slouch when it came to fighting and the two were evenly matched. There were no adults in the room to stop them.

Peggy was terrified and ran screaming to a corner, where she crouched down, hiding her head. A little girl with dark hair left the others, came over to her and put her small arms around the sobbing child. "Don't cry, please don't cry. They're only fighting. Boys are always fighting. Boys are awful. Here, sit on my knee."

The girl sat down on the floor and Peggy climbed onto her knees. She played with a long, dark ringlet hanging down near her face, and laughed when she pulled it and it bounced back up again.

The girl smiled happily. "You're like a little doll. I've never had a doll, but I've seen them. And you're better than a doll, because you're real, and dolls are only pretend. Will you be my friend? My name's Jane, and I'm four. What's yours?"

Peggy didn't say anything, but her tears stopped. Jane sat quietly, cuddling Peggy, and laughing to herself as she watched the fight.

The boys were roughly the same weight, but Frank had the advantage of cold, calculated fury and his need to defend his sister. He glanced at the other boys who were egging them on, and knew instinctively that if he lost this fight, Peggy would never be safe from their torments.

After a few minutes Frank's adversary was on the floor in a corner. "Truce. Give in. Hold 'im off," he called out.

Frank turned to face the others. He raised his fists defiantly. "Anyone else want a go?"

No one stepped forward.

Frank swaggered over to the corner where Peggy sat on Jane's knee. "Thanks," he said. "She's only two, and she's scared. Her name's Peggy and I'm Frank."

The girl had a merry laugh, open features and piercing blue eyes. Frank liked her, he liked the way she was nursing Peggy, and he saw the contentment with which the little girl responded to the older one. He knew that he could trust her. "Let's be friends," he said.

Over the next few weeks, the reality of his mother's death dawned upon Frank.

He would never see her again and pain inside reduced him to tears. Other boys laughed and jeered at him, but he only had to stick out his jaw and raise his fists aggressively, and they quickly backed off. Peggy did not seem as unhappy, because Frank was always there for her. Also, Jane had taken to her and petted and fussed over her, calling her "my little doll". Jane was indisputably the leader among the girls, so her protection meant a good deal.

Jane was good for Frank also. He liked her with the instinctive affection that recognises a kindred spirit. He approved of her gentle ways with Peggy, and he also liked her naughtiness. She was always playing tricks and pranks, making everyone laugh. She would jump out from behind a door when the officer opened it, shouting "boo", and then run away laughing. She was always caught and smacked, but nothing seemed to quench her high spirits. The day she climbed the water pipe in the playground and sat on the gutter and wouldn't come down was one of the funniest things Frank could ever remember. Fat old Officer

Hawkins had been on duty that day and got onto a ladder, then lumbered up it, with all the boys crowding around underneath, trying to see her knickers. When she finally got Jane down, she thrashed her soundly in the playground, and then again in the evening before bedtime, but Jane just rubbed her bottom, shook her curls defiantly, and did not seem to care.

The night times were the worst for Frank. Alone in a small, hard bed, with darkness all around, he sobbed silently for his sweet mother, whom he had adored with all the passion of boyhood. He missed the warmth of her body, he missed the smell of her skin, the touch of her hand, the sound of her breathing. He would creep over to Peggy's bed and get in beside her, where the smell of her hair would numb his pain, and they would sleep together till morning. This became their one comfort in the first months of their life in the workhouse.

A year passed. After breakfast one morning, Frank and two other boys were taken to the Matron's office. She said abruptly, "You are big boys now that you are seven, and we are taking you to the boys' section today. Wait in the hallway, and the van will come for you at nine o'clock."

The boys did not know what she meant, and the three of them sat on the bench, engaged in mock fights and ribaldry.

At nine o'clock, a man entered the front door and enquired, "Are these three to go?"

They were taken outside to a green van and told to climb in the back. It was all very exciting. They had never been in a van before, so they clambered in willingly, ready for adventure. The van started with a jerk, and they were thrown off the bench onto the floor. They shrieked with laughter. This was going to be a good day. A ride in a van! You wait till we get back and tell the others. The van stopped twice, and other boys of their own age climbed in. Soon there were eight boys, all shouting and skidding around the floor of the van as they turned corners, or pressing against each other to see out of the small back window in order to wave at people as they passed. Everyone turned to look, because motorised transport was comparatively unusual in those days. The boys felt very privileged, and infinitely superior to the people walking or travelling in horse-drawn carts and wagons.

Eventually the van stopped and the back door opened. Frank saw a very large, grey-stone building in front of him, and he did not much like the look of it.

"Where am I?" he asked.

"This is the boys' section. You come here when you are seven and stay until you are fourteen," said a tough-looking man, who was a workhouse officer.

"And where's Peggy?" he demanded.

"I don't know who Peggy is, but she's not here."

"Peggy is my sister and I look after her. My dad told me to."

The officer laughed. "Well, someone else will have to look after her. There's no girls allowed in here."

Still Frank did not understand. He was unsure, frightened, and he felt like crying, but he wasn't going to let the other boys see him, so he squared his shoulders, clenched his fists and put on a swagger as they were taken to the Master's office.

The interview was brief. They were told that they must obey the rules, obey the officers at all times, and that if they did not do so they would be punished. The Master then said, "You will be given your duties and lunch is at one o'clock. You will start school tomorrow."

Frank had wanted to ask about Peggy, but the Master so terrified him that he did not dare speak. He followed the officer to the dining hall with a feeling of panic in his heart that he had not known since the night when he had awoken to find his mother's side of the bed empty.

Lunch in a huge refectory with about a hundred and fifty other boys, some of them very big, was terrifying and he could hardly eat. He ate half a potato and drank some water, but it nearly choked him, and he could not stop his tears from falling. Some of the bigger boys pointed at him and sniggered. None of the male officers showed any sympathy. The three new boys who had come together were all considerably more sober now. The fun and high spirits of the van ride evaporated as the reality of the situation began to dawn upon them. They had left the small world and comparative kindness of the nursery, where there were women officers and nurses, for the harsh, often brutal world of the workhouse proper, where, for the next seven years, they would encounter only male officers.

Back in the nursery, after breakfast, Peggy looked around for Frank, but could not find him. She looked in the lavatory and the washroom, but he was not there. She looked in the classroom and under the stairs, but he was not in those places either. Bewildered and frightened, she stood on the bottom stair hugging the banister, and stamped her feet. An officer came up to her, but she screamed and stamped her little feet even faster.

"Poor little thing," remarked the officer to a colleague, "she's going to miss her brother, they were very close. She'll just have to get over it in her own time. There's nothing we can do."

Peggy was three years old and Frank had been with her all her life. She had not noticed the loss of her father, when she was eighteen months old, and had only the vaguest memory of her mother. But Frank was her world, her life, her security and she was utterly devastated. All day she stood on the bottom step, hugging the smooth, round balustrades, sometimes silent, sometimes sobbing. Sometimes she kicked the stairs and hurt her toe. Twice she wet herself, but still she wouldn't move. Jane tried to talk to her, but Peggy shook her shoulders and screamed, "Go away."

"Leave her alone," said an officer to Jane, "she'll get over it in a day or two."

Towards evening Peggy started to bang her head on the balustrade. It hurt, but she wanted it to. Perhaps Frank would come when he knew she had hurt herself. When he didn't come, she sobbed uncontrollably, then slipped down onto the stairs in a deep sleep. A nurse picked her up, carried her to the dormitory and put her to bed.

For the next three months, Peggy hunted for Frank every day. She always expected to find him, but never did. She asked everyone: "Where's Frank?" and was told that he had been transferred to the big boys' section, but she did not understand. She developed the habit of sitting alone in a corner and rocking herself. A nurse, who knew that this was a particularly frightening development in a lonely, insecure child, tried to comfort her. But Peggy would not be comforted. Each lonely night, she sucked her thumb and rocked herself and cried for Frank to come to her. But he didn't come.

As time passed, she stopped looking for Frank and asked for him less, until eventually she stopped asking. It was assumed that she had forgotten all about him.

It was to be nine years before brother and sister saw each other again, and by that time they did not recognise each other.

BILLINGSGATE

At the age of seven, Frank had entered an all-male world of petty rules, upheld by harsh, uncompromising discipline and gratuitous tyranny. Many of the workhouse officers were men who had been brought up in a workhouse themselves during the nineteenth century, when conditions for paupers were simply appalling. A child had to have a very strong constitution to survive the brutality, the work, the cold, and near-starvation. These men knew of no other way of life, and to them it was only natural to impose the same sort of regime on the boys in their charge.

Frank was immediately set to work on one of the numerous tasks assigned to paupers: cleaning potatoes, cutting cabbage, scrubbing out the huge cooking vats (only the smallest boys could get inside them), burnishing the stoves, cleaning the brass, and hosing down the vast stone floors of the kitchen – and woe betide any boy who got himself wet! The list was endless and the day long, starting as it did at 6 a.m. The boys also went to the local council school, so the work had to be done before or after school. Frank found that if his tasks were not finished before he went to school, he got a beating from the officer in charge, and if he stayed behind to finish the job, he got a beating from the schoolmaster for being late!

Small boys quickly learned to hide their tears. They knew that any sign of weakness would be seized upon by a bigger boy and mercilessly exploited. Bullying, constant intimidation and jeering were the only response a smaller boy would gain from tears.

Once, and once only, Frank asked an officer where Peggy was. The man must have told one of the older boys, perhaps maliciously, knowing what would happen. The same day, in the washroom, a chorus went up. "Peggy, Peggy, who's Peggy?"

"Peggy's his tart. What a fart!"

"Peg, Peg, peg your nose, what a pong!"

"Peggy's a stink."

"He has to put a clothes peg on his nose 'afore he can touch 'er."

Frank burst into tears, and a big boy came and pushed him over onto the slippery floor.

"Garn, you ain't got no tart, yer titch," said the boy, squeezing Frank's testicles so hard that he screamed with pain.

The officer came in and the big boy swiftly merged into the crowd, looking innocent.

The officer looked round and asked no questions. "Get up," he said curtly to Frank, "get washed and go to the dormitory."

Frank crept into bed and cried, as he did every night, for his mother and his sister. He had learned to make no sound when crying, so as not to attract attention, and to keep very still, so that he seemed to be asleep. But he often lay awake for hours, his heart bursting.

During these wakeful hours he often – nearly always, in fact – heard movements and soft footsteps, grunting and puffing and cursing sounds, as iron bedsteads rattled and straw mattresses squeaked. Each dormitory had an officer in charge who had himself once been a workhouse boy. The officer slept in a closed cubicle at the end of rows of beds, and each night a boy would slip quietly out of bed and go into the cubicle.

What can one expect if a crowd of boys are thrown together, with no escape and no female influence? All the boys were lonely. All of them were motherless. They had only each other in whom to find comfort and, let us hope, a little happiness because for them life would be short. From 1914 to 1918 the older boys in Frank's dormitory – those born in the 1890s – were destined to be sent straight from the workhouses of England to the trenches of France, to die as cannon-fodder in defence of King and Country.

★

It was September 1914. A costermonger by the name of Tip called at the workhouse and asked to speak to the Master. The Master was prim and pompous; the coster flashy and talkative. He explained, in a husky voice inclined to sudden squeaks, that his lad had gone off to the war, and he had been left without a boy, and a coster must 'ave a boy, how else was he goin' to do his trade, like, an' what he was lookin' for was a sharp little lad of about eleven or twelve, eleven being the preferential age, seeing as how they learns quickest, a boy who was a good worker, an' quick, an' it didn't matter about no book learning, because he never could see no use for that in the fish trade, and them as 'ad book learning never seemed to get on spectackiler in the trade, but he, Tip, would edicate the boy himself an' make a right sharp coster out of him, as how he could earn his living honest-like, an' keep his head up with the best, an' he would supply his lodgins an' his victuals, least as to say his doxy would, an' 'ad the Master got such a boy, who was hard-workin' an' willin'?

The coster delivered all this in a curious voice that growled and gurgled sometimes, and squeaked and whistled at others. The Master paused to think, and the coster, who never paused and could not conceive of anyone else doing so, started again, "An' he's gotta be strong, 'cause its no place for a wimpish lad, an the doxy'll feed him well an' keep his strength up, an' —"

The Master held up his hand to silence the man. "Just wait here, will you?" he said, as he left the office.

Workhouse masters were encouraged to off-load inmates in order to reduce expenses, but they were not allowed to turn them out onto the streets unless provision for their maintenance was assured. The apprentice system was the answer.

The Master thought carefully about the coster's request, and his mind fixed on Frank — he was eleven, he was strong, he was hard-working, he was obedient, and he was, according to his school reports, one of the "has ability but must try harder" type — the despair of every honest schoolmaster.

The boys were at tea, and Frank was called out.

"Now stand up straight, look lively and don't answer back," said the Master as he cuffed him round the ear. "There's a man here wants to see you."

They entered the office, where the coster was whistling. He had a beautiful, mellow whistle that seemed a most unlikely adjunct to his peculiar speaking voice.

"This boy seems to answer your requirements. I give you my assurance that he is hard-working. All our boys are trained to work."

The coster looked Frank up and down and sucked his teeth. He had only two, one in the upper and one in the lower jaw, both at the front, so he was able to vary his sucking with singularly comic effect.

He pinched Frank's ear. "You're a skinny li'l sprog. Can you lift a box of herrings?"

Frank didn't dare to answer back in front of the Master, so he just nodded.

"Ain' chew got a tongue, ven?" demanded the coster.

Again Frank nodded.

"Yes, he has and he can use it to good effect when he wants to," answered the Master.

"Vat's what I needs, a boy as can holler good and loud like, an' make 'em all sit up."

"This is the boy for you, then. He's got a voice like a foghorn," said the Master conclusively.

"I'll take 'im. An' if he don't come up to scratch, I'll bring him back next week."

Before Frank had time to say a word, he was whisked off to the clothes cupboards, his workhouse uniform removed, and ill-fitting street clothes put on him. The coster took him by the hand and they stepped out into the road together.

Tip was a flashy dresser. Not for him the drab greys and browns of working men. He wore green corduroy trousers and a shirt of vivid blue. His shoes were tied with enormous bows which bore no resemblance to the humble shoelace, and at his throat was tied a silk neckerchief of red and blue. His cap was not your ordinary cloth cap, as worn by the English, nor the beret favoured by the French, yet it bore a close similarity to the French style. Tip's cap could be described as a very large beret, made of the best velvet, and the colour, neither blue nor green, seemed to change with the light and movement. Tip considered himself a real swell, and his doxy admired him prodigiously.

He glanced down at Frank and his masculine vanity acknowledged that the boy was taking in his elegance. "You gotta look sharp in our trade, titch. No use lookin' like a bag 'o dirty washin'. The ladies don' like it. An' it's the ladies as wha' does the buyin', see? So you gotta please the ladies. That's rule number one. We'll 'ave to get you some new clobber. Can't 'ave you goin' round lookin' like vat, queering my pitch. The ladies would run away fritted, vey would. I knows of a Jew as what can fix you up cheap and natty like."

Tip had started the sentence in his baritone voice, but as he came to the end of it, the words came out in a series of high, unexpected squeaks. Aware that Frank was listening with puzzled attention, he explained.

"It's the toobs. The toobs what wears out with all that 'ollering. They gives out if you're a good coster, like what I am, 'cause they're too delicate to stand all that 'ollerin'. Vat's what I needs a boy for, to 'oller, along with other fings, lots of other fings, all of which I'll teach you, but 'ollerin' will be one of your first jobs. Now let's 'ear you 'oller. See vat li'l lad over there, playing in vat puddle? Well, you call out, loud as you can now, 'Hey, mucky, your mum's comin'.'"

Frank caught the spirit of things, and bellowed the words out with all his strength. The boy jumped up and ran round the corner like a greyhound.

Frank roared with laughter, and squeezed Tip's hand. "Vat's what I needs," said Tip. "Reckons as how you'll suit me, an' if you can pick up ve other tricks of the trade quick like, we'll get on famous. Now we're gettin' to my lodgings, an' my doxy's

Doll see, and Doll, she's a rare 'un, but she won' stand no lip from boys, see, so don' you give her no lip an' you won't feel the back of 'er 'and." Tip rubbed the side of his chin reflectively and muttered, "An' you don't wanna feel the back of 'er 'and, I can tell yer."

They climbed a dark and foul-smelling staircase to the fourth floor. A large and shapely woman ambled towards them. She wore a red skirt, frayed and dirty at the hem, and a purple blouse, high at the neck, with a row of jet buttons down the front against which a full bosom pressed, screaming for release. Black jet beads hung to her waist, and heavy black hair hung down around her shoulders. When she smiled, her teeth were also black, as though they had been painted to match her outfit. She looked at them both, then cried out, "Is vis the li'l workhouse kid, ven? Oh, look, he's thin, the pet," and she pressed Frank's head to her bosom, an experience which he found to be not unpleasant, though the smell could have been sweeter. "We'll 'ave to give 'im some pie dahn Dill's, eh Tip?"

"Let's ge' goin' ven," said Tip with a leer.

Doll twisted her hair up on top of her head in a fashionable coil (Frank watched, fascinated) and stuck several pins in. One of them had a bird on the end and this she settled on the top of her head.

"You bet, squire," she said with a wink. Then she leaned down to Frank. "He's a nice-lookin' li'l lad, bu' thin like. Oh, I don' like 'a see 'em so thin. What's yer name an' all, eh? We'll ge' choo some pie, ven. Howzat?"

It was nearly seven o'clock and the streets were filled with people. Apart from marching to school in a crocodile, Frank had not been outside the workhouse gates for years. He was filled with wonder and to linger was irresistible. Here, a family was fighting, the man and woman threatening each other with equal fury; there, some boys were playing skittles; yonder a woman was fetching water from the pump whilst a crowd stood around with their buckets, gossiping as they waited. Frank had not seen women for years, and couldn't take his eyes off them, until he realised with alarm that Tip and Doll were almost out of sight, and he had to run to catch up with them. They sauntered along, greeting people, chaffing children, Tip pinching the cheeks of young girls, Doll screaming across the street to another woman. They both dressed in a more gaudy fashion than any of their neighbours, and Frank felt proud to be with them, although neither looked round to see if he was still there.

They entered a beer shop, high-ceilinged, bare-walled, with a wooden floor. The serving counter was at one end next to a raised platform with a piano on it. The room was not particularly full, and Tip and Doll seemed to know everyone. Frank was all eyes and ears. This was the high life indeed!

"You standin' a top o' reeb [*pot of beer*], Al?"

"Sey [*yes*], I done a doogheno flash [*good deal*] today. But kool 'im [*look at him*]. Who's he?"

"My wen dal [*new lad*] Give 'im some reeb an' rater" [*beer and water*].

Frank took his beer and sipped it, puzzled. Conversation continued.

"Jack, 'e 'ad a regular tosseno tol [*bad luck*]. 'Ad a showful [*bad money*]. Bigger loof [*fool*] 'im."

"He musta bin flash karnurd [*half drunk*] at ve time."

"On [*no*], just a dabeno [*bad debt*]."

Costers in those days spoke to each other almost entirely in back slang, incomprehensible to an outsider. This continued until well after the Second World War.

Frank's eyes rested on each of these big, confident men as he spoke, but none was as flamboyant or assured as Tip, and the seeds of hero-worship were sown in this young heart.

He drank his beer. No one seemed to notice him. He was hungry, and Doll, who was flirting with a man sporting a walrus moustache, appeared to have forgotten the pie she had promised him.

The beer shop filled up, cards were brought out and men sat

down to the serious business of gambling. A group of boys in a corner were engaged in the equally serious business of 'three ups'. A piano player started a tune, and everyone sang along, getting louder and louder at each chorus. A girl leaped onto the stage and started dancing with more energy and vigour than grace, accompanied by shouts and catcalls from the audience. The beer flowed and the laughter swelled. Exhausted, Frank fell asleep on the floor.

He was awakened by Doll, screaming, "Oh, the poor li'l nipper. 'Ere, Tip, you'll 'ave to carry 'im."

"Take me for a monkey?" said Tip, scornfully. He shook Frank hard and pulled him to his feet.

"Come on, there's a day's work ahead."

Doll was the worse for wear and hung onto Tip's arm as they walked through the streets. Frank, more asleep than awake, kept close behind them. They climbed the endless steps to the fourth floor, and a straw mattress and a blanket were pulled out from behind the big feather bed and put on the floor under the table for Frank, who was only too thankful to lie down anywhere. He went to sleep to the comforting and familiar sounds of grunting and puffing and rhythmic bed rocking.

Frank was awakened by a flannel soaked in cold water being thrown on his face. He leaped up and banged his head on the table. Stunned, he gasped: "What's up? Where am I?"

Tip spoke. But it was a very different Tip from the evening before. Gone the flashy clothes, gone the easy swagger and pleasant bonhomie. The morning revealed Tip the coster, Tip the businessman, Tip of the calculating, clever, ruthless eye for a bargain. "Out o' bed, sharp now. There's work 'a be done. Billingsgate opens at four, and it's three o'clock, an' we've gotta get the barrow an' the gear, an' be there. Get some clothes on, an' follow me."

Tip was already in his work trousers and was pulling on his heavy boots. Frank felt the urgency and leaped out of bed. He was still dressed from the night before and had only to find his boots. He pulled them on hastily and stood up straight.

"Good. Now take vat bag, an' we're off."

Out in the night air, Tip was electric with energy. He kept doing little runs and skips and punching the air with his fists. He gave several short, barking shouts, took in great lungfuls of air and blew it out noisily. He was working himself up to a fever pitch, and Frank caught the energy. He sensed that something significant was happening, and he ran along the dark, quiet street, alive to everything, tingling with anticipation.

They went to a tunnel under a bridge. Other men were there already and each man had a boy. They greeted each other in their own lingo. A door was opened, revealing a pitch-black cavern, and a naptha flare was lit with a match. The flame leaped up, revealing a stack of barrows, trucks, handcarts, donkey carts, bridles, hooks, chains, ropes, tarpaulins – a medley of wood and metal.

Tip growled to Frank, "Watch wot I takes, and be sure you remembers it. If you don't ge' the right gear, you can't do yer job, an' the tally bloke there, he'll cheat you if 'e can."

He selected what would be needed for the day, and paid the rental to the man with the flare. "Push this 'ere, an' let's get goin'."

A boy called out, "Hey, yennun – you."

Frank took no notice.

The boy kicked him hard. "Don't you answer ven, yennun?"

Tip explained. "He means 'new one'. That's you, see? Take no notice, we got work 'a do. You'll pick up ve lingo in no time."

In pain, and limping, Frank pushed the barrow. He had learned to hide all signs of weakness in the workhouse and it had stood him in good stead.

"Now, we mus' get a move on." Tip leaned his weight on the barrow and it sped over the cobbles, rattling on solid, iron-framed wheels.

Billingsgate was London's fish market, and lay on the north

bank of the Thames, east of the Monument. Fishing boats came in throughout the night and the market stalls, laden with fresh fish, were ready for business when the market opened at 4 a.m.

Tip's electric excitement is, if anything, intensified and every nerve in his body seems to be quivering. A fishy, seaweedy smell hits his nostrils, and he inhales deeply. "Beautiful, be-ooootiful," he murmurs appreciatively.

The noise all around is intense. Above the babble of voices Frank can hear the shouts of salesmen, standing on boxes or tables, roaring out their merchandise and their prices. A Babel of competition.

"'Andsome cod, best in the market – all alive."

"Fine Yarmouth bloaters – oo's the buyer?"

"Eels O! Eels O! Alive O!"

"Wink, wink, winkles, best for tea."

"'Ere you are, guvner, fine brill, come an' look at 'em, guv. You won't find better."

"Over 'ere. Finney 'addock. 'Ad – 'ad – 'ad – 'addy 'addock.

"Now or never – whelks, whelks, whelks, I say."

On all sides everyone is asking "What's the price?" whilst shouts of laughter from salesmen and customers, bargaining and bantering, pepper the noise of the crowd.

Frank can see, in the semi-darkness of the sheds, the white bellies of turbot shining like mother-of-pearl; living lobsters, their claws flailing helplessly in the air; mounds of herrings with scales glittering like sequins; huge baskets piled with grey oysters, blue mussels, pink shrimps, sackfuls of whelks, their yellow shells piled up high; buckets of grey-and-white eels slithering and sliding all over each other.

Frank sees porters in strangely shaped leather helmets, rather like squashed pagodas, carrying fish baskets on their heads. Eight hundred tons of fish pour in and out of Billingsgate every day and all of it, down to the last herring, is unloaded and portered in this way. A man whose neck is 'set' can carry sixteen baskets, each weighing a stone, on his head. These powerful men are the backbone of the fish market, and their history is one of high romance. The quinquereme of Nineveh, laden with spices and precious oils, was unloaded in exactly the same way in medieval London. Caesar's galleys, rowed up the Thames by chained men, were berthed here, London's most ancient port, and unloaded by men such as Frank sees.

Frank flattens himself against a wall as one of these giants passes, shouting: "Move over – make way, please – gangway."

A thin man, trembling under the weight of his load, mutters, through clenched teeth: "Shove to one side, can' choo?"

Everywhere ragged, desperate-looking men and boys are clamouring for the job of porterage, hoping to earn a shilling or two before the day's end.

Through the arches of the open end of the huge covered building, silhouetted against the grey sky of dawn, Frank can see the masts and tangled rigging of the oyster boats and lobster trawlers. Sails, black against the skyline, shift and tremble. He sees the red caps of sailors as they draw in the sails. He hears the chug-chug of primitive engines as a throttle is opened. He hears the shouts of men as they unload their vessels.

"Keep close beside me," Tip growls, "an' listen to everyfink. Don't miss nuffink, see? You gotta learn how to buy."

He assumes a nonchalant air and saunters down the gangway, whistling as though he were on holiday. He passes through the arches onto the quayside, where the river glides black and secretive, and silver threads of light pierce the wakening sky. They clamber over ropes and rigging to the long row of oyster boats moored close along the wharf – known as "Oyster Street" in the trade – where the fishermen sell direct from their boats.

"No middlemen here. Best prices," hisses Tip out of the corner of his mouth.

Each boat has its blackboard and the master, in his white apron, walks up and down calling his prices. The holds are filled with oysters and sand, which a man turns over with a spade, rattling the masses of shells.

Tip discusses price with the master, shakes his head and walks away, saying loudly to Frank, "I knows of better oysters dahn ve sewers."

The oyster merchant shouts after him. Tip ignores the shouts, and clambers over shrimp nets and weights to reach a fisherwoman, with huge muscular arms, shouting the price of shrimps. The master of the vessel is behind her, filling a jug with shrimps and letting them fall back like a shower of confectionery. Tip breaks the head off one, and sniffs it.

"I wouldn't give that to my dog," he says and hands it to Frank, who doesn't know what to do with it.

Clambering over ropes, rigging, sails, cans of engine oil, netting, lobster pots, gangplanks, ladders, baskets, trays – all littered over the quayside in a seeming mass of confusion, Tip and Frank scramble the whole length of Oyster Street. Nothing is bought.

Six o'clock is approaching. Tip snaps into action, his nonchalance leaving him as fast as he had assumed it. He returns to the fisherwoman, and buys shrimps at half her asking price, oysters for a third. Brill and dab he buys, which he had earlier disdained as "poison", with a bucket of eels added, "to clear 'em".

Buying is over and the excitement has passed.

Tip hired a porter – a starved-looking man of sixty – and refused to pay the sixpence the man asked.

"Three pence, then," said the man, humbly.

"I'll gi' yer tuppence, take it or leave it. I can soon find another, stronger'n you, you miserable ol' skele'on."

The man took it, and staggered out of the gate to where Tip and Frank had left the barrow.

"An' now for breakfuss," said Tip.

A COSTER LAD

The woods are lovely and dark and deep,
But I have promises to keep,
And miles to go before I sleep.
Robert Frost

"Betty, my dear, I say, Betty, why you look charming' this mornin'. I'll draw up my chair here an' get close in by this nice, invitin' fire. An' you, Betty my love, can 'ave the infinite pleasure of supplyin' me with some good 'am an' heggs an', if you got some nice 'ot muffins an' butter, I'll 'ave 'em an' all, an' some of yer best Rosie Lee, good an' strong. Betty, my love – why you do look ravishin' this fine morning – you can look after vis young lad, like wot he was your own son. Bring him the same, cause 'e's new, an' there's a hard day's work ahead, an' likewise a man can't go to work on an empty stomick, no more can a boy."

Tip leaned back in his chair, put his feet on the table, and placed his order, with an expansive wave of the hand. Frank sat down to the best breakfast he had ever had in his life. After years of workhouse bread and margarine it tasted like nectar. The muffins oozed butter down his chin as he sank his teeth into them; the yellow yolk of the egg ran over the pink ham and he dipped his bread into it. He ate with concentrated enjoyment. Men and boys came in and sat down. Betty rushed around serving. The fire crackled and tobacco smoke filled the air. Voices merged into a quiet hum, and Frank fell asleep, his head on the table.

A heavy hand hit his shoulder. "Right now. It's eight o' clock, an' we gotter get a-goin' on the round."

Tip walked swiftly out into the yard and Frank staggered after him, rubbing the sleep from his eyes. They arranged the cart together, Tip instructing every move, securing the sides, the shafts, the step, placing the trays, the weights and measures, the knives, bags and torn newspapers. At each move, he would say: "Now don't forget this one."

They started the round. If Frank thought that life in the workhouse was hard, that was because he had not experienced life as a coster. From that day on he never stopped working and he never stopped loving every minute of it.

He hollered his way down the streets, bawling out the day's catch. Shrimps, mackerel, herrings, whelks – his high-pitched voice carried from one end of a street to the other. He learned quickly, and within a month he could gut a fish so fast you wouldn't see him do it. He charmed the ladies with his appealing eyes, so that they bought things they didn't want. He flicked a mussel from its shell with a twist of the knife, faster even than Tip. He could worm a whelk before it knew what had hit it.

The round was about ten miles' walking distance. Tip usually closed the barrow at about three o'clock in the afternoon. Anything left over was Frank's to sell. A tray was suspended round his neck and he went out alone. Tip would size up the value of the fish on the tray and say what he wanted Frank to get for it. Anything over that amount was commonly known as a "bunt", or "bunce", and the boy could keep the money. This was regarded as a coster boy's pay, because they received no wages for their work, food and lodgings being regarded as quite sufficient recompense for a day's labour.

Frank quickly discovered that this was to be the hardest part of his day's work. The tray was heavy and his legs soon felt heavy too. Buying was mostly over for the day, and customers were few, so they had to be first attracted, and then persuaded to buy. The fish was getting stale and nothing can disguise the smell or look of stale fish, especially in summer. Frank often had to trudge several miles before he had sold his stock and gained the money Tip demanded for it. Frequently there was nothing at all left over for his bunt. But on other occasions there was, and Frank was ecstatic at having earned himself sixpence or a shilling – a fortune for a boy who had never had anything of his own. To earn his bunt became his main aim, and often he did not return to the lodgings before nine or ten in the evening. He would then crawl under the table, dog-tired, and sleep until 3 a.m., when he was wakened to go to the market.

Frank picked up the lingo within a few weeks, and was soon talking fast and confidently in the incomprehensible jargon costers proudly shared. He assumed the devil-may-care swagger of the other coster lads. He copied Tip's easy-going banter with the ladies. He also copied Tip's flamboyant style of dress, achieved with a few cut-downs from the master-dresser and a few bits such as a neckerchief and shoelaces which he had bought himself with his bunts. His ambition in life was to buy himself a flashy cap.

He adopted the costers' attitude to money: "Spend it while you've got it, tomorrow you may die." He saw that costers worked very hard and that a good trader earned a lot of money. He saw this money being thrown around each evening in the pubs and taverns with extravagant ease. Any man who had had a good day wouldn't hesitate to spend his entire profit on drinks for his mates. If he'd had a bad day, another coster would buy for him. If any coster was in hard street, or was turned in by the police, there would be an immediate whip-round for him. No coster saved a penny, not even a halfpenny, for the future.

Costers didn't live in homes; they lived in lodgings, where they dossed down for a bit, and then moved on. The lodgings were always unspeakably squalid and cheerless, because costers and their women were hardly ever in them. Life was lived in the streets, the markets, the pubs, the penny hops, the penny gaffs, at the race tracks and in the bawdy houses. Life, with all its richness, was lived outside. Costers went back to their lodgings only for a few hours' kip, before the next day dawned and the markets opened.

Above all, Frank learned the trade. Unless he had been trained from boyhood, no man had the slightest chance of becoming a successful coster. The tricks and dodges, the graft and guile, were just as important to learn as the skills of buying and bartering. Frank learned all this lore from the other coster lads as they went around in the early evenings, selling off the day's 'left-overs' and trying to earn an honest bunt. He learned to cover his fish with parsley, to keep it smelling nice. He learned to squeeze a lemon over it, to improve the taste. He added a few nuts to his store, to increase his range. He learned to sell four pints of whelks as five, by taking a bit off the top of each. He learned where he could sell fish heads and tails, and the best times to find the buyer. He learned to mix dead eels with live ones to increase his stock by five to one, and "they don't notice one's dead until vey gets vem 'ome". He made the acquaintance of an unscrupulous pieman who would take eels that had been dead for two days for ready money. He learned that herring and mackerel look fresher by candlelight, so he carried a candle stuck in a turnip for dark evenings. He learned to wheedle and whine, saying his master would knock him about if he didn't sell his wares. He always sold.

By the age of twelve, Frank was as sharp as a terrier. He was up to every dodge in the business, and there were some who said he was as clever a man as Tip. He spent long hours in the markets, he knew the price of everything and forgot nothing. An expert in slang, he conducted all his business in the lingo. He could chaff a peeler so uncommon curious that the only way to stop him was to let him off. He was a master of his trade.

At the age of thirteen Frank decided it was time to go it alone. He wasn't going to give the best years of his life to a master, not he. He'd be his own master, do his own buyin' and sellin', and keep his own profits He'd show them how it was done.

He left Tip and Doll and moved into a common lodging house for men – the back room of a public bar that was open only to the water's edge. The floor was rough stone, the ceiling and walls unplastered. For twopence a night he could hire a straw mattress and a blanket on the floor. Any other lodgings would cost him tenpence a night. So Frank took it, reckoning that he would hardly be there anyway, and why waste good money on a place he only slept in?

The men were rough, obscene, vicious, and put the fear of God into the lad, but he was growing fast, was quick on his feet and good with his fists. He coped, but only just. His greatest terror was of being robbed. He had seen it happen more than once. A sobbing lad of about twelve stuck in his mind. The boy had been skinny and pale and had lost all his stock money overnight. If a lad can't buy, he can't sell. Frank gave him a shilling to buy some walnuts for the theatre trade, and learned to keep his stock money safe. He kept it in his socks and slept each night with his socks and boots on, and the boots tightly laced.

Most of the men in the lodging house were casual labourers, picking up a day's work if and when they could. All were unskilled. Frank considered himself an aristocrat, being skilled in the fish trade. He hired his own gear, bought his own stock, and sold in the streets, keeping all his profits which he spent on flashy clothes, fancy food, beer, girls, the penny hops, the penny gaffs and gambling ... gambling.

By the age of fourteen, it would be safe to say Frank was a desperate gambler. All the coster men and boys gambled, but none more seriously than Frank. The love of the game was first in his thoughts and dreams, and not a spare moment would pass but he would toss a coin and invite a bet on it. He did not care what he played for, or who he played with, as long as he had a chance of winning. Every day he worked untiringly, spurred on by the thought of the money he would earn, which he could lay against the odds with the next gamester he met. Many a time he lost not only his money but his neckerchief and jacket as well, but nothing could dampen his ardour for the game, a run of continual bad luck making him more reckless than ever.

The coster boys would meet at various points to pitch against each other. They met under railway arches, in pub yards, on the quayside of the river, or even on the shingle when the tide was out. If ever a group of boys' backs and heads were seen crouching in a circle, it would be safe to say that it was a group of gamblers, and ten to one Frank would be in the middle, calling the loudest, the quickest, the fiercest.

"Sixpence on Tol."
  "Sixpence he loses."
  "Done."
  "Give 'im a gen [*shilling*]."
  "Flash it them [*show it*]."
Tol wins and the loser bears his losses with a rueful grin.
Now Frank goes into the ring and takes up a stance to toss his coins. His face is scornful.
  "Sixpence on Frank."
  "A gen he loses."
  "I take that one."
  "Owl [*two shillings*] on Frank."
  "Kool Tol, he's fritted [*Look at Tol, he's afraid*]. Done."
Frank is cool and determined. He plays three up, and calls "Tails." The three coins fall, all tails up. Frank takes his winnings.
Betting starts again. Tol throws, calling "Heads." The coins fall, one head, and two tails. He throws again. The coins fall, showing three tails. Frank takes his winnings. Tol curses and spits, and throws again. "Heads." Again they come down tails. Frank wins. He stares hard at Tol.
  "An half-couter [*half sovereign*] next throw."
A gasp goes up from the onlookers, and they bet among themselves for or against Frank.
  "Done," says Tol defiantly.
Frank tosses. "Heads," he calls. The three coins fall, all heads up.
  "You stinking fish," screams Tol, and pledges his jacket and his boots to honour the debt. He is getting aggressive, and the crowd presses closer. Tol jerks his elbow savagely. "I wish to Christ you'd stand back." Tol's lips are pressed together, his eyes anxious and watchful.

The tense atmosphere has attracted men to the scene, who start their own betting on the two gamesters.

Tol adopts new tactics to bring back his luck. He pushes aside the onlookers and shifts his position a quarter-circle to the right before throwing.

"I'll have it off you. A half-couter," he cries with bravado, knowing full well that he is pledging half his stock money.

"Done," says Frank, confidently.

Betting amongst the onlookers continues and Frank and Tol know that sovereigns are being placed on one or other of them.

Tol spits on the coins, then takes a halfpenny and tosses it on his hand to see what he should call. He then spits again on the three coins and shifts his feet defiantly on the cobbles. He tosses his three coins, calling out "Tails." The coins fall, all tails up. His features relax, and he looks round the circle with a triumphant grin. He puts on his jacket and boots with a triumphant air. Money changes hands among the spectators.

That throw marks the end of Frank's luck for the day. He tosses again and again and, four times out of five, loses. He can hear the bets of the men going against him, and grinds his teeth in fury. If it were an accepted part of gambling to murder your opponent, he would do so. Tol calls again and again. Every time Frank accepts and challenges in return. He loses all his winnings, all his earnings, his neckerchief, his jacket, he even pledges his magnificent velvet cap, vowing it will bring him luck. It doesn't, and he loses it.

With the cap in his hands, Tol stands up. He casts a contemptuous look at Frank, spits on the cap and throws it in the river.

"I'm off now to get a liner [*dinner*]."

He swaggers away to the admiring gasps of the boys and the amused shrugs of the men.

Seething with fury Frank vows revenge. "You wait, you scab, I'll 'ave you to rights. I'll muck you, you scurf, you," he screams.

The men laugh and saunter off. The boys lose interest. A new game starts.

Frank tried to strike a jaunty pose as he stood up, but with no jacket, no neckerchief and no cap, he didn't feel like the cold, calculating gamester any more. He turned quickly and walked in the opposite direction from Tol.

He walked for hours, not feeling the keen wind blowing off the Thames, his mind full of the next game, when he would get even. He'd show 'em. He'd 'ave the houses [*trousers*] off that lousy skunk. He'd get 'is money back, an' more. Hatred filled his heart when he remembered the insult to himself and his trade. Being called a stinking fish was more than a man could stand. He'd get even. His luck'd be back next week. Not for an instant did it occur to him that he had been a fool. The passion for gambling had him in its obsessive grip.

In anger and resentment Frank trudged on, unaware of his surroundings, hating everyone, scowling at those who passed. Ahead of him was a two-bit jerk of a little nipper in baggy trousers, and shoes down on the uppers, leading a little girl, not yet out of nappies, by the hand. He hated them both. The little girl was laughing as she toddled along on unsteady legs. Suddenly she fell and let out an exaggerated howl of pain. The boy bent down and helped her up. He wiped her eyes with his sleeve, and rubbed her knees, spitting on his fingers in order to clean them. He laughed and said: "All better now," but the little girl wouldn't be consoled. She rested her blonde head on his shoulder and put her arms around his neck. He picked her up and carried her into a court, and Frank saw them no more.

Life turns on little things. The momentous events in history can leave us untouched, while small events may shape our destinies.

Frank stood quite still in the street, suddenly feeling cold. The heat of revenge left him, and a cold uncertainty entered his heart. He shivered and leaned against the wall, feeling unexpectedly dizzy. What was it? Everything seemed so cloudy, so misty. What could it be? He didn't seem to be real any more. He touched his face and felt tiny soft arms around his neck. He breathed in and could smell the lovely scent of a baby's hair. Stunned, he wanted to run after the boy and the little girl, to find out who they were. But they had gone. Had he really seen them – a boy in baggy trousers and a tiny girl with blonde hair – or were they ghosts? He shivered and rubbed his eyes, trying desperately to recall something. But the mists of forgetfulness swirled around, and he could not remember what it was.

He made his way back to the lodging house, his mind in turmoil. He was Frank the coster; Frank the rising man; Frank the desperate gambler, feared by all. What did those kids in baggy trousers and nappies mean to him? Nothing! He tried to shake off the image. All right, he had a sister and she was in the workhouse. So what? That wasn't his fault, was it? Let her look after herself, like he'd done. Anyway, he hadn't thought of her for years, and, likely as not, she'd forgotten all about him. He hadn't asked his father and mother to die, that was their lookout, he'd got on all right without them. He shook off the thought of the boy and girl, and whistled his way back to his lodgings. He'd had nothing to eat all day, because he had lost his money, but he wrapped himself up in his blanket in defiance of hunger, and lay down on his palliasse. Sleep evaded him, however.

He heard the other men coming into the lodging room. He heard their cursing and swearing, their belching and farting, and he hated them. How could they be like that? A ghost of a man crept up to his bed, a big man who was strong and gentle. This man looked after his wife, who was frail and coughing. The ghost merged into the farmyard sounds and smells of the men around him, and Frank fell into a light sleep. For the first time in years he dreamed of his mother, whom he had loved so passionately. She was leaving him to go to work. With a cry of anguish he sat up in bed. He felt all over the bed for her, but she wasn't there, and then he remembered where he was and wept bitterly. He remembered now that terrible night when she had not returned, and he remembered holding little Peggy in his arms until the next day when they had been taken to the workhouse.

Memories came flooding back as he lay staring into the darkness: the court where they lived, the room they shared, his mother laughing and singing to him, or his mother coughing and his father anxious. The big ghost hovered over the place, but never quite materialised. He remembered the tiny baby, born not much bigger than a teacup. He thought of the times they had washed her, he and his mother, and put baby clothes on the little creature that were far too big for her. He remembered his mother feeding her, and he wept afresh at this strange and beautiful memory. He buried his face in the straw palliasse, as he had done so often in the workhouse, to muffle the sounds of his sobs. The ghost came nearer and seemed to want to speak to him but did not.

Frank woke at the sound of the other costers getting ready to go to market. What a crazy night! What had been going on? This was the real world. He threw a boot at his mate, and asked him for the loan of some stock money for the day. He knew that costers always helped each other out when one of them hit hard times.

At Billingsgate he was the cool, hard, professional buyer again. His eyes never missed a trick. His ears didn't miss a sound. He hollered his way through his round with double the usual energy and was sold out by 2 p.m. He found his mate to repay the loan. It was a point of honour for costers to repay a debt.

He counted his earnings. There was enough for stock money for tomorrow, and a tightener [*dinner*] today. He went to Betty's and ordered the best Kate and Sidney [*steak and kidney*], with spuds and two doorsteps [*thick lumps of bread*], followed by spotted dick [*currant pudding*] and custard, and a pint o' reeb [*beer*]. No. He thought again. Make that two pints o' reeb.

That's what a man needed inside im, some good grub. He hadn't eaten since breakfast yesterday, what with the game, and queer goings on. No wonder he'd felt funny. A man couldn't keep goin' without a good lining to his stomach. He sat down with his back to the door. Betty brought his food and pinched his ear, but somehow he didn't feel like responding and she retired, offended.

A big man came in. He had hired a boy to hold the bridle of his horse, and called out to the boy as he entered, "You look after her, lad, while I'm away."

Frank heard the words, and the ghost came back and sat down beside him. He remembered, at first dimly, and then as clearly as though it were yesterday, that he had promised his father that he, Frank, would look after his mother and his sister. The spotted dick nearly choked him, and he could eat no more. Did Betty hear him mutter, "I'm sorry, Dad, I'm sorry," as he glanced sideways, or was she imagining it? She certainly saw him brush a tear from his eye with his sleeve, and said to Marge, the cook, in her motherly way, "Vere's somefink up with vat young 'un. Can't eat 'is spotted dick, an' all. Sumfing's up, I tells yer."

Frank sat at the table for a long time, unable to move. The ghost left him, but the memories remained. His mother was dead but his sister, as far as he knew, was alive and in the workhouse. He thumped his fists on the table and dug his nails into his hands as he remembered the tyranny and cruelties he had endured. He prayed that it had not been as bad for his sister in the girls' section. Perhaps they were kinder to girls. He remembered the time they had spent together in the infants' section, and carrying her to his bed when she cried at night. He recalled fighting a bully who had called her "baldy", and he grinned with satisfaction. He remembered a little girl called Jane, who was a friend to them both, and he prayed that Jane had looked after Peggy when he had been transferred to the boys' section. He had never prayed before, but now he did so, and he vowed to heaven, his teeth and fists clenched, that if his sister was still alive he would find her and get her out of the workhouse. He would look after her as he had promised his father.

Betty came over, concerned, and cleared the table.

"How about a nice cup o' Rosie Lee, luv, good an' sweet? On the 'ouse, o' course."

PEGGY

Frank found himself in the workhouse once more. This time he was waiting in the Master's office. He had smartened himself up, as best he could in a communal lodging house, and was waiting with dread in his heart. Was she still alive? Children died in workhouses. He had seen it himself, and had heard stories from people he had met. If Peggy had died, he'd kill those responsible and swing for it. Footsteps came along the corridor, and he stood up.

Frank's first surprise at meeting the Master after nearly four years was how little he was! He had a childhood memory of a large, terrifying man, whose word was absolute law and who had the power to beat and flog for the slightest misdemeanour. Yet here was this flabby little man, about a head shorter than Frank himself, who looked as if he hadn't the strength to lift a bit of cod off a plate, never mind a box of them off a slippery quayside. Frank looked at his puny muscles and compared them in his mind with the lean and muscular men he had worked with for years, and nearly laughed out loud. Was this the terror of the workhouse, this pathetic-looking jellyfish?

But he had come for a purpose, and must be polite. He enquired about his sister: was she still alive? Yes, the Master replied, without giving anything away, she was. Frank gave a huge, shuddering sigh of relief. Where was she, then? The Master replied, guardedly, that she was in the girls' section, where she was well cared for. Frank's joy was unconfined. Here, in this very building? Could he see her, then? His eyes were eager. The Master was prim. No. Boys were not allowed in the girls' section.

Frank was nonplussed. "But I can't help bein' a boy," he blurted out. "If I was 'er big sister you'd let me see 'er, wouldn't you?"

The Master smiled, and agreed, but rules were rules, he said, with such finality that the interview ended.

Frank's joy at knowing she was alive was greater than his disappointment at not being allowed to see her. But he would see her – damn the Master – and he changed his round so that he would be near the workhouse gate at 4 p.m. when the girls returned from school. He hung around, shouting "whelks and eels" as the crocodile of girls marched past him. But he couldn't pick her out. There were a couple of dozen little girls with blonde hair, about the age that she would be, but even though he went every day for a fortnight and looked carefully at them, he couldn't recognise his sister. Several of the bigger girls giggled and nudged each other, winking at him as they marched past. Normally he would have flirted back, but he had no heart for flirting now. He changed his round again.

He sought another interview with the Master. On this occasion he had carefully prepared his questions. If he couldn't see his sister because of the rules, what were the rules about taking her away altogether? The Master was surprised at the boy's persistence and explained, condescendingly, that any relative could apply for the discharge of an inmate and, provided the applicant could prove that he could provide adequately for said inmate, the application would be considered favourably.

Frank's quick brain translated. "You means, if I can support my sister, I can get her out of 'ere?"

The Master nodded.

"An' what would you means by 'support'?"

The Master looked at the eager fourteen-year-old sitting before him, and smiled at the impossibility of his hopes. "I would say, firstly, that the applicant must be of good character and must have decent accommodation. He must prove himself able to support the inmate for whose discharge he is applying, and should have a reasonable sum of money saved against illness or loss of work."

"An' 'ow much would you call a 'reasonable sum'?"

The Master tapped his pencil, and smiled archly.

"Oh, I would say twenty-five pounds. That is a fair sum."

Frank swallowed. Twenty-five pounds! Ask a working boy today to save £25,000 and he might swallow and turn pale, just as Frank did.

The Master concluded the interview and assumed that he would see no more of the boy.

Frank dragged his feet miserably back to the lodging house. The obstacles seemed insurmountable. Why couldn't he just take her? When he entered the squalid doss-house, in which about twenty men slept and ate, he realised the Master was right. He couldn't possibly bring a girl here. He would have to be able to provide for her and find somewhere decent to live.

Frank then worked as he had never worked before, spurred on by necessity. He did his fish round, as ever, but instead of knocking off when he had sold it all, he looked into the fruit-and-nut trade, and hawked them around the pubs and theatres and music halls until ten or eleven at night. He doubled his income. He changed his habits and became something of an outcast from his old mates, because he never gambled, never flashed his money around by joining them in the tavern. They resented it and ridiculed him. He opened a Post Office National Savings Account. No coster ever saved. Conspicuous spending each evening in the pubs and taverns was their habit. But Frank wasn't interested in what the others did. He had opened the account because he knew that in a communal lodging house he would eventually be robbed. When he learned that he would earn four per cent on his investments he was thrilled and carefully worked out how many pennies that would be to every pound saved. By the age of fifteen he had saved eight pounds.

There is no doubt about it, Frank was a brilliant and imaginative coster. He went into the fried-fish market, arranging for the fish to be cooked at a baker's and employing a lad to hawk it around at a fixed rate, plus the bunting system. He looked into the roast-chestnut market and worked out that the hire of the gear would pay for itself around Christmas time. He was right.

By the age of sixteen he had twenty-five pounds in his Post Office account.

He then looked round for a room to rent for himself and Peggy. It had to be a decent room – on that point he was determined. His sister was not going to be dumped in any old hole. She would be twelve years old now, quite the young lady. He had not seen her since she was little more than a baby, but he visualised her as petite and pretty, and felt sure she looked like his mother. Mother and sister merged into each other in his imagination, a numinous female ideal, the guardians of his hopes and longings.

He found a room on the top floor of a house at eight shillings a week, plus two shillings for the rent of furniture. It was an upper-class house, he felt. There was a gas stove on the middle landing for everybody's use, and a tap in the basement, There was even a lavatory in the yard. He was well satisfied.

Frank stood again in the Master's office. He had on his best clothes and his Post Office book was in his pocket. The Master had not expected him, and was astonished when he saw the proof of twenty-five pounds saved in only two years. How had a boy of sixteen achieved it? He looked at him with new respect and said: "Your request will have to be considered by the Board of Guardians. They meet in three weeks' time."

He gave Frank the date and time of the Guardians' meeting and told him to come back on that evening.

Frank asked if he could see his sister, and was told curtly that he would see her in three weeks' time. Seething with frustration, he looked at his powerful fists and nearly knocked the man down. But he remembered he had to be "of good character", so thrust his hands behind his back. He would never get Peggy out if he hit the workhouse master!

The Guardians debated the application. It was unusual, but they agreed to release the girl, if she wished to go with her brother. Frank was called into the boardroom and interrogated.

They seemed satisfied and were especially impressed by the Post Office book. They told him to stand by the window, and Peggy was called away from her evening duties.

Peggy was in the washhouse, helping to prepare the younger girls for bed. It was a duty she loved – better than scrubbing the greasy old kitchen floors, or putting out smelly dustbins. She could play with the little girls, and there was always laughter when Peggy was putting them to bed. They had to laugh quietly, so as not to get into trouble, but, somehow, a bar of soap slithering across a stone floor seemed even funnier if you had to stuff a towel into your mouth to stop shrieks of laughter. Suppressed giggles double the fun for young girls.

Peggy was flushed with the steam and the laughter. Her blonde hair was damp and the wispy bits around her forehead curled upwards. Her apron was wet, and her arms soapy.

An officer came in. "The Guardians want to see you. Come with me."

She didn't know what the summons meant and had no time to feel alarm. She was shown into the big boardroom, where a group of gentlemen sat around an oval table.

Frank, standing inconspicuously by the window, watched her every step. She was taller than he had expected. He had imagined a tiny creature, because he remembered a tiny baby. But this was a grown girl in early puberty. He liked her dishevelled hair and laughing features, still damp from the washhouse. He saw, with a stab of pity, the fear and uncertainty as she stepped towards the oval table.

The Chairman said, not unkindly, "Your brother has made an application to remove you from the workhouse."

"My brother?" Peggy looked bewildered.

"Yes, you have a brother. Didn't you know?"

She shook her head. The anguish inside Frank made his legs turn to jelly. He leaned against the wall.

"Well, you have, and he asks permission to take you out of our care and to look after you himself. Do you wish to go with him, or do you prefer to stay here with your friends?"

Peggy didn't say anything, and a member of the Board said sharply, "Speak up, child, and answer the Chairman when he is good enough to speak to you."

Peggy's lip trembled and she began to cry, but still she said nothing. Frank's anguish had turned to dread. What if she did not want to come? It was a possibility he had not even considered.

The Chairman, who was kindly, with daughters of his own, said gently, pointing to Frank: "This is your brother Frank. It is to be regretted that you have not seen him since you were three years old, but now he has applied for your discharge and we, your guardians, are satisfied that he can provide for you. Do you wish to go with him?"

Peggy looked over towards the window, and saw a tall stranger. He did not mean a thing to her. Insecure children are terrified of change. She thought of the happy laughter in the washhouse, and her friends at school and in the dormitory. She stared at this unknown, unknowable young man, and her heart was set on her friends and the routine she had always known.

Frank saw rejection in her eyes and panic spurred his movements. Before she could speak, he stepped swiftly across the room.

"Stay where you are, you have no right—" shouted the Master.

Frank took no notice. He walked straight up to Peggy and stood looking down at her. Everyone in the room was hushed as brother and sister looked at each other for the first time in nine years. Then, slowly, he extended the little finger of his right hand and curled it round the little finger of her right hand. He held it close and grinned. "Hello, Peg."

The action stirred her memory as nothing else could have done. Holding little fingers was a special and intimate gesture from a childhood almost lost to her now. No one else had ever done that to her. She had forgotten all about it, but now she remembered. A dim, far-off memory of loss and longing stirred within her. She looked at this tall lad and the love that she had not known for years flooded her heart.

She squeezed his little finger in return, and smiled a smile of secret understanding. He saw the dimples in her cheeks, and knew that he had seen them before. Then with sudden, impetuous warmth, she threw her arms about his neck and leaned her head on his shoulder. The Guardians watched with breathless wonder. Even the Master was silent. The intoxicating smell of her hair sent a thrill through Frank's tense body and he relaxed, knowing that she was his sister, and that all would be well.

She did not hold him for long, but turned to the Chairman and curtsied. "I will go with my brother, if you please, sir."

Memories of early childhood dwell in a limbo that is neither forgetting, nor quite remembering. As Peggy danced along the pavement, looking up at Frank, she tried desperately to recall him, but could not. She looked up at his face, his hair, his smile, and tried to persuade herself that she knew him and could remember him when they were little, but she had to admit to herself that he was a stranger. Yet somehow he wasn't. His big, rough hand grasping her own felt familiar, his arm round her shoulders as he led her down a dark street was familiar too. Something in his touch struck a chord within her that she knew and responded to.

Frank was jubilant. He felt like a king. None of his mates could have done what he'd done. He had got her out of that place, his little sister, and he would never let her go back. She did not look as he had imagined, but that did not matter; she was better than he had imagined. He greeted several of his friends, who nudged each other and shouted, "Who's yer tart? Where'd 'ja find 'er? Any more like 'er fer us?"

Frank replied, good humouredly, "She's my sister, and there's no one in the whole world like her."

He took her back to the lodgings – in a respectable street, he pointed out. He was proud to show her the facilities of the house.

He led her up to the second floor and showed her the last word in luxury: the gas stove on the landing, where she could cook. They climbed two more flights of wooden stairs, and he proudly flung open the door.

It was a small attic room with a sloping roof and a garret window, in which a broken pane had been patched up with cardboard. The walls were unpainted and bits of plaster were falling off. The ceiling was yellow and stained with damp. The furniture, rented for two shillings a week, consisted of a rough wooden table and chair, a narrow iron bedstead with coarse grey army blankets, a wooden box, a candle stuck in a milk bottle, a jug and washbowl and a chamber pot. It looked fairly bleak, but children like small rooms, and to Peggy it seemed like heaven.

She threw her arms around Frank. "It's lovely, lovely. Are we really going to live here?" Her eyes filled with uncertainty. "Will I have to go back? Don't let me go back. I want to stay here with you." He folded her in his arms and said fiercely, "You'll never go back. Didja hear me? Never. Not as long as I can see to it. We'll be together, always. Vat's a promise, an' all. Now, let's see vat smile o' your'n, so I can see them dimples."

She smiled with trusting confidence, and he put his little fingers into the dimples.

"You'll 'ave to smile a lot more offen, yer know."

He brought in some wood and lit a fire in the narrow grate. Red and yellow flames leaped up, filling the little room with colour. He had bought some muffins and some real butter, and they sat on the floor by the fire, toasting the muffins on the end of a knife. They were so delicious she couldn't stop eating them and the butter ran down her chin. He chuckled and wiped it off with his finger. She took hold of his hand and licked the butter off his finger, looking up at him with melting eyes. A thrill ran through him, and he did not know what to say.

She murmured, "Muffins. Muffins and butter. Better than nasty smelly old bread and margarine. Can I eat muffins for evermore, Frank?"

"Course you can. Thousands of 'em. I'll see to that, you'll see. Muffins every day, if you wants 'em. An' candy, an chocolate, an' cakes an' all."

"And can I have jam and honey and cream?"

"Wha'ever you wants, my li'l sister, you can 'ave. You'll see."

"And pretty dresses?"

"Loads of 'em."

"And a carriage with four horses?"

"Of course. Six 'orses, and a coachman, an' all."

Peggy sighed with happiness. But something inside her stirred, and she clung to him. "But you won't go away? You won't let them take me away from you again, will you?" Her eyes were wide with terror. His eyes were serious and his voice firm. "No one can take you away from me, not no one, never. I've promised, haven't I? We'll be together always."

Satiated with muffins and warmth and the emotion of the day, her eyes began to close. Frank watched her closely, thinking he had never seen such a pretty face. She was so much prettier than the coster girls most of his mates had. They were rough-looking girls with loud voices and dirty hair. He leaned forward and touched her hair. It was like silk, and so fine he had to blow it, just to watch it move. She felt his breath on her face, and opened her eyes.

"Come on, little girl, it's time for you to go to bed."

Frank used the words he had used when he was six and she was two. A distant memory stirred and she giggled, and leaned back against the wall, kicking her heels against the floor.

"Can't make me."

He leaned towards her and took off her boots and socks, saying as he did so, "This little piggy goes to market. This little piggy stays at home."

She caught the rhyme and finished, "And this little piggy goes wee, wee, wee, all the way home. Home, Frank, not the workhouse but home, with you."

He undressed the sleepy young girl just as he had done nearly ten years before. He put her into the bed and she fell asleep straight away, snuggled into the warm blanket that he pulled around her.

He threw another log on the fire. He did not feel sleepy. He felt wide awake, teeming with emotions that tumbled into his conscious and subconscious mind. He had done it! He'd got her out. Out for good an' all. Hadn't that stinking workhouse master sat up when he'd showed him the Post Office book, and told him there were respectable lodgings to take her to? Frank looked proudly round the little room. This was real swell, this was.

He stroked the hair of the sleeping child, and a wave of tenderness swept over him. This was his sister. Was she really like their mother? He couldn't say. Already the shadow of his mother was fading as the reality of Peggy grew more distinct. How soft and pretty girls were. He stroked the smooth white skin of her arm and compared it with his own, all covered with black hairs. He took up her hand, then noticed with fury that it was all red and rough, her nails short and broken, with little cracks at the fingertips. The bastards. They'd got her scrubbing and doing heavy washing already! They'd better not come his way again, or he'd murder them! No – that was too good for them. He'd get the Master and the lousy officers scrubbing the floors themselves. They could scrub for years. That'd learn 'em! He swore angrily to himself, and vowed that Peggy would never have to work so hard again.

He got up and turned the log with his boot. Sparks shot up the chimney and the embers glowed red, making the meagre little attic look cosy. He looked around, and thought of the squalid men's doss-house on the waterfront where he had lodged for two years. Disgusting! Men were always coughin' an' spittin'. Men were always fartin' and belchin' an' swearin'. Always fightin' over nuffink, they were. It wasn't just Peggy who'd been rescued. Rescuing her had rescued him from that lousy, flea-ridden dump, and he was never going back. Never.

He sat down again beside her and listened to her quiet breathing. Men snored! Leastwise, all the men he'd ever known had snored like elephants. Enough to keep a person awake all night. Peggy let out a tiny puff as she moved in her sleep, and he held his breath. Was that how girls snored? The workhouse dormitory with seventy boys and an officer came to his mind, and he shut the thought out quickly. He didn't ever again want to think of it. It was too awful. They were both out now and they'd stay out. They belonged together. His jaw was set with determination as he looked into the future.

She would have to go to school. His sister was going to have a good education and grow up to be a lady. He'd see to it, he would. His sister wasn't going to be a common coster girl, like them poor little kids. Half-starved, half-frozen, unwanted kids, sent out for hours and hours to sell a few lousy apples or rotting pears that no one would buy and then they'd get beaten because they hadn't sold a thing. His sister would be a lady with book-learning and a posh accent.

The log shifted on the fire, and the sound broke his train of thought. Perhaps he'd better get some shut-eye. He'd have to be up at three to go to the market. It was more important than ever that his trading showed a profit. He could think about schools tomorrow. But he didn't want to disturb the magic of the moment. The firelight was fading, but he could see the dark curve of her lashes against her pale skin. He could see the slender white shoulder against the grey blanket. He leaned over and kissed it, very gently, so as not to disturb her. This was the best day of his life.

Quite suddenly he felt really tired. The excitement of the day had caught up with him at last. He pressed the log down into the ashes, undressed, and crept into bed, hoping not to wake her. But the bed was so small that he had to push her over to make room for himself. She sighed, and stretched out a sleep-warmed arm, which, feeling his body, curled around his neck and drew him towards her. She murmured: "Is that Frank? Is that really Frank, my lovely brother? Oh, I love you so much."

He kissed her eyes, her hair, her face, her mouth. He passed his hands down her slender body, and fire ran through him as he felt the circle of her tiny firm breasts and buttocks. She was neither asleep nor awake, but she loved him with all her heart and mind, with all her soul and her body. Their union was as inevitable as it was innocent.

TILL DEATH US DO PART

Peggy was singing her way through her scrubbing and polishing at Nonnatus House. It was always nice to hear her. Sister Julienne casually remarked, "You sound happy. How's Frank these days?"

"Frank? Well, he's had a bit of a stomach ache recently, but a dose of Epsom Salts will soon see that off."

A few weeks later she confided to Sister, "Frank's still got the stomach ache, Sister. Salts don't seem to do him any good. What else can I give him?"

Questioning revealed that Frank's stomach ache had lasted for six weeks. Sister advised seeing the doctor, but Frank would not go to the doctor. Men like Frank never do.

"I've never bin to a sawbones in me life, an' I'm not startin' now. I'll work it off, you'll see."

But he couldn't work it off, and a couple of weeks later he had to shut up his stall in Chrisp Street Market at 11 a.m. leaving half the fish unsold – something unheard of. He took a couple of codeine and slept when he got home, and felt sufficiently well to go to Billingsgate at 4 a.m. the next morning.

"There, I said I'd work it off, didn' I?" he said as he kissed Peggy goodbye.

But some of his mates brought him home at 7 a.m. The pain had got so bad that he couldn't continue. Peggy put him to bed and called the doctor, who examined him and advised hospital. Frank refused. The doctor assured him it would only be for a few days for tests. Peggy insisted and finally Frank acquiesced. Tests revealed the early stages of carcinoma of the pancreas. They were told it was inflammation of the pancreas and radium treatment was advised.

At Nonnatus House Peggy sought reassurance. "It's only

inflammation, and what's the pancreas, anyway? It's only a tiny organ in the body, they tell me; it's not like the liver or the stomach. The radium treatment will get rid of it in no time, I suppose. After all, the pancreas is not much bigger than your appendix, and thousands of people have their appendix out, don't they?"

We reassured her. What else can you do? We did not say that, in those days, no one had ever been known to recover from cancer of the pancreas. Frank was given the choice of hospitalisation for the radium therapy, or an out-patient visit twice a week. He stayed at home. He handed over the lease of his stall to a mate of his for three months, saying he would want it back when he had had a good rest and was better. He told Peggy not to give up any of her work, because he didn't want to be fussed. However, Peggy did give up most of her work, arguing that this would be the only time in their lives when he was not working six days a week, and they could treat it as a holiday. A bit of radium therapy would hardly get in the way and they could go out and about on the other days and have a good time.

However, Peggy continued her work at Nonnatus House. Perhaps she needed the proximity of the Sisters for reassurance and advice. She did not appear anxious, saying things like, "He's getting on nicely now, thank you, Sister," or, "We haven't been out anywhere, really. The radium seems to make him tired, so we stay in, and he likes to hear me reading to him. It's better than going out, we reckon."

One day she said, "He seems to get pain at night, but they've given him some tablets, and that'll do the trick, eh, Sister?" Another time she said, "He's lost a bit of weight. Good thing too, I tell him. 'You were beginning to get quite a paunch on you,' I said, and he laughed and said, 'You're right there, Peg.'"

Within a few weeks we were requested to take Frank for home nursing. Sister Julienne and I went to assess him.

Peggy and Frank lived in a prefab on the Isle of Dogs. These were small, ready-made buildings erected in huge numbers after the war, to house some of the thousands of people whose homes had been destroyed. The prefabs were put up as an emergency measure and intended to last only four to five years, but many of them lasted forty to fifty years. They were very pleasant, cosy and greatly preferred to the terraces that had been destroyed by the bombs. As we approached the prefab estate in the morning sunlight, it looked charming, with the low buildings, leafy trees full of sparrows and the river lapping in the background. It always surprised me that only a short distance from one of the biggest commercial ports in the world such quietness and peace could prevail.

Their tiny garden, about six to ten feet of space all around the house, was well tended, with flowers and cabbages and runner beans growing well. A vine was trained up the south wall and I wondered if they ever got any grapes worth eating. The front door opened straight into the sitting room, which was comfortable and pretty. It was also spotlessly clean. Peggy was obviously very house-proud.

She greeted us with her usual happy smile. "It's good of you to come," she said as she took Sister's cloak and hung it up. "He's in bed at the moment, but he's getting along nicely. He's had two weeks of the radium treatment now and he's getting stronger all the time. He says he'll be back at the market in no time."

We went into the bedroom and I was thankful that Sister Julienne was with me. Had I been alone, my reaction at seeing Frank for the first time in about three months would probably have betrayed my shock. He looked ghastly. He lay in the middle of the big double bed, his eyes sunken, his skin grey. He had lost so much weight that his flesh hung in wrinkles and he had lost most of his hair. I doubt if any of his mates at the market would have recognised him.

Sister went straight up to him, with her gentle warmth. "Hello Frank, how nice to see you again. We miss you at Nonnatus House, and look forward to your return. The other man's good, we've no complaints, but it's not the same as having you."

Frank smiled, and the skin pulled tight across his nose and cheek bones. His eyes, sunk deep into their bony sockets, gleamed with pleasure. "I'll be back right enough, Sister. It's only a few more weeks of this radium, an' I'll be on me feet again."

"Are you sure you won't go into hospital for the remainder of your treatment? It would be more restful, you know. The ambulance journey back and forward can be very tiring, especially after the treatment."

But Frank and Peggy were both adamant that he should remain at home.

Sister examined him. She carefully moved his emaciated body, the arms and legs that seemed to have insufficient muscle to lift their own weight. Was this the man who had lifted a hundredweight box of cod only a few short weeks ago? I went to the other side of the bed and caught in my nostrils the smell of death as I leaned over him.

Strangely enough, Peggy did not seem to notice how desperately ill he was. She seemed perfectly happy, and kept saying things like: "He's getting on fine," "He's getting stronger each day," or, "He ate all the milk pudding I made for him. That shows he's getting well, doesn't it?" I was struck by the fact that we all see what we want to see. Peggy appeared to have closed her mind to the reality of Frank's condition, to the extent that she literally couldn't see it. To her, Frank was exactly the same as he had always been, her brother and her lover. He was the beat of her heart, the blood in her veins, and the physical changes, obvious to anyone else, she just did not see.

It was arranged that I should call for home nursing twice a day, and that Sister would come any time that Peggy requested.

I do not know whether or not Sister Julienne noticed the sleeping arrangements in the little house. The prefabs were constructed in a rectangle with a single large room and two small rooms leading off it. These were intended as bedrooms, but one of the rooms in Frank's house was a dining room, which we could see through the open door. The only room used for sleeping had a double bed in it. If Sister Julienne noticed these things, and put two and two together, at no time did she say so. The Sisters had seen it all before, many, many times. In cramped living conditions, where a family of ten, twelve, fifteen or more lived in one or two rooms, incest was hardly surprising. Families kept their secrets and the Sisters did not comment or judge. I felt that there was nothing in human life that they had not witnessed in the seventy years they had worked in Poplar.

Later Sister said to me, "We will have to keep up this pretence that he is going to get better. The charade has to go on – treatments that will do no good, drugs that are useless – to give, the impression of medical competence and nursing care. 'Hope' lies in those treatments and, without hope for the future, most of our patients would find themselves in torment at the end."

One day when I called they were studying travel brochures received from Thomas Cook. Frank was very alert in his mind. His speech was slower and quieter, but his eyes were bright, and he seemed almost animated.

"Peg an' me, we thinks we'll go to Canada for a good 'oliday when the treatment's done an' I'm on me feet again. She's never bin abroad afore. I was in France and Germany in Hitler's war, an' I never wants 'a go near Europe agen. But Canada, now – big clean open spaces. Look a' this 'ere, nurse. Lovely pictures, aren't they? We reckons Canada's just the place for us, don't we, Peg? Who knows, we might stop there if we likes it enough, eh, Peg?"

She was sitting on the edge of the bed, her eyes glowing with happy anticipation. "We'll go on the Queen Mary," she agreed. "First Class, like a couple of swells."

They both laughed and squeezed hands.

Together Peggy and I helped him to the bathroom. It was difficult, but he still had the strength to get there. She washed him all over, because although he could get into the bath, he did not have the strength to get out. In clean pyjamas he sat in the sitting room looking at the plaster ducks flying across the wall, whilst Peggy and I changed the bed with the text over it, executed in big, childish embroidery stitches, 'God is Love'.

We had taught Peggy many essentials in the art of nursing, such as treating pressure points and dealing with pain or nausea. She was quick to acquire any small skill to make Frank more comfortable. I enquired about appetite, pain, bowels, vomiting, headaches and fluid intake, and left them happy with their plans for Canada. Should it be Vancouver or the Rockies? They couldn't decide.

The air was sweet as I left the little house, and the sounds of the huge cargo vessels, the cranes, the lorries, seemed far off. I thought of the thousands of powerful men working ceaselessly in that great port, and the fragility of life. Health is the greatest of God's gifts, but we take it for granted; yet it hangs on a thread as fine as a spider's web and the tiniest thing can make it snap, leaving the strongest of us helpless in an instant.

Frank received a six-week course of radium therapy and was taken twice a week by ambulance to the hospital. Both he and Peggy expressed wonder and a touching appreciation that all this was free on the new National Health Service. "It's lucky I got ill now, an' not a few years ago. I could never 'ave paid for all this expensive treatment." They seemed completely confident that it would be effective, probably because it was so elaborate. That he was getting weaker every day was put down to the temporary effects of the radium, which would pass when the treatment was completed. Everyone – that is, all the medical and paramedical staff, which must have totalled at least thirty people – kept the illusion going, though there was no corporate decision to do so.

Nausea is an unpleasant side effect of radium treatment and was something that Frank had been warned about in advance. He attributed his weakness and weight loss to the fact that he could not eat much. 'Cos a man's gonna get thin like, if he's not eatin' like what I'm not. Once I get some good grub inside me, an' keep it down, I'll pack the old weight on, you'll see."

Pain was another matter. The control of pain is the first

responsibility of anyone involved in the care of the dying. Pain is a mystery that we cannot fathom, because there is no measure. Everyone's tolerance of pain differs, therefore the correct dose of analgesic will differ. One must balance the strength of analgesic to the level of pain perceived and not allow the pain to develop beyond the patient's tolerance.

Frank was having half a grain of morphine three times a day. Later this was increased to four, then six times daily. It was sufficient to dull his pain to an acceptable level, but did not impair his faculties. He was interested in everything.

He once said: "Every mornin' I hear the fishin' boats come up the river. Can't get out of the 'abit of wakin'. In my mind I can see the sails, dark against the red sun, like wot' they used to be like, comin' quietly out of the morning mist. Boo'iful they was, just boo'iful. You've gotta have seen them sailin' boats to know wot' a lovely sight it was. Now I listen to the sounds of ve engines. I can tell you by ve sound if it's an oyster smack or a mackerel trawler. I can even tell you 'ow many deep-sea vessels from the Atlantic come in. It'll be good to be back at Billingsgate."

Peggy and I agreed that it wouldn't be long. He was getting on famously.

Peggy had given up all work now and never left his side, except for essential household duties. She spent hours reading to him. Frank had never learned to read fluently, and could barely write.

"Book-learnin's never been my strong point – but Peg, she's the scholar. I love to 'ear her read. She's got a lovely voice."

Peggy read about half a dozen of Dickens's novels in this way, sitting close to him, outwardly reading but inwardly attentive to every mood and movement. She was conscious of every shade in her loved one, ready to close the book if she sensed tiredness, or to change his position if she saw discomfort. Peggy knew almost before he knew himself what his needs were going to be.

Love permeated every nook and cranny, every corner and crevice of that little house. You could feel it as soon as you entered the front door, like a presence so tangible you could almost reach out and touch it. If there is one thing that a dying person needs more than relief from pain, it is love. I have seen, later in my career when I was a ward sister at the Marie Curie Hospital in Hampstead, unloved, unwanted people dying alone. Nothing can be more tragic or pitiful. And nothing is more hopeless or intractable for the nursing staff to deal with.

Love prompted Peggy to sing to Frank every evening, the old songs, the folk songs and hymns that they had both learned in childhood. Love prompted her to move the bed so that he could see the masts and funnels of the boats as they approached the docks. Love told her which visitors to admit and which to turn away from their front door. They grew even closer. They had always been one flesh; now they were one spirit, one soul. And all the time she kept up the pretence that he was going to recover. If she cried alone in the kitchen, he never saw it.

It was Frank who first startled me. We had just finished a blanket bath (he no longer had the strength to get to the bathroom) and he had asked Peggy for a hot drink and a hot-water bottle. As soon as he heard the kitchen door close, he said, "Nurse, you must promise me you won't let on to Peggy. It'll break her heart. Promise, now."

I was putting things away in my bag and my back was turned towards him. I didn't move or breathe. I had to respond in some way, but I couldn't find my voice.

"I want you to promise, now."

"What do you mean?" I said, eventually. I had to turn round, and he was looking straight at me, his sunken eyes bright in their dark sockets.

"I mean I'm not gonna get better an' I don't want Peg to know until she has to."

"But Frank, what makes you think you won't recover? The radium treatment ends next week and then you will begin to feel stronger."

I hated myself for this pathetic falsehood. I felt degraded by it. Why do we have to be like this? In India, apparently, a man often predicts his own death, says farewell to his family, goes to a holy place, and dies. Yet we cannot admit to someone that he is dying, so we have to play false, and I have been as big a deceiver as anyone.

He didn't say a word, but closed his heavy eyes. We heard the kitchen door open. He hissed fiercely, "Promise. Promise you won't tell her."

"I promise, Frank," I whispered.

He sighed with relief.

"Thank you." His voice was husky. "Thank you, now I can rest easy."

The radium treatment halted the malignant growth for a while, but could not be continued beyond six weeks, as it would destroy other organs. Frank's deterioration was rapid when treatment stopped. The pain became more intense, and the morphine was increased to one grain, then two grains every four hours. He could barely eat, and Peggy sat beside him feeding semi-solids into his unwilling mouth.

"There, Frank love, just another little spoonful, put some strength into you."

He would nod, and try to swallow. She washed and shaved him, turned him, cleaned his mouth and his eyes. She dealt with his urine and his bowels, and kept him clean and comfortable, all the while humming the songs he liked. He no longer looked at travel brochures, nor had the mental strength or interest to listen to Dickens, but he seemed to like to hear her singing. He rarely spoke and was drifting in and out of consciousness.

Frank was quietly slipping away into that mysterious border land between life and death where peace and rest and gentle sounds are the only needs. One day, in my presence, he gazed at Peggy for a long time as though he did not recognise her and then said, quite clearly: "Peggy, my first love, my only love, always there, always when I need you." He smiled and drifted away again.

More than anything else a dying person needs to have someone with them. This used to be recognised in hospitals, and when I trained, no one ever died alone. However busy the wards, or however short of staff, a nurse was always assigned to sit with a dying person to hold their hand, stroke their forehead, whisper a few words. Peace and quietness, even reverence for the dying, were expected and assured.

I disagree wholly with the notion that there is no point in staying with an unconscious patient because he or she does not know you are there. I am perfectly certain, through years of experience and observation, that unconsciousness, as we define it, is not a state of unknowing. Rather, it is a state of knowing and understanding on a different level that is beyond our immediate experience.

Peggy was aware of this and, in ways that neither she nor anyone could explain, she entered into Frank's mental state in the last few weeks and days of his life.

One day, as I was leaving, she said, "It won't be long now. I shall be glad for us both when it's all over." She did not look unhappy. In fact she looked as serene and as confident as ever. But all pretence was gone.

I asked her, "How long have you known that he was going to die?"

"How long? Well, I can't say exactly. A long time, anyway. From the time the doctor first said he should go into hospital for tests, I suppose."

"So you've known all the time, and never let on?"

She did not reply, but stood on the doorstep, smiling.

"How did you guess?" I asked, intrigued.

"It wasn't a question of guessing. I just knew, quite suddenly, as though someone had told me. I've had so much happiness in life with Frank, more happiness than anyone can expect. We're more than brother and sister, more than husband and wife. How could I fail to know that he was going to die?"

She smiled, and waved to a neighbour who was passing, and

replied to her enquiry, "Yes, he's getting on nicely, thank you; he'll be up and about soon, you'll see."

The last evening of his life came surprisingly quickly. Rash is the professional who will predict death. The young can die while your back is turned, yet the old and frail, who you think will die in the night, live on for weeks.

The late summer evening was beautiful as I approached the prefab estate. Long shafts of sunlight glimmered on the river and made the little buildings glow like pink marble.

Peggy greeted me at the door with the words, "He's changed, nurse. About an hour ago he just changed. Something's different."

She was right. A deep motionless stupor had come over Frank. He did not appear to be in any discomfort or distress. In fact I have never in all my experience known anyone to die in a state of distress. "Death agony" is a common idea, but I have never seen it.

Frank's breathing had changed. It was very slow and deep. I counted the breaths and there were only six per minute. He was slightly blue around the mouth, nose and ears. His eyes were open but unseeing. Peggy took his hand and grasped it firmly. She stroked his forehead with her other hand and leaned over him whispering, "I'm here, Frank. It's all right, my love, I'm here."

He seemed quite unconscious, but I saw his hand move as he gripped hers more firmly. What is this mystery we call the unconscious? I felt sure he knew she was there. Perhaps he could even hear her and understand her words. I felt his nose, his ears, his feet. They were quite cold. I felt his pulse; it was only twenty beats per minute. I whispered, "I'll stay here quietly. I'll sit over by the window."

She nodded. I sat down to contemplate them both. She was completely calm and relaxed. She did not look unhappy or even anxious. Every nerve of her concentration was focused on the dying man. She was with him in death as she had been in life.

His breathing rate dropped to four per minute and the hand

holding Peggy's fell limp. I felt his pulse again, but could not locate it, and when I did it was a feeble eight or ten beats per minute. I sat down again, and Peggy continued to stroke his face and his hands. The clock ticked steadily, and quarter of an hour elapsed. Frank gave a deep, deep breath, which made a rasping sound as it passed through the collapsed throat muscles. A little fluid oozed out of his mouth and trickled down the pillow. His eyes were still open, but a white film was collecting over them.

Peggy whispered, "I think he's gone."

"I think so. But wait quietly for a minute."

She sat unmoving by the inert body for about two minutes. Then, to our surprise, he took another huge, rasping breath. Would there be another? We waited for a full five minutes, but he did not breathe again. There was no pulse or heartbeat.

Spontaneously Peggy said, "Into Thy hands, Oh Lord, I commend his spirit." Then she recited the Lord's Prayer, in which I joined her.

Together we straightened and laid out the dead man's body. We closed his eyes. We could not keep his mouth shut so I tied the chin with a bandage to keep the lower jaw in place. We could take it off when rigor mortis had set in. We had to change the bed linen completely, because at the time of dying his bowels and bladder had emptied.

We washed him all over, and I said, "We will leave him in a shirt, put on back to front. The undertakers will bring a shroud."

She replied, "I've got one. I got it several weeks ago. I couldn't have left him indecent could I?"

She fetched a chair and climbed up to a small cupboard high above the gas meter. There was a box in it from which she extracted a shroud. We put it on him. I asked her if she would like me to contact the undertakers. She thanked me, and said she would be grateful. "But tell them not to come till tomorrow morning, will you, please?"

That was perfectly normal. In those days the deceased often lay in the house for a day or two as a mark of respect for the dead. Family and neighbours would come in to "pay their respects".

Throughout, Peggy was completely calm and tranquil. Her face and voice betrayed no sign of sorrow or loss. In fact I would have said she had an almost ethereal quality about her. I left her with a feeling of admiration.

At the door, she said, "If you see anyone, any neighbours, don't tell them Frank's died, will you? I'll tell them tomorrow. I want to tell them myself."

"Of course not," I reassured her, although I would have to report it at Nonnatus House.

Her anxiety passed.

"That's all right. It's just the neighbours, I don't want them to know yet. They can come tomorrow to pay their respects. But not tonight."

We smiled at each other, and I squeezed her hand. No one would come barging in tonight, not the undertakers, nor the neighbours, nor anyone. She could be alone with her thoughts and her memories. Would she like a couple of sleeping tablets?

She thought for a second. Yes, that would be a very good idea. I opened my bag and handed her a couple of Soneryl.

Peggy shut and locked the door when I left. She sat for many hours on the edge of the bed, unable to take her eyes off Frank, their life together tumbling through her mind. Her happiness had been perfect and complete, she had always known that, and now she was not going to be parted from him.

She pulled up a chair and climbed again to the cupboard above the gas meter and took out two more boxes, one very small, the other larger. She undressed and brushed her hair. She opened the larger of the two boxes and took out a white shroud, which she put on, tying the ribbons carefully at the back. She opened the small box and tipped out fifteen grains of morphine, to which she added the two Soneryl. She took a bottle of brandy and a glass from the bedside cabinet, and swallowed all the tablets in two or three gulps. She continued drinking brandy until she could no longer sit up.

When the undertakers arrived the next morning they could not get in. They broke the window and saw her dead, her arms around her brother.

AND THE MEEK SHALL
INHERIT THE EARTH

The Reverend Thornton Applebee-Thornton had been a missionary in Sierra Leone for twenty-five years. He was enjoying a six-month furlough home in England, which he tried to spend mostly at the Applebee-Thorntons' country house in Herefordshire. This was not always easy, because his father, a widower of ninety who was looked after by two ladies from the village, was a retired Indian Army colonel who had never been able to understand his only son's priestly persuasion. In fact, he despised it, despised his wet and wimpish ways, and secretly felt aggrieved that he should be afflicted with such offspring. His only son, he grumbled to himself, might have had the decency to turn out to be more of a man than that poor thing with his dog collar and his sermons, a missionary pandering to the blasted natives.

"Bah!" he would shout, "kick hell out of the blasted wogs. That's the only way they will respect you. It's the only language they understand."

At which point his reverend son decided that perhaps it was time to visit his cousin Jack at his farm in Dorset; but cousin Jack had just retired to the South of France, leaving his son Courtney in charge of the farm and yes, of course, (the letter read) cousin Thornton would be more than welcome to stay if he could accommodate Fiona's busy programme at the riding school that they had just opened. A week at the farm convinced the Reverend Mr Applebee-Thornton that all this horsey stuff was not for him. Equally, the young couple decided between themselves that the poor old boy was really a frightful bore and they couldn't be expected to introduce him to their circle; perhaps Africa was the best place for him.

So he visited old school friends, and students from his days at theological college. They were delighted to see him, but sadly, after they had exhausted the shared experiences of thirty to forty years ago, found they had little to say to each other.

Perhaps a couple of weeks in Brightlingsea – or did they call it Brighton these days? – would be pleasant. The Metropole was comfortable and he enjoyed the sea breezes, but, as he sat on the front watching life pass by, he was forced to conclude that he had spent so long in Africa and given so much of his mind and energy to the mission that he had lost touch with the changes in England. Expecting the customs and manners, dress and behaviour of the 1920s, he was a little shocked, and more than a little pained by what he saw.

The Reverend Mr Applebee-Thornton was a bachelor – not, he was quick to assure his friends, by choice. He greatly admired, indeed revered, the fair and gentle sex, and would very much have wished the solace and companionship of a loving wife, joined in the felicity of holy matrimony as vouchsafed to his more fortunate friends and colleagues; but the fair ideal had not come his way. The truth is that the reverend gentleman was essentially a one-woman man, and the only woman he had ever fancied was, unfortunately, a nun. He had never spoken to her, beyond the sacramental words: "This is the body of Christ, take this … " as he gave her the consecrated bread; but she was enshrined in his heart and when he was moved to another mission her memory went with him. But that was all a long time ago, he mused, as he watched the boys and girls flaunting themselves half-naked on Brighton beach, and times had changed. Perhaps one was out of touch?

He pulled a letter from his pocket. One of his old friends from theological college was the rector of All Saints', Poplar. The Rector would be delighted to see him, the letter read, and to show him around the parish. Would a couple of weeks be sufficient?

This was how the Reverend Thornton Applebee-Thornton came to be in Poplar at the time of which I write. As the mission in Sierra Leone was planning to introduce a midwifery service, the Rector suggested that his old friend might like to study the work of the Sisters of St Raymund Nonnatus. It seemed like an invitation not to be missed. Accordingly, the Rector contacted Sister Julienne, and arranged that conducted tours of our practice would start the following day, with visits, by arrangement, to some of our patients.

The Reverend Mr Applebee-Thornton came to lunch at Nonnatus House. We were about twelve at table that day. We were accustomed to luncheon visitors, mostly clergymen and sometimes retired missionaries, and it was always a pleasant change. The Reverend was a tall, distinguished man of around fifty. He was good-looking, with fine, slightly sharp features and a sensitive mouth. He had a full head of pure white hair and sun-weathered skin. He was very thin and I thought this was probably due to repeated bouts of dysentery and other intestinal infections. He ate heartily of the lamb stew provided by Mrs B, our cook, complimenting her with loquacious courtesy upon its excellence. He had a deep, kindly voice and kindly eyes that looked at each person around the table with intelligent understanding. If he spoke directly to anyone his attention was so focused, and so penetrating, that he seemed to be able to read the mind and character of the person he was speaking to.

Conversation was general. Sister Julienne asked him to tell us about the mission at Sierra Leone and he expounded on the size of the Christian community, the dire poverty of the natives and the work being done to found schools and hospitals. He spoke with fluency and charm, with not a trace of self-aggrandisement, to which he would have been entitled, having been a pioneer in a challenging and hostile environment.

He was fascinating. We all hung on his words, especially Chummy, our nursing colleague, whose burning ambition – in fact her only reason for training as a nurse – was to be a missionary. Eagerly she asked him about the plans to start a midwifery service, to which he smilingly replied that he hoped she would honour the mission by being their first trained midwife. Chummy's huge shoulders expanded with pride and joy. She closed her eyes and exclaimed, "Oh, I will, I will. You can rely on me."

He looked at her quietly and carefully, his pleasant eyes taking in her youthful enthusiasm. Many people reacted to Chummy's massive size and awkward gestures with ill-concealed humour, but not this gentleman. He leaned towards her and said softly, "I am quite, quite sure that we can rely on you."

Chummy's breath quivered out of her in a series of happy gasps and she could bring herself to say no more.

The Reverend Mr Applebee-Thornton turned to Sister Julienne. "Which brings me to the purpose of my visit today. What with the charm of the company and the excellence of the luncheon, I had almost forgotten that I was here to be shown around your district nursing and midwifery practice."

Was it an accident? Was it coincidence? Was it a mistake? Or was it devilish cunning? With a perfectly straight face, saucy Sister Julienne, whose eyes never missed a trick and whose mind was everywhere, looked coolly at him and lied through her teeth, without so much as a blush.

"I very much regret that none of the Sisters will be available to escort you on a tour of the district. I cannot express my regret too strongly, but we all have other duties this afternoon."

He looked disappointed and everyone else looked surprised. "It is a busy time for us," she continued, "and unfortunately none of my trained nurses can be spared for the purpose either."

The poor man looked uncomfortable, as though he were superfluous to requirements, and ought to be going.

"However, Jane is available this afternoon . . . "

At this poor Jane nearly fell off her chair, knocking over a salt pot and a dish of mint sauce, which slid greenly across the table. Sister Julienne appeared not to notice.

". . . And Jane, who knows the district well – perhaps better than any of us – would be delighted to accompany you."

She rose to her feet, and we all got up with her and stood

behind our chairs as she said grace. My eyes were lowered, but I glanced up and looked across the table at Jane. Her hands were not folded; they were clinging to the back of her chair and she was panting. Little beads of perspiration had broken out on her forehead and all in all she looked as if she were on the point of collapse. What on earth was Sister doing, I wondered. This was sheer cruelty.

In the hallway I heard Sister suggesting to Jane that she could take the Reverend to the Manchester Road and the Dockland areas first. Then they could look at Bow, Limehouse and the other parts of the district another day.

Jane went to fetch her coat and her legs were shaking. I saw the Reverend Mr Applebee-Thornton watch her closely as she walked in front of him. His face was thoughtful. Jane reached to take down her coat, but her hands twitched so convulsively that she could not take it off the peg.

"Allow me," he said courteously, and helped her to put it on. He put his hand on her arm and led her to the door. He turned and thanked Sister for allowing him such an excellent guide, who he was quite sure would be most helpful and informative. He opened the door for Jane with a slightly old-fashioned bow and murmured: "After you, madam."

They returned at tea time and he was full of praise, saying how informative Jane had been, and how greatly he valued the time she had so graciously spared him. Asked if he would like more conducted tours of the district, he said that there was no limit to his thirst for knowledge. Asked if he was quite happy with Jane as his escort – would he prefer a trained midwife on another occasion – he became profuse in stating his preference for Jane, who, he declared, was the perfect guide. Her erudition and encyclopedic knowledge of the topography and sociology of the area were more than he had dared hope for.

Jane appeared to accept her new role as guide for the Reverend Mr Applebee-Thornton, and carried out her duties with her

SHADOWS OF THE WORKHOUSE

customary attention to detail. Sister Julienne advised her to take a map, and to keep notes of what they had seen.

A week or two later, at lunch, Sister enquired how things were going. Jane replied eagerly, "Well, Pippin wants . . . "

She turned a deep red and her hands flew to her mouth. Stuttering, she tried to excuse herself. "I don't mean to be impertinent, Sister, but he asked me to call him Pippin. I said I couldn't presume to be so familiar, but he said that all his friends call him Pippin, and he would be hurt if I didn't."

To this. Sister replied, with exaggerated solemnity, that Jane had done the right thing, and must certainly call him Pippin, if that was his wish.

That same evening we were in the bicycle shed. Sister Julienne was mending a puncture, and I was tightening my brakes. To my great surprise, she said, "Where do you get your clothes from, Jennifer?" With the tyre lever grasped firmly in her small hand, Sister ripped off the outer tube.

"Well, I have a dressmaker. I don't usually go for off-the-peg stuff."

"But what store would you recommend for good clothes?"

I thought for a while. Sister plunged the inner tube into a bowl of water. "Liberty's, I suppose, in Regent Street."

"Ah yes, Liberty's. That sounds most suitable." She was turning the inner tube thoughtfully in the water, looking for bubbles.

"Jane needs some new clothes. I am going to tell her to get some. I wonder, Jenny, would it be too much to ask you to go with her? I'm sure she would value your advice. You need spare no expense, because Jane earns money but she never spends it."

No one could ever resist an appeal from Sister Julienne – certainly not me. More surprises were in store.

"And who is your hairdresser?"

"I always go to Chez Jacques in Regent Street, which just happens to be opposite Liberty's."

Her eyes lit up. She had found the puncture now; the water

was bubbling. But her real interest seemed to be in my hairdresser.

"Just opposite! Now, that's marvellous. It couldn't be more convenient. If you are in the area, could you take Jane to the hairdresser? She always cuts her hair herself, but I am sure she would look prettier if a good hairdresser attended to her."

Now, none of my nearest and dearest would suggest that I am quick off the mark when it comes to matchmaking. My poor mind doesn't work that way. Slow, they call me. But on that occasion the penny dropped. "It would be a pleasure, Sister. Just leave Jane in my hands."

Jane was dingy, drab and plain. Her clothes were about the worst I have ever seen. Her shoes were heavy, black lace-ups. Her stockings − tea-coloured lisle − were baggy. Her hair always looked a mess, and her skin was grey and deeply lined. To smarten her up would be quite a job.

After breakfast the next morning, Sister Julienne said: "Jane, you need some new clothes. Go with Jennifer this afternoon and she will choose some for you. You also need a haircut."

Jane meekly replied: "Yes, Sister."

It may seem extraordinary to speak to an adult in such a manner, but there was no other way of dealing with Jane. She was incapable of making even the smallest decision for herself and had to be directed in everything. I took my cue from Sister. I had thought carefully, and decided that a new look for Jane would have to be subtle. If I tried to dress her up like a fashion plate, the result might be disastrous. But first, the hairdresser.

Jane had never before been inside a West End hairdresser's and she hung back timidly at the door. But I only had to say, "I've made an appointment for you; you've got to come in," and she obeyed meekly.

I had a quiet word with Monsieur Jacques: "A gentle style, to frame the face, nothing exaggerated, no backcombing, something to suit a mature lady of quiet habits."

Monsieur Jacques nodded gravely, and took up his scissors.

As every woman knows, it's the cut that counts, and Jacques was a master-cutter. Had he ever achieved anything as spectacular as his reinvention of Jane? Perhaps the enormity of the challenge inspired him, for the result was little short of a miracle. Her natural curls moved in all the right places, her dingy greyness was now a confident iron-grey, with a softening of white at the temples. Jane looked at herself with astonishment in the huge mirrors, and as he flicked a wayward curl with his tail-comb, she actually smiled. Some of the worry left her face and she giggled. "Ooh, is that me?"

At Liberty's I looked out for a sales assistant who would not intimidate Jane. Some of them can be so smart and sharp they set the teeth on edge. A languid young woman with a drainpipe figure and a contemptuous eye shimmied across the carpet, but I steered Jane towards a homely-looking soul with a tape measure round her neck.

I explained the requirements, and she murmured reassuringly, "The unconscious elegance of a Hebe-Sports, with a little blouse or two. Leave everything to me." She deftly applied the tape measure to Jane's bony frame.

As promised, Jane emerged from the changing room transformed by a tailored suit in elegant grey. The tape measure breathed, "The iconic statement of the suit is in keeping with modom's splendid height. The subtle moulding of the skirt lends softness to the hips. Observe the detail of the pockets, rounding and moulding the line of the hips. Notice how the curve of the collar flatters modom's superb shoulders."

All of which was another way of saying that Jane's gaunt figure and prominent bones had somehow been concealed by the cut of the suit. She stood, meek and silent, passively allowing the collar to be adjusted a fraction of an inch.

One would have thought that the tape measure had by now exhausted her repertoire, but not at all. She was just winding herself up for a virtuoso performance.

"The slender figure and sublime height of modom are perfection for the timeless beauty of the true suit. Observe the effortless grace of modom's posture —" (Jane was drooping as usual.) "Good clothes reflect the creativity of their creator, striving for the zenith of creation. The true suit is visionary, in a restrained and dignified mode. Modom's intuitive understanding of the truly chic speaks volumes for her ineffable vision."

Jane looked utterly bewildered, and even I felt as though I were sinking out of my depth.

The tape measure cast a swift, professional eye over us both, absorbed the fact that we were floundering, and swiftly came in on the attack. "Observe how the silken threads pick out a million dancing lights, and enhance the flickering shades in modom's beautiful hair."

I had to agree that the colour certainly matched Jane's hair, although she stood silent, having no opinion on the subject.

The tape measure now turned to the drainpipe, who had joined us. "And now we must consider the passive and perfect necessity of the little blouse. Quintessentially, tara lawn is the first essential. Such a fine fabric – wouldn't you agree?"

"Oh, quintessentially essential," the drainpipe gushed as we crossed the floor to a room filled with blouses.

"The colour at the throat is all important. Modom requires understatement. The bold gesture is not for modom. Dusty pink, I think."

She pulled from the rail a pink blouse and held it against Jane's scrawny throat. The result was undeniably pleasing.

"Whilst the blue – muted, of course – draws attention to modom's fine eyes." A second blouse was held up. It was true. I had never before noticed how blue Jane's eyes were.

The tape measure drew forth yet another. "And what does modom say to mellow yellow?"

Jane had nothing to say, but the drainpipe ventured to suggest that perhaps mellow yellow was a little over-emphatic in its proclamation, and would not the merest whisper of lilac speak with quiet authority?

The tape-measure raised her manicured hands. "Lilac! Heavenly lilac! How could I forget?"

She signalled to the drainpipe, who trickled away and returned with a third blouse, of perfect fit and colour. Jane looked charming in all of them.

The tape-measure was rhapsodic. "Ah! the perfection of lilac. Queen Mary's favourite colour, and modom's truest friend. Lilac is a poem, a fragrance, a hint of nothingness. Modom cannot possibly miss heavenly lilac from her wardrobe."

These women certainly gave value for money and we took the lot.

Shoes, gloves, handbag and some decent stockings were all chosen in the same manner, and we were on our way east of Aldgate, back to Poplar.

Was Pippin likely to be aware of all the intense female activity that had been going on for his delight and diversion? Was he likely to see any difference? The sad answer to both these questions was probably "No". I have yet to meet a man who can give you even the vaguest description of what a woman was wearing ten minutes after she left his company. He would probably say, with an airy wave of the hand, "Oh, she was looking lovely in a green floaty thing," when she was wearing tight-fitting blue!

Jane changed for lunch and therefore it was to an all-female audience that she displayed the results of our outing. Cries of "Lovely", "transformed", "fab hair-do", went up all around, and Jane looked surprised, quietly gratified by all the compliments. Sister Julienne allowed herself a meaningful wink as she whispered to me, "Well done."

Pippin came at 2 p.m. prompt, and exhibited no surprise at Jane's appearance. Perhaps he saw no change! They left together for Mile End, the northerly border of our district.

Let us not enquire too closely into these guided walking tours, conceived and executed with a view to benefiting the native people of Sierra Leone. To do so would be a lapse of good taste.

Suffice it to say that the two-week stay at the Rectory was lengthened to six and that, day by day, bit by bit, Jane began to look more relaxed and happy, and less chronically nervous.

Pippin came to lunch one Sunday a few weeks later, and towards the end of the meal he said, "I will have to be leaving you all soon. My six-month furlough draws to its close, and I must return to the duties God has been pleased to entrust to me in Sierra Leone. Before I leave England I must spend a few weeks with my aged father in Herefordshire. These visits are not always easy for me, because we do not always see eye to eye, especially over the treatment of the native African. My father, now aged ninety, was an army officer in the African wars of the 1880s, and his principles I regard as harsh, whereas he regards mine as weak and mollycoddling. It can be very difficult."

He turned to Sister Julienne. "I was wondering, Sister, if you could possibly spare Jane for a couple of weeks to come with me? I feel that a feminine influence would ease the tension in an all-male household. With her charm and tact, and her gentle disposition, I feel that she could mollify my father in ways that I never could with my blunderings. Jane has already agreed to come if you can spare her. And I, for my part, would be eternally grateful." Jane's hand was resting on the table; he touched it lightly, and gave it a little squeeze.

She blushed and murmured: "Oh! Pip."

The visit started badly because the old colonel called Jane "a raw-boned horse" and Pippin was furious and would have walked out of the house without even unpacking. But Jane laughed and said she had been called worse than that in her time. Pippin raged on about "that impossible old man" until Jane went up to him, placed her fingers on his lips, and whispered: "Just be thankful that you have a father at all, dear."

In an agony of self-reproach he caught hold of her wrists and drew her to him. "May God forgive me. I am not worthy of you." He kissed her gently. "All my sins will be redeemed by your suffering, my wise and perfect love."

Later that evening the Colonel returned to horses when he referred to "that little filly of yours". Pippin stiffened, but his father carried on, "She's got good legs. Always a sign of pedigree in a horse or a woman. You can tell the breeding by the shape of the ankle."

The weeks passed well and the Colonel took to Jane. Her quietness appealed to him and he approved of her self-effacing habits. He barked at his son one evening: "Well, there's one thing to say. That little filly of yours is not going to drive you mad with a lot of silly chatter. Never could abide those magpie women, m'self; yackety-yackety-yak, all day long."

His son smiled and said, "I take it that we have your blessing, then, sir?"

"Whether you have my blessing or not, my boy, I can see you are set on the filly and nothing will make any difference. Go ahead, go ahead; your mother would have been pleased, God rest her soul."

The Reverend Mr and Mrs Applebee-Thornton returned to Poplar for a few days before they sailed for Sierra Leone. I have never in my life seen a woman so changed. She was tall and regal, her eyes were smiling, and calm confidence seemed to spring from deep within her. Pippin hardly took his eyes off her, and always referred to her as "my dear wife", or "my beloved Jane".

Of course, we had to have a party. Nuns love a party. They are very sedate affairs, ending at 9 p.m., in time for Compline and the Greater Silence, but they are fun while they last. Mrs B provided excellent cakes and sandwiches, to which we added a little sweet sherry, compliments of the Rector. The invitation was open to anyone who had known Jane and wanted to wish the happy couple well in their new life. About fifty people came, and some boys from SPY (the South Poplar Youth Club) provided music with their guitars and drums, which was considered to be very risqué. Pippin gave a delightful speech. The length of the phrases and the extravagance of the language – about pearls of great price, and the best wine being served last – was lost on many people; but the gist of the message was that he was the luckiest man alive, and everyone cheered.

Dancing had just begun when the telephone rang. I was first on call.

"Yes ... yes ... This is Nonnatus House. Mrs Smith ... What address, please? How frequent are the contractions? Have the waters broken? Keep her in bed, please. I'll come straight away."

Part II

THE TRIAL OF SISTER
MONICA JOAN

SISTER MONICA JOAN

Sister Monica Joan did not die. She developed severe pneumonia after wandering down the East India Dock Road wearing only her nightie one cold November morning, but she did not die. In fact, the incident seemed to rejuvenate her. Perhaps she enjoyed all the extra pampering and cosseting supplied by her Sisters and Mrs B, the cook. No doubt she enjoyed being the centre of attention. Perhaps penicillin, the new wonder drug, had pumped fire into her old heart. Whatever the reason, Sister Monica Joan, at the age of ninety, enjoyed a new lease of life, and was soon to be seen trotting all over Poplar, to the great rejoicing of everyone who knew her.

The Sisters of St Raymund Nonnatus was an Anglican order of fully professed nuns. The Sisters were all trained nurses and midwives, and their vocation was to work amongst the poorest of the poor. They had maintained a house in the London Docklands since the 1870s, when their work was revolutionary. Poor women in those days had no medical care during pregnancy and childbirth, and the death rate was high.

Midwifery as a profession did not exist. In each community local women, in a tradition passed on from mother to daughter, went around delivering babies. Such a woman was called 'the handy woman' and her practice usually consisted of 'lying-in and laying-out' (i.e. lying-in after childbirth and laying-out of the dead). Some of these women were good at their trade, and were caring and conscientious, but they were untrained and unregistered.

Against relentless parliamentary ridicule and opposition, many inspired women, including the Sisters of St Raymund Nonnatus, fought to have midwifery recognised as a profession, and for midwives to be trained and registered. Eventually, after a series of bills were defeated in the House, the women won, and the first Midwives Act became law in 1902. The Royal College of Midwives was born, and from that moment maternal and infant deaths began to fall.

The Sisters were true heroines. They had entered slum areas of the London Docks at a time when no one else would go near them, except perhaps the police. They had worked through epidemics of cholera, typhoid, tuberculosis, scarlet fever and smallpox, careless of being infected themselves. They had worked through two world wars and endured the intensive bombing of the Blitz. They were inspired and sustained by their dual vocation: service to God and service to mankind.

But do not imagine for one moment that the Sisters were trapped by their bells and their rosaries, and that life had passed them by. The nuns, collectively and individually, had experienced more of the world and its ways, more of heroism and degradation, of sin and salvation, than most people will experience in a lifetime. No indeed, the nuns were not remote goody-goodies. They were a bunch of feisty women who had seen it all, lived and loved and suffered throughout, and remained true to their vocation.

Nonnatus House was situated just off the East India Dock Road, near Poplar High Street and the Blackwall Tunnel. It was a large Victorian building and sat next to a bomb site. A third of all Dockland dwellings had been destroyed by the Blitz, and most of the derelict buildings and rubble had not been cleared away. Bomb sites became children's playgrounds during the day and dormitories for meths-drinkers overnight.

Overcrowding had always been chronic in Poplar, and it was said that Poplar housed 50,000 people per square mile. After the Second World War the situation was even worse, because houses and flats had been destroyed and rebuilding had not yet commenced, so people just moved in with each other. It was not unusual to find three or four generations of one family living in a small house, or fifteen people living in two or three small rooms in the tenements – the Canada Buildings or the Peabody Buildings or the notorious Blackwall Tenements. These were Victorian buildings constructed on four sides around a central courtyard, with inward-facing balconies which were the arteries of the tenement. There was no privacy. Everyone knew everyone else's business, and terrible fights would occur when the tensions of overcrowded family life erupted into violence. The tenements were bug-infested and insanitary. Some of the better ones had an indoor lavatory and running water, but most of the buildings had neither and infections spread like wildfire.

Most of the men worked in the docks. Thousands poured through the gates when they opened each day. Hours were long, the work was heavy, and life was hard, but the Cockney men knew nothing else, and they were tough. The Thames was the backdrop of Poplar, and the boats, the cranes, the sound of the sirens, the whisper of the water all formed part of the tapestry that had been woven into its cloth for generations. The river had been the people's constant companion, their friend and enemy, their employer, their playground and frequently, for the destitute, their grave.

Cockney life, for all its poverty and deprivation, was rich – rich in humanity and humour, rich in drama and melodrama, rich in pathos and, unhappily, rich in tragedy. The Sisters of St Raymund Nonnatus had served the people of Poplar for several generations. The Cockneys did not forget, and the nuns were loved, respected, even revered by the whole community.

During the time of which I write, an incident occurred that shook the very foundations of Nonnatus House. In fact, it shook the whole of Poplar, because everyone got to hear about it and for a time the local people could talk of little else.

Sister Monica Joan was accused of shoplifting.

My first intimation that something was wrong occurred when I returned from my evening visits, wet and hungry, and wondering why anyone was ever fool enough to be a district midwife.

What about a cushy little office job? I thought to myself as I pulled the bag from the carrier of my bike, knowing it would take me an hour to clean and sterilise all my instruments and repack the bag ready for use the following morning. Yes, that's it, I thought for the umpteenth time, a soft, cosy office job, with regular hours and central heating, sitting behind a nice smooth, desk, tapping at my Olivetti, and thinking about my date that evening; a job in which the maximum responsibility would be to find the minutes of the last meeting, and the biggest disaster a broken fingernail.

I entered the front door of Nonnatus House, and the first thing I saw was a great number of wet dirty footprints all over the fine Victorian tiles of the hallway. Large footprints in a convent? They were certainly very big, far too big to be those of a nun. Could it be that a group of men, had recently entered? It seemed unlikely at seven o'clock in the evening. And if the rector or any of the curates had called they were unlikely to leave dirty footmarks. If any tradesman had called in the morning and left such an unseemly visiting card, the mess would have been cleared up before lunch. But there they were – large dirty footprints all over the hall. It was inexplicable.

Then I heard Sister Julienne's voice coming from the direction of her office. Sister's voice was usually quiet and well modulated, but now it had a slight edge to it, either through anxiety or nervousness, it was hard to tell. This was followed by men's voices. It all seemed very strange, but I didn't want to linger, knowing that I had my bag to prepare before I could get anything to eat, so I made my way to the clinical room, where I found Cynthia and Trixie and Chummy deep in conversation.

Chummy had opened the door, apparently, to a sergeant and a constable who had asked to see the Sister-in-Charge. Chummy was all of a flutter, because she always went to pieces when any man entered the room, but chiefly because the constable was the policeman she had knocked over when she was had been learning to ride her bicycle. Intense embarrassment at the sight of him had rendered her speechless. The men had entered the hallway, and in her awkward confusion she had banged the front door so hard that it had sounded like a gun shot. Then she had tripped over the doormat and fallen into the arms of the policeman she had injured the year before.

Chummy was still in a state of such nervous distress that it was hard to get a word out of her, but Cynthia, apparently, hearing the bang of the front door and the noise of poor Chummy falling over, had come to see what it was all about. It was she, apparently, who had taken the policemen to the office and called Sister Julienne.

No one knew much more than that, but female speculation can make a great deal out of very little. Whilst we boiled our instruments, cut and folded our gauze swabs and filled our pots and bottles, our imaginations ranged over everything from arson to murder. Chummy was convinced the visit had something to do with her assault on the policeman, but Cynthia gently calmed her down, saying that there was no way a charge would be brought a year after the event, and his coming to Nonnatus House must be a coincidence.

We went to the kitchen for supper, deliberately leaving the door open, of course. We heard the office door open and heavy footsteps. We all pricked up our ears, but heard only a quiet: "Good night, Sister. Thank you for your time, and you will be hearing from us in morning." The front door closed, and four inquisitive girls were left in a state of unbridled curiosity.

It was only after lunch the following day that Sister Julienne asked us all to remain in our seats as she had something to say. Fred the boiler man and Mrs B the cook were also asked to the dining room, because the matter had to come out into the open, and Sister did not want rumours flying around that would undoubtedly be exaggerated.

Apparently, Sister Julienne told us, Sister Monica Joan had been in Chrisp Street Market and the owner of a jewellery stall had seen her fingering several items. He had heard from other stall-holders that one of the Sisters was "light-fingered" so he watched her, but pretended not to be doing so. He saw her pick up a child's bracelet, look around her and then deftly tuck it under her scapular. Then she had assumed her usual haughty aspect, head held high, and attempted to walk away. But the stall-holder stopped her. When he asked to see what she was holding beneath her scapular, she was extremely rude to him, telling him not to be so impertinent, and calling him a "boorish fellow". A crowd, of course, had gathered. The man grew cross, called her a "scraggy old God-botherer" and said she'd better hand it over, or he'd get a peeler. Whereupon Sister Monica Joan had flung the gold bracelet across the stall with a contemptuous gesture, crying: "You can keep your tawdry trinkets, you loutish lump. What do I want with them?" and stalked off with an expression of offended dignity on her fine features.

Mrs B exploded: "I don't believe a word of it. Not a word. He's a liar, vat bloke. I knows him, an' I knows as what he's a liar, I do. You won't get me believing a story like vat about Sister Monica Joan, you won't, love 'er."

Sister Julienne silenced her. "I'm afraid there is not a shadow of doubt about the truth of the matter. Several people are ready to testify that they saw Sister Monica Joan throw the bangle across the stall before she stalked off. But I'm afraid that is not all. There is worse to come." She looked around at us, sadly and we held our breath.

The costermonger, probably enraged at having been called a "boorish fellow" and a "loutish lump" went round other stall-holders who had talked about a "light-fingered Sister" and collected eight men and women who claimed that they had strong suspicions about her having stolen from them, or who had positively seen Sister Monica Joan take something small and hide it under her scapular. Collectively they had gone to the police.

Sister Julienne continued, "The police were here yesterday and this morning. I felt bound to confront Sister Monica Joan with their report, but she wouldn't say a word to me. Not a single word. She just looked out of the window as though she had not even heard me. I told her I was going to look in her chest of drawers, and she just shrugged her shoulders dismissively, and pursed her lips and said, 'Pooh to you.' I must say her attitude was extremely annoying, and if she behaved in that way to the coster, it is not surprising that he was so enraged."

Sister Julienne produced a suitcase from under the table, saying: "This is what I found in Sister Monica's chest of drawers," and she withdrew several pairs of silk stockings, three egg cups, a great quantity of coloured ribbons, a lady's silk blouse, four children's colouring books, an ornate hairpiece, a corkscrew, several small wooden animals, a tin whistle, a quantity of teaspoons, three ornamental china birds, a bundle of knitting wool all tangled up, a necklace of gaudy beads, about a dozen fine lawn handkerchiefs, a needle case, a shoe horn and a dog collar. All of the items were unused, and some of them still had a label attached.

There was really no need for Sister Julienne to say, "I'm afraid this has been going on for some time." It was painfully obvious to all of us and Mrs B burst into tears. "Oh, the love, bless 'er, oh the poor lamb, she don't know what she's doin', she don't. Wha's going to 'appen to 'er, Sister? Vey wouldn't lock 'er up, not at 'er age?"

Sister Julienne said she didn't know. Prison seemed an unlikely outcome, but the costermonger was definitely bringing a charge, and Sister Monica Joan would be prosecuted.

Sister Monica Joan was a very old nun born into an aristocratic family in the 1860s. She had obviously been a strong-willed young woman who had rebelled against the restrictions and narrow self-interest of her social class, because she had broken away from her family (a shocking thing to do) around 1890 in order to train as a nurse. In 1902, when the first Midwives Act was passed, Monica Joan trained as a midwife and, shortly after, joined the Sisters of St Raymund Nonnatus. Her profession to a monastic order was the last straw for her family and they disowned her. But Novice Monica Joan didn't care a hoot and carried on doing her own thing. When I knew her, she had lived and worked in Poplar for fifty years and was known by virtually everyone.

To say that by the age of ninety she was eccentric would be an understatement. Sister Monica Joan was wildly eccentric to the point of being outrageous. There was no telling what she would say or do next, and she frequently gave offence. Sometimes she could be sweet and gentle but at other times she was gratuitously spiteful. Poor Sister Evangelina, large and heavy, and not gifted with verbal brilliance, suffered most dreadfully from the astringent sarcasm of her Sister-in-God. Sister Monica Joan had a powerful intellect and was poetic and artistic, yet she was quite insensitive to music, as I witnessed on the occasion of her shocking behaviour at a cello recital. She was very clever – cunning, some would say. She manipulated others unscrupulously in order to get her own way. She was haughty and aristocratic in her demeanour, yet she had spent fifty years working in the slums of the London Docklands. How can one account for such contradictions?

Whilst being a professed nun and a devout Christian, in her old age Sister Monica Joan had become fascinated by esoteric spirituality, ranging from astrology and fortune-telling to cosmology and centric forces. She loved to expound on these subjects, but I doubt if she knew what she was talking about.

At the time I knew her, she was verging on senility. The focus of her mind seemed to come and go, to shift and change. Sometimes she was perfectly rational, while at others it was as though she were seeing the world through a mist, trying to grasp, things half-seen. Yet I suspected she knew her mind was going, and occasionally used the fact to get what she wanted. Somehow she had a magnetic quality about her and she fascinated me. I loved her dearly and enjoyed spending time in her company.

When Sister Julienne solemnly told the group in the dining room that Sister Monica Joan would be prosecuted for theft, a wave of shock had rippled around the table. Novice Ruth cried quietly.

Mrs B protested vociferously that she wouldn't believe it. Trixie said she wasn't surprised. Sister Evangelina snapped, "Be quiet, we'll have none of that," and sat very still, staring down at her plate, but her temples were twitching, and her knuckles went white as she gripped her hands together. Sister Julienne said: "We must all commit Sister Monica Joan to our prayers. We must seek God's help. But I will also engage a good lawyer."

I asked if I might visit Sister Monica Joan in her room that afternoon, and permission was readily given.

As I mounted the stairs, my mind was in a turmoil. How would I be received by a lady who had been visited by the police, from whose chest of drawers numerous stolen items had been extracted, and who had been told that she would be facing prosecution?

Sister Monica Joan's room was not the customary cell of a nun, bare and plain. Hers was an elegant bed–sitting room with all the comforts due to a distinguished old lady. These were probably a great deal more than any other nun might expect, but Sister Monica Joan had a knack of always getting her own way. Since the pneumonia she had spent more time in her room, and I had been a frequent and happy visitor. But on this occasion, my heart was pounding with anxiety.

I knocked, and heard a sharp: "Enter. Come in, don't just stand there. Come in."

I entered, and found her at her desk, notebooks and pencils all around her. She was scribbling away furiously and chuckling to herself.

"Ah, it's you, my dear. Sit down, sit down. Did you know that the astral permanent atom is equivalent to the etheric permanent atom and that they both function within the parallel universe?" She seemed to have no recollection of what had been going on, for which I was profoundly relieved. If she had been in a state of remorse it would have been hard to know what to say.

I grinned and sat down. "No, Sister. I didn't know about the parallel universe, nor the permanent atoms. Do tell me."

She started to draw a diagram for my benefit. "See here, child, this is the point within the circle, and these bands are the seven parallels that are the unifying stability within the atoms that are the essence of the parallel universe wherein men and angels and beasts and others . . . I think."

Her voice trailed away as she scribbled furiously, her mind obviously racing ahead of her pencil. Suddenly she cried out, her voice squeaking with excitement: "I have it. Eureka! All has been revealed. There are eleven parallels. Not seven. Ah, the perfection of eleven. The beauty of eleven. All is revealed in eleven."

Her voice dropped to a whisper, and she raised her eyes to heaven, her features radiant. I felt again the magnetism of this woman, who could hold me in a spell just by moving her fingers or lifting an eyebrow. Her skin was so fine and white that it seemed barely sufficient to cover the fragile bones and blue veins that meandered up her hands and arms. She sat perfectly still, a pencil poised between two fingertips, the first joint of which she could bend independently of the rest of the finger. With eyes closed, she murmured, "Eleven parallels, eleven stars . . . eleven crowns," and I was bewitched all over again. I knew that many people could not stand her. They found her arrogant, haughty, supercilious and too clever by half – and, I had to admit, with some justification. Many thought she was an affected poseur, playing some sort of role, but I could not agree with that. I thought she was absolutely sincere in everything she said.

That she was utterly unpredictable was agreed by all, but now, it seemed, she was a shoplifter! I felt quite sure that she had no recollection of what she had been doing, and could not be held accountable for her actions. She was still murmuring, "Eleven stars . . . eleven spheres . . . eleven teaspoons."

Suddenly she opened her eyes and snapped, "Two policemen were here this morning. Two great big clomping fellows with their boots and their notebooks, going through my drawers, as though I were a common criminal. And Sister Julienne took it all away. All my pretty things. My colouring things, my ribbons, eleven teaspoons. I had been collecting them – eleven – just think, and I needed them, every one."

Grief seemed to overcome her. She didn't cry, but she seemed frozen with terror, and murmured: "What is going to happen to me? What will they do to me? Why do elderly, respectable women do this sort of thing? Are we tempted, or is it a sickness? I don't understand ... I don't know myself ... "

Her voice faltered, and the pencil dropped from her trembling fingers. She knew all right. Oh yes, she knew.

PHOSSY JAW

Nonnatus House was subdued and saddened as we awaited the prosecution of Sister Monica Joan for shoplifting. Even we young girls, always ready to giggle and joke about almost everything, were more restrained. We somehow felt it unseemly to laugh when the Sisters were suffering. Sister Monica Joan spent more of her time in her room. She did not go out of the house at all, seldom came down to the dining room, and really only left her room for Mass and the five monastic offices of the day. I sometimes saw her entering or leaving the chapel, but she hardly spoke to her Sisters. They treated her with gentleness, but she returned their smiles and kindly glances with a toss of her proud head as she went to her pew to kneel in prayer. We are all complex creatures, but prayer and downright rudeness seemed incompatible.

The only people she consistently spoke to were Mrs B and myself. Dear Mrs B, whose love of Sister Monica Joan was unconditional and unreserved, and who still didn't believe a word of it, was up and down the stairs all day, pandering to her every wish. Sister Monica Joan treated her more like a personal lady's maid than she had any right to, but Mrs B seemed perfectly happy with her new role, and nothing seemed to be too much trouble. She was heard muttering to herself in the kitchen one day: "China tea. I though' as 'ow tea was just tea. But no. She wants China tea. Now where am I goin' to get vat?" None of the grocers in Poplar seemed to stock China tea, so she went all the way up West to get it. When she proudly presented a cup to Sister Monica Joan, Sister sniffed it and sipped it, then declared that she didn't like it. Anyone else would have been furious, but Mrs B took no offence: "Not 'a worry, my luvvy. You just 'ave a slice o' vis honey-cake I made this mornin', while I run along and make you a nice pot o' tea, jus' as 'ow you likes it."

Sister Monica Joan could out-queen the Queen when she chose. Her attitude was serenely gracious as she inclined her head. "So kind, so kind." Mrs B glowed with pleasure. Sister broke a piece of honey-cake with her long fingers and delicately raised it to her lips. "Delicious, quite delicious. Another slice, if it's not too much trouble." Mrs B, fairly bursting with happiness, ran downstairs for the umpteenth time that day.

Sister Monica Joan fascinated me as she did most people. But she never treated me as a lady's maid. No doubt her instinct told her that it just would not work. We understood each other as equals and found endless pleasure in each other's company. During the uncertain weeks of waiting we had many conversations in her pretty room just after lunch, or before Compline. We talked for hours. Her short-term memory was faulty – often she did not know what day or month it was – but her long-term memory was excellent. She could clearly recall facts, incidents and impressions from her Victorian childhood and her working life in the Edwardian era and the First World War. She was highly intelligent and articulate and could express herself vividly, often in beautiful language that seemed to come naturally to her. As I wanted to learn more about old Poplar, I tried questioning her. But this did not work. She was not easy to pin down, and often took no notice of what I had said or asked. She had a habit of making statements unrelated to anything that had been said beforehand, like: "That rapacious old mongrel!" And then no more! The old mongrel had obviously come into her mind unbidden and then slunk away, his tail between his legs.

Sometimes she developed her thoughts and her words flowed easily. She would make a dramatic statement: "Women are the cohesive force in society." She picked up a pencil and balanced it delicately between her two fingertips, those astonishing fingers that she could bend at the first joint. Would she continue? To say a word might break her thoughts.

"And 'woman' in the slums is capable of taking on almost superhuman responsibility, from a very young age, that would crush most of us. Today they live in luxury – look at all the giddy young girls around us – they have no memory of how their mothers and grandmothers lived and died. They have no understanding of what it took to raise a family twenty or thirty years ago."

She glanced at the pencil and twisted it round with her thumbs. Privately I questioned the "luxury" in the tenements, but said nothing for fear of chasing away her memories. She continued.

"There was no work, no food, no shoes for the children. If the rent was not paid the family would be evicted. Thrown onto the streets by the law of the land."

She paused, and a memory flashed through my mind of something that I had seen only a few weeks earlier, when I was cycling back from a night delivery.

It had been about three o'clock in the morning, and I saw a group of people, a man and woman and several children, coming towards me, keeping close to the wall. The woman was carrying a baby and a suitcase. The man was carrying a mattress on his head, a rucksack and several bags. Each of the children, none of them over ten, was carrying a bag. They saw the headlights of my bike and turned their faces to the wall. The man said, his voice quite distinct in the darkness: "Don' chew worry. It's only a nurse," and I cycled past, not realising at the time that a dramatic and tragic event was taking place; an event that used to be referred to light-heartedly as a "moonlight flit". The family were anticipating eviction and fleeing unpaid debts. God only knows where they ended up.

Sister Monica Joan was staring at me, hard, and then she narrowed her eyes. "You remind me of Queenie – turn your head."

I did so.

"Yes, you look just like her. I was so fond of Queenie. I delivered her three children and I was with her when she died.

She was no more than your age, but she died trying to avoid eviction."

"What happened?" I whispered.

"She went into the Bryant and May factory that made matches. They were a lovely family, and I knew them well. No fights in that family. Her husband was no more than a boy when he was killed in a riverboat accident. What could Queenie do with three little children? The Parish would have taken them from her, but she wouldn't have it. She went into the match factory because they offered higher pay than anywhere else. Danger money, they called it, and wriggled out of any responsibility by saying the women accepted the danger when they accepted the pay. Wicked it was. Wicked. Death money it should have been called. Queenie worked there for three years and kept a roof over their heads and just enough to eat. We thought she would escape phossy jaw. But it got her, yes, it got her, and she died a terrible death. I was with her at the end. She died in my arms."

Sister Monica Joan said no more. Could I risk a question?

"What is phossy jaw?"

"There you go. What did I say? Young girls have no idea how women had to live and work. The matches were made from raw phosphorus. The women inhaled the vapour, and the fumes got into the mucous membrane of the mouth and nose. The phosphorus penetrated the bones of the upper and lower jaw. The bones literally sloughed away. In the dark you could see the woman's jaw glowing with a bluish light. There was nothing that could be done for these women and they died a slow and agonising death. Don't ask me again what phossy jaw is, you ignorant girl. It's what Queenie died of, trying to provide for her children, trying to avoid eviction."

She glanced at me, and clamped her teeth together.

"That's what we fought for. Girls like Queenie, hard-working, loving, young women full of life, who were driven to their deaths by the system. I was with her when she died. It was ghastly. The bones of her lower face crumbled away, and she suffered weeks of agony. There was nothing we could do. Her children went to the workhouse. There was nowhere else for them."

The rain fell quietly on the window, and she sat quite still. I could see the pulse beating sluggishly in her long neck, carrying the life-giving blood to her brain. "Draw the curtains, please, dear." I did so, hoping she would continue, but she only murmured, "It seems like yesterday, no time at all." And there was no more.

The memories of people like Sister Monica Joan should be cherished. I sat on the edge of her bed, my legs drawn up underneath me, and tried to interpret from her sensitive features what was in her mind. I did not want Queenie to fade from her memory, so I asked about the children going to the workhouse, but she became irritable and snappy.

"Questions. Always questions. You give me no peace, child. Can I not expect a little repose in my old age?"

She threw her head to one side with an affected sigh. At that moment the bell sounded for Compline. "There now. See what you have done. You've made me late for my religious duties."

She swept past me without a further glance and made her way to the chapel.

That evening I attended Compline. The lay staff at Nonnatus House were not bound to do so – we were not professed religious – but we could attend any offices if we wished to. I particularly loved the words of Compline, the last office of the day, and had been very affected by the story of Queenie, so I followed Sister Monica Joan into the chapel. Her behaviour was atrocious! She entered without so much as looking at anyone else, and did not take her usual pew but went straight to the visitors' seats, took a chair and sat with her back to her Sisters and the altar. Sister Julienne quietly came up to her and gently tried to draw her into the group around the altar, but Sister Monica Joan rudely pushed her aside and even drew her chair further away so that she was looking directly at the wall. Compline proceeded in this fashion.

Sister Julienne was obviously saddened, and the love and pity in her eyes showed that she knew something strange was going on in the mind of the old lady, which she was trying to understand. Perhaps it was advancing senility, or perhaps one of those mental illnesses that make people turn away from, and become aggressive towards, the people who have been closest and most dear to them. Quietly the Sisters left the chapel. The Greater Silence had begun. After that evening Sister Monica Joan always sat with her back to her Sisters, even at Mass.

The following afternoon I went to Sister Monica Joan's room after lunch, hoping that she would not turn against me as she had against her Sisters. She had enriched my life so much with her friendship, and I knew it would be greatly impoverished if that friendship were suddenly withdrawn.

She was sitting at her desk, alert and busy with her notebooks and pencil. She turned. "Come in, my dear, come in. This will interest you. The hexagon meets the parallel" – she was drawing a diagram again – "and the rays combine here ... Oh bother!" Her pencil broke. "Fetch me my pencil-sharpener, will you, dear? The second drawer down in my bedside cabinet." She continued tracing the lines across the paper with her forefinger.

I went across the room to her bedside cabinet, happy that she was not excluding me from her affections. What made me pull open the third drawer down? It was not intentional, but it almost paralysed me, and for several seconds I thought I would choke. The open drawer revealed several gold bangles, two or three rings (one of the stones looked like a sapphire), a small diamond watch, a pearl necklace, a ruby pendant on a gold chain, a gold cigarette case, a couple of gold cigarette holders studded with stones, and several tiny gold or platinum charms. The drawer was only about two inches deep and no more than ten inches wide, but it must have contained a small fortune in jewellery.

Sudden silence can attract immediate attention. She turned round and saw me transfixed, looking into the drawer. At first she did not say anything, and the silence developed an ominous quality that was broken by her hissing: "You wicked girl, prying into my affairs. How dare you? Leave the room immediately. Do you hear? Withdraw, at once."

It was so shocking, I had to sit down on the edge of the bed. Our eyes met, mine full of grief and hers flashing with anger. Gradually the defiance crumbled away, and her old, old face assumed a tired, almost pathetic quality. She whimpered, "All my pretty things. Don't take them away. Don't tell anyone. They will take them all. Then they'll take me away, like they took Aunt Anne. All my pretty things. No one knows about them. Why shouldn't I have them? Don't tell anyone, will you, child?" Her beautiful hooded eyes filled with tears, her lips trembled, and the toll of ninety years descended on her as she crumpled into a sobbing wreck.

It took only a second to cross the room and hold her in my arms. "Of course I won't tell anyone. No one will ever know. It's a secret, and we won't tell anyone, I promise."

Gradually her tears dried, and she blew her nose and gave me one of her saucy winks. "Those great clod-hopping policemen. They'll never know, will they?" She raised one eyebrow and chuckled conspiratorially. "I think I will take my tea now. Go, child, and tell Mrs B that I will have some of that delicious China tea."

"But you didn't like the China tea."

"Of course I liked it. Don't be silly. You are getting muddled up, I fear!"

Laughing, I kissed her goodbye and made my way down to the kitchen to deliver the message to Mrs B.

It was not until later that evening that the awfulness of the dilemma hit me. What on earth was I going to do?

MONOPOLY

A promise is a promise, but theft is a criminal offence, and my pledge to Sister Monica Joan that I would not tell anyone about the stolen jewellery weighed upon me so heavily that I could hardly keep my mind on my work. Purloining a few pairs of silk stockings and handkerchiefs was naughty, but stealing jewels, some of them very valuable, is a serious offence. Normally nothing disturbs my sleep, but this did. If I told Sister Julienne, she would call the police again, and they would search Sister Monica Joan's room a second time, more thoroughly than before. Perhaps there would be other things hidden away, in a box maybe, or in the bottom drawer of the bedside cabinet. The gravity of the offence might be more than doubled. They might arrest her on the spot, old as she was. I blocked out such a thought. Sister Monica Joan must be protected at all costs. I would not tell anyone.

Antenatal clinic was particularly trying that week. There were too many women, it was too hot, and there were too many small children running around. I felt like screaming. We were clearing up afterwards. Cynthia was cleaning the urine-testing equipment, I was scrubbing the work surfaces.

She said: "What's up? You've not been yourself lately."

Relief swept over me. Her deep slow voice acted like a balm to my troubled spirits. "How do you know? Is it that obvious?"

"Of course it is. I can read you like a book. Now come on, out with it. What's up?"

Two of the Sisters were still in the clinic, packing up the antenatal notes and filing them away. I whispered, "I'll tell you later."

After Compline, when the Sisters had gone to bed, Cynthia

and I sat in her room with an extra helping of pudding left over from lunch. Briefly I told her about the jewellery.

She whistled. "Phew! No wonder you have been quiet recently. What are you going to do?"

"I'm not going to tell anyone in authority. I'm only telling you because you guessed something was up."

"But you can't keep it to yourself. You've got to tell Sister Julienne."

"If I do, she'll tell the police and they might arrest Sister Monica."

"You're not being rational. They won't arrest her. She's too old."

"How do you know? This is big stuff, I tell you. It's not just pinching a few crayoning books."

Cynthia was quiet for a while. "Well, I don't think they will arrest her."

"There you are, you don't know. You only think, and you might be wrong. If they arrested her it would kill her."

There was a bang on the door. "I say, you chaps, how about a game of Monopoly, what? No one in labour. All the babies tucked up in bed. What say you, eh?"

"Come in, Chummy."

Camilla Fortescue-Cholmeley-Browne. Descended from generations of High Commissioners of India, educated at Roedean and polished by a Swiss finishing school, Chummy represented the upper crust in our small circle. She had a voice that sounded like something straight out of a comedy and she was excessively tall, which caused her to suffer much ragging. But she took it all with sweet good nature.

Chummy tried the handle. "But the door's locked, old bean. What's going on? Something rummy's afoot, or I'm a brass monkey."

Cynthia laughed and opened the door. "We've got some pudding in here. If you want some go and get a dish, and while you're about it, tell Trixie."

When she had gone, Cynthia said to me, "I think we had better tell the girls. Neither of them is in authority so the police won't be called, and they might help. Chummy's father was a District Commissioner or something in India and Trixie's cousin is a solicitor, so they might know something about the law."

I agreed. It was a relief to be sharing the responsibility after all my silent anguish.

Both girls came in with a dish and a spoon, Chummy bearing the Monopoly board. We shared out the pudding. Cynthia sat on the only chair and three of us sat on the bed. The Monopoly board was laid out on the bed, supported by books to stop it sagging. I had been against playing Monopoly, but Cynthia said it would help relieve the tension, and she was right.

We sorted out our money and tucked it in piles under our knees while Cynthia told them the story.

Trixie burst out laughing. "What a scream! So the old girl's been pinching things left, right and centre. Tucking them under her scapular and no one would ever suspect. The cunning old vixen." She roared with laughter.

"You cat. Don't you call Sister Monica Joan names or I'll—"

Cynthia intervened. "I won't have you two squabbling in my room. If you want to start a row you can go elsewhere."

"Sorry," I muttered reluctantly.

"I'll be good," added Trixie, "I won't even call her a female fox. But you must admit it's a scream. I can just see the headlines: 'The Secret Life of a Naughty Nun'."

Trixie threw the dice. "Two sixes. I start."

"That's just the sort of thing I'm not going to allow to happen," I snarled. "The police are not going to be told." I moved my piece. "Liverpool Street. I'll buy that." I laid down my money with determination and took the card.

Chummy threw her dice. "This is a Council of War, and I'm with you, old horse. The important thing is to protect Sister Monica Joan from the machinations of the Constabulary, what? Mum's the word, I say. What ho! Not a syllable. Lips sealed."

Cynthia shook the cup slowly and thoughtfully, and rattled the dice. "Well, someone's going to find out, even if *we* don't say anything. The police will search her room again; they are not fools, you know."

"I've thought of that," I said. "Perhaps we could take the jewels out of her room and hide them."

"Don't be a fool." Trixie was always too sharp for my liking. "Then you'd be an accessory."

"What's that? I thought accessories were things like gloves and handbags."

"Accessories are the law. You can be an accessory before the fact, or an accessory after the fact. It doesn't matter if it's before or after; either way you'd be in for it." Trixie pushed the dice to her neighbour as she spoke.

Chummy shook the dice. "I'd say she's got to the root of the matter. If the jewels were in your possession, the Robert Peelers would say you'd egged the old lady on. Bally awkward situation, and you'd be as sore as a gumboil. No. We've got to prove that she didn't know what she was doing." Chummy moved her piece, but decided not to buy.

Trixie jumped on it in a flash. "I'll buy that. Come off it. That old girl's as sharp as a razor. She's got it all weighed up. No one suspects a nun, so she's in the clear – that's what she thinks."

"I'm not so sure." Cynthia moved her piece. "The Angel Islington. I'll buy that. I like the blue properties. I think her mind is definitely disturbed."

"Don't give me that one," Trixie snapped. "She's as crafty as they come. Look how she manipulates everyone to get her own way. She knows exactly what she's doing. Another visit from the police would do her good. I'll put a house on each of my properties please, Bank."

Chummy was Bank and sorted out the high finance. "Well, I can't agree, old sport. I think another visit from the police would give her a stroke."

"Of course it would." I threw the dice so hard they overshot the board and landed on the floor. "The police will never know. I'll see to that."

Cynthia, who, as the room-owner, had the right to sit on the only chair, retrieved the dice. "I have a feeling it's not as easy as that. You have to tell 'the whole truth and nothing but the truth'."

"That's only in court," I said, "and we're not in court . . . yet. Park Lane – I'll buy that."

"You're not thinking straight, idiot, I've already got Mayfair. It won't do you any good. Anyway, if you end up in court giving evidence, you'll have to tell the whole truth."

I decided not to buy Park Lane and Trixie gleefully snapped it up.

"If you don't, it's called 'obstructing the course of justice'. I've heard my cousin talk about that."

It was Chummy's throw. "I've heard of that one, too. It's the same sort of thing as 'withholding evidence', which is a serious offence. I say, this pudding's no end good. Is there any more, madam hostess?"

"No, but I've got some biscuits here in my wardrobe. Just let me move the chair and I'll get them. How about a coffee?"

Trixie shook her head. "I've got a much better idea. My brother bought me a couple of bottles of sherry for Christmas; he thought I needed cheering up, stuck in a dreary hole like a convent. We'll have them now. It will help the discussion. We've got to come to a sensible decision about this. Get your tooth mugs, girls."

Trixie slid off the bed and Chummy remembered some chocolates and crystallised ginger left over from a previous occasion. I ran down the passage to get my tooth mug and some figs and dates, to which I was partial.

We settled down again around the Monopoly board, which had wobbled with all the movement on and off the bed. After some argument about whose piece was where, and which houses were on whose properties, we poured the sherry, took handfuls of food, and continued the game.

Trixie was clearly winning. She had houses on Park Lane and Mayfair, and the dice fell in her favour. Everyone seemed to stop there and had to pay rent. Groans all round. The sherry slid down nicely, assisted by all the sweet food. Chummy made a general point that had been in all of our minds.

"Where do you think, the old lady got all those sparklers from? I say, this sherry's going down a treat. I always say sherry tastes so much better out of a tooth mug than one of those bally little glasses, what? Perhaps the dregs of toothpaste in the bottom of the mug give it that special flavour. I did a cordon bleu course, you know, but the teacher never mentioned that. If I ever go back there, I'll recommend it. Hell's bells! Go back five places – that puts me in jail!"

Trixie giggled. "We'll get Sister Monica Joan in jail before the night's out. Sorry! Sorry! Don't take on so. Just stirring it up. Have another sherry!"

Cynthia filled my mug. "Yes, where did she get it from? There's nowhere in Poplar that sells expensive jewellery."

Trixie had the answer – inevitably. "I reckon she's been going to Hatton Garden. It's not far from here, only a short bus ride. A pious-looking old nun going around the shops and warehouses. Easy. No one would think to suspect her, the wicked old thing."

"She's not wicked," I shouted. "Don't you dare. She's—"

"Now, now, you two. My turn and I collect £200 for passing Go. Come on, Bank. Wake up. I want my money."

Chummy jerked herself upright. "I'm beginning to think the police have to be told because of this business of withholding the course."

"The what?"

"The course of evidence, of course."

"You're not making sense."

"Yes I am. You're not listening."

Cynthia was carefully tucking her £200 down her bra. "I think you mean the course of justice."

"That's what I said."

"No you didn't. You said the course of evidence."

"Well, same thing, and it's an offence."

"What is?"

"Holding the evidence, old bean. And it's not allowed."

"You mean withholding the evidence."

"That's what I said."

"No you didn't. You said holding it."

"Look here, this is going round in circles. Anyway it's my turn." Trixie picked up a card from the pack. "So you reckon we've got to get the police in again?"

"Yes, because of obstructing, old thing."

"No you don't. You want to get the police in again because you fancy that policeman."

"I don't. Don't you dare." Chummy gulped down her sherry and went bright red.

"Yes you do. You're sweet on him. I've seen you go all coy and giggly when he comes to the house."

"You're a regular shower. You've no right to come out with whoppers like that, you gumboil, you."

Poor Chummy looked as if she were on the verge of tears, so Cynthia came to her rescue.

"You're just stirring it up again, Trixie. You haven't looked at your card yet. Turn it over."

Trixie did so, and gave a howl of anguish "I'm ruined. I'm bankrupt. This isn't fair. Make repairs on all your houses. I shall have to sell. Give me another drink. I've got to think about this one." She took another mug of sherry and another chocolate.

"I'll take Mayfair and Park Lane off you at half-price," I said magnanimously.

"No you won't. I'm not selling at half-price."

"You've no option."

"That's what it is – obtion." Chummy was obviously thinking deeply, as she gazed into her mug. "Obtion – the course of justice. And it's an obtion, and you mustn't do it."

"There's no such thing as an obtion."

"Yes there is, and you mustn't obtion the justice of the course. I know it. My father told me. Someone he knew obtioned the justice course, and I can't remember what happened, but it happened."

"Well thanks for nothing. A lot of help, I'm sure. Look, I'm going to auction these. Does anyone want these priceless properties? I'll take eighty per cent. You won't get a better chance. All right then, seventy per cent, I'm not going to sink to half price, I'll have to do something else."

At that moment Chummy's legs got the cramp. They were too long to be kept in a confined space, and with a groan she stretched out, knocking the board for six.

"Well, that's that," said Trixie with satisfaction. "I'm the clear winner."

"No you're not. You haven't made repairs to your houses."

"I don't have to."

"Yes you do."

"Now don't you two start that again. Help me to clear up the board and the pieces. Chummy doesn't look as if she's going to be much help. There's a drop left in the bottom of this second bottle. Do you want to share it between you? I've had enough."

We did. Cynthia was shaking Chummy.

"Look, this is my bed. You go to your own bed."

Suddenly Trixie grabbed Cynthia's arm. "Oh my God! I've just had a dreadful thought."

"What?" we said in chorus.

"Chummy's on first call tonight."

"Never! Oh no! What's to be done?"

The three of us gazed at Chummy stretched full length, smiling sweetly and fast asleep on Cynthia's bed. We looked at each other, and looked again at the sleeping form.

Cynthia spoke. "I'll take first call tonight. There's nothing else for it. Trixie was out last night, so I'll take it if a call comes in. I've had less than you two anyway. We might as well leave Chummy here, and I'll sleep in her room. We must throw away these bottles and open the windows to let in some fresh air, in case one of the Sisters comes up here tomorrow. Go and open the windows on the landing, at both ends, and in the bathroom. We've got to get a good draught blowing through."

Thankful for Cynthia's common sense I went to open the windows. The cold air hit me like a pain, and my head began to reel. The window flew out of my grasp and struck the brickwork. Cynthia came up and secured it.

"I'm going to wash these mugs and wash out the bottles too, to get rid of the smell. You had better go to bed. You'll be on duty at 8 a.m. Don't listen for the telephone. I'll take any calls."

She went to Chummy's room and I to mine. For several nights I had lain awake, but that night I slept like a baby.

AUNT ANNE

As I entered Sister Monica Joan's room she glared at me. "I'll murder that fellow one of these days. You see if I don't. The dirty old goat!"

Strong language for a reverend Sister. It was intriguing, but I knew from experience that straight questions seldom got straight answers. However, if I entered Sister Monica Joan's world and, as far as possible, relived it with her, she would often recall whole scenes from long ago. So I said, "He's always up to something. What is it this time?"

"You've seen him at it?"

I nodded, and waited.

"He's always there. Lah–di–dahing around the factory gates in all his finery – silk shirt, bow tie and gold watch chain. I'll give him a silk shirt – I'll strangle him with his silk shirt, the old rascal."

This was going to be rich. She needed no prompting to continue. "Those poor girls in the shirt-making factories. They are the lowest paid of all the workers, and they work the longest hours, too. There's a grass bank outside the factory gate – you know the one I mean?" I nodded. "Well, he stands there in all his finery, twirling his moustache, and as the girls come out of the gate he throws coins, mostly copper, some silver, up the bank towards the wall, shouting. 'Scramble, girls, scramble for it.' And up the grass the girls go, shouting and pushing and laughing. There might even be a fight to get at a silver sixpence. The dirty old man."

I was beginning to wonder why such a philanthropic act should provoke such vitriol.

Sister Monica continued even more angrily. "It's degrading

them. Those girls wear no knickers, you know. How can they afford such a luxury? That's what he's after, the debauched old satyr. And when they are menstruating they have no protection. The blood just runs down their legs. The smell is supposed to be enticing. I don't know, perhaps it is. But it's degrading for those poor girls who scramble for a penny that will buy them a bun or a drop of milk. I can't bear to see women exploited in that way."

I finally understood what she was on about. "But women have always been exploited for their sexuality."

"Yes, I suppose so, and always will be, I fear. And no doubt some of them want to be. I dare say half the girls scrambling up the bank and sliding down with their skirts around their necks know what they are doing. But it pains me to see them degraded."

She did not continue with her thoughts, but asked me to go and see Mrs B about tea, which I did. When I returned to the room, Sister Monica Joan was not there. The jewels had been uppermost in my mind for days, so quietly I looked into the bedside cabinet. The drawer was empty.

As she had made no reference in the past few days to my earlier discovery, I had assumed that she had forgotten all about it. Perhaps I had fondly imagined that she had forgotten about the jewels. But now I knew she had not forgotten a thing and had taken the precaution of hiding them elsewhere. But where? Had she tucked them into her mattress? She was quite capable of cutting a small hole, stuffing them in and sewing it up neatly. No one would ever know.

Trixie's image of a crafty old vixen came to mind. Perhaps she was. Perhaps she was piling up wealth for some hidden purpose of her own. But at the age of ninety? It was hardly likely.

She swept back into the room in high spirits. No remorse, no shame that she had been caught stealing, no fear of future discoveries. Perhaps she had hidden them in the lavatory cistern or behind the bath.

Her opening comment was, as usual, quite baffling. "Twenty-seven dinner services, each with ninety-six pieces. I ask you, my dear, what sensible family could possibly need twenty-seven dinner services?"

Such a question requires a little thought before it can be answered.

Whilst I hesitated, she continued, "And fourteen sets of silver-plated cutlery. Would you believe it, every single piece, every fish fork or sugar tong, had to be counted and checked before it could be put away. Have you ever heard such nonsense? And they thought I would be content to spend my life counting fish forks."

I was beginning to understand. One had to get used to following sideways the many strands of Sister Monica Joan's thoughts. Perhaps the dinner services and the fish forks related to her family and her girlhood in the 1870s and 80s.

Her next statement confirmed this. "My poor mother was a slave to such possessions. For all her finery and 'Your Ladyship' she was more of a servant than her own servants. I doubt she knew a day of real freedom in her whole life. Poor woman. I loved her, and pitied her, but we never understood each other. My father ruled her life. Every move. Do you know, my dear, he had all her hair cut off and her teeth pulled out when she was less than thirty-five?"

I gasped: "How? Why?"

"She was never strong, always ailing. I don't know what was wrong with her, except perhaps that her corsets were too tight." Corsets. The accepted instrument of torture for women

"I remember it quite well. I was only a little girl but I remember my mother lying in bed with doctors present. One of them told my father that all her strength was going to her hair and her teeth and that they would have to go. She was never consulted in the matter, she told me many years later. Her head was shaved and all her teeth extracted. I was in the nursery and heard her screaming. It was barbaric, my dear, and ignorant. I was frightened when I saw her later: her face swollen; blood all over her pillow and sheets; a bald head. She was crying, poor woman. I was about twelve years old and something happened to me in that moment.

Something revolted inside me and I knew that women suffered through man's ignorance. As I stood by her bed, I changed from a carefree little girl into a thinking woman. I vowed I would not follow the pattern of my mother, my aunts and their friends. I would not become a wife whose husband could order that her teeth be pulled out, or who could be locked up like poor Aunt Anne. I would not spend my life counting fish forks. I would not be dominated by any man."

Sister Monica Joan's face assumed an expression of haughty defiance. The young can be very lovely, but the faces of the old can be truly beautiful. Every line and fold, every contour and wrinkle of Sister Monica Joan's fine white skin revealed her character, strength, courage, humanity and irrepressible humour.

I said, "Several times you have mentioned that your Aunt Anne was locked up. Why was this?"

"Oh my dear, it was iniquitous. Aunt Anne, my mother's sister, was put into a lunatic asylum because her husband was fed up with her!"

"What! You are joking," I retorted

"Don't you accuse me of joking, you saucy girl. If you are going to be rude to me you can leave the room." She turned her head and arched her eyebrows, slightly dilating her nostrils, the epitome of offended dignity, although I had a feeling she was putting it on for effect.

"Oh, come off it, Sister. You know that was just an expression. What happened to Aunt Anne? – that's what's important."

She turned to me and giggled like a child caught doing something naughty. But her expression quickly changed.

"Aunt Anne, dear Aunt Anne. She was my favourite aunt. Always pretty, always sweet and gentle with a soft laugh. When she visited the house she always came up to the nursery to spend time with us, to tell stories and play games with us. We all loved her. Then suddenly she came no more. No more."

Sister Monica Joan sat as still as a statue, gazing out of the window. The sun was shining and she moaned, "It's too bright, it hurts my eyes. Draw the curtain across, will you, child?"

I did so and when I returned she had her handkerchief to her eyes. "We never saw her again. When we asked our mother she just said, 'Hush, dears, we don't talk about Aunt Anne.' We kept thinking she would come back with her games and her stories; but she never did."

She sighed deeply and balanced her chin on her long fingers, lost in thought. "Poor woman, poor dear woman. She was defenceless."

"Did you ever find out what had happened?" I enquired.

"Yes, years later I found out. Her husband tired of her and wanted another woman. So he quite simply spread the story around that she was weak in the head and going mad. Perhaps he ill-treated her; perhaps his repeated insinuations really did unbalance her mind, so that she began to doubt her own sanity. We don't know, but it is not difficult to drive someone mad. Eventually her husband persuaded two doctors to certify that she was incurably insane. It would not have been difficult in those days. Perhaps the two doctors were cronies of his. Perhaps they were paid to certify. I do not suppose she was ever examined properly by an independent and impartial psychiatrist, as she would be today. It would have been very easy for him to choose his own doctors and the certificate was irreversible. Aunt Anne was taken away, taken from her children, who from then on were motherless. She was locked up in an asylum, where she remained for the rest of her life. She died in 1907."

"That is one of the most shocking stories I have ever heard," I said.

"It was not uncommon. It was a very clever way for a rich man to get rid of an unwanted wife. He had to pay for the asylum, of course, but that would not trouble a rich man. After a period of years, I don't know how many, he could get a divorce with no scandal. Easy!"

"And did the woman have no one to speak for her?"

"Oh yes, her father or a brother could, and probably would. It was not always plain sailing for an unscrupulous husband. But my grandfather, Anne's father, was dead, and there were no brothers, only four daughters in the family. So poor Anne had no one to protect her."

"Could her mother or sisters not speak for her?"

"Women had no voice in any matter. It had been the same for centuries. That is what we fought for." Her eyes flashed and she banged the desk. "Independence for women. Freedom from male dominance."

"Were you a suffragette?" I asked.

"Bah! Suffragettes. I've no time for suffragettes. They made the biggest mistake in history. They went for equality. They should have gone for power!" With a dramatic gesture she swept her arm across the desk, scattering pencils, papers and notebooks to the floor. "But I broke the mould in my family when I announced that I was going to be a nurse. Oh, you should have heard the rumpus. It would have been funny if it had not been so deadly serious. My father locked me in my room and threatened to keep me there indefinitely. Then he tried to insinuate that I was mad and should be confined to an asylum like poor Aunt Anne. But times were changing. Women were beginning to break the chains of their bondage. Florence Nightingale led the way and many others followed. I wrote to Miss Nightingale from my prison in my father's house. She was quite an old lady by then, but she was very powerful. She spoke to Queen Victoria on my behalf. I don't know what they said, but the result was that I was released from captivity. My poor docile mother never really recovered from the shock of having a rebel daughter. Nonetheless, I was thirty-two before I could break away from my father's domination and start nursing. That was when my life began."

The chapel bell rang for Vespers.

Sister Monica Joan took up her black veil and adjusted it over her white wimple. She turned to me with a naughty wink. "If my father had seen me as a nun, he would have had a stroke. But mercifully he was spared, because he died the same year that the old Queen died. Hand me my prayer book, child."

It was on the floor, along with the other items that had been pushed from her desk. I retrieved everything that was scattered around, placed them all on the desk and handed her the prayer book.

"Now for it," she said, her head held high, her eyebrows arched in a slightly supercilious curve. A mischievous grin crinkled the corners of her mouth and eyes. "Now for it," she said again as she swept out of the room.

There was nothing cringing or pathetic about Sister Monica Joan. She was going to battle it out to the end. If she couldn't face her Sisters in chapel, she would sit with her back to them, and if they didn't like it, they could lump it.

After the evening visits we took supper in the kitchen. This was a meal prepared by ourselves, because we all came in at different times. We were looking the worse for wear, particularly Chummy, who couldn't hold her drink but did not want to admit it, and had been protesting all day that she thought she had a touch of flu. Chummy was, in addition, torn by a feeling of guilt because she was supposed to have been on first call that night and it had been Cynthia who had gone out at the bleakest hour before dawn, 3 a.m. We sat down around the kitchen table, eating our peanut-butter sandwiches.

"They've gone," I whispered, in case any of the Sisters were in the hallway.

"What's gone?"

"The jewels, they've gone. They are not in the drawer."

Trixie eyed me dubiously. "Are you sure they were there in the first place? After all, we've only got your word for it. Perhaps you dreamed the whole thing. Sister Evangelina calls you Dolly Daydream, and not without reason."

"I did not dream it. I tell you, I saw them and now they've gone."

"Well she must have hidden them somewhere else, the cunning old—"

Cynthia stopped her. "Don't you two start on that again. I'm too tired to put up with you squabbling like a couple of children. Pack it in."

Chummy groaned and spoke in a weary voice: "I second that motion, Chairman. My poor bally head feels like a suet pudding that's gone cold and been warmed up again for the servants. Did I hear you say that the jewels have gone?"

"Yes."

"Well strike me pink."

Trixie was quick off the mark. "She's hidden them. It's as clear as daylight. She knows she's been rumbled, so she's hidden them again. You can't tell me she doesn't know what she's doing. Of course she does." Trixie cut another slice of bread and dug her knife into the jar.

Cynthia was less emphatic. "Well, this does throw rather a different light on things. I still don't think she knows what she's doing."

"Oh, go on with you. She pulls the wool over everyone's eyes. But she doesn't fool me for a moment," said cynical Trixie.

Chummy was licking the peanut butter off the knife.

"Premeditation. That's what the constabulary will be after. Were her actions premeditated or were they not? If we're going to protect Sister Monica Joan, Counsel for the Defence, that's what we've got to prove. But at the moment, my poor bally head aches so much I can't think straight. I'm going to bed. Who's on first call?"

"You are."

"Groan, groan and thrice groan. That settles it. I must get in a bit of the old sweet slumber before that accursed bell pitches me out onto the floor. Nighty-night all. Sweet dreams."

Cynthia stood up. "And I'm going to bed too. Don't you two start quarrelling as soon as you're alone."

Trixie looked at me when they had gone. "I reckon there's not much more to say. Chummy hit the nail on the head. Was it, or was it not, premeditated? Come on, let's do the washing up."

RECREATION HOUR

Recreation in a convent is a time when the nuns can let their hair down – metaphorically, of course. Usually the recreation hour lasts from 2 p.m. to 3 p.m. With the morning work completed, lunch taken and no religious duties to perform until Vespers at 4.30 p.m., the nuns are free. But "free" only within the discipline of the order. At Nonnatus House, during the recreation hour, the nuns withdrew collectively to their sitting room, where they would engage in needlework and polite conversation.

How these reverend ladies found time for it defeats me to this day. Each of the nuns seemed capable of packing forty-eight hours of work into every twenty-four and each of them did it with serenity and grace. Sister Julienne, for example, who was Sister-in-Charge, was not only the senior nurse and midwife with overall responsibility for the practice, but she was also in charge of the smooth running of the house. She was accountable for maintaining the monastic tradition of religious observance, instructing the novices, teaching the student midwives, acting as hostess to numerous house guests, handling convent finances and keeping the accounts. She took her fair share of district visits, including night calls, as well as finding time to engage in needlework and polite conversation during her brief hours of recreation when most people would want to lie horizontal with their feet up.

It was their practice, as I have said, for the nuns to retire to their sitting room after lunch. But occasionally Sister Julienne would say at lunch time, "I think we will take recreation in the nurses' sitting room today," whereupon the Sisters would look with a particular benevolence upon us girls, as though they were granting us some special favour. The nuns would then go to their cells (nuns sleep in cells, not bedrooms) to collect their work, and we would rush to our sitting room to clear away dirty plates, mugs, ashtrays, magazines, glasses, empty chocolate boxes, biscuit tins, hairbrushes, medical books (yes, occasionally, we put in a bit of study), and all the paraphernalia essential to the life of the average young girl.

The Sisters entered and we smiled sweetly, as though we hadn't been frantically clearing things away for the past five minutes. Sister Evangelina, not famous for her tact, glared around her, growling, "Well, Nurse Browne, I believe your mother is coming to visit you at the weekend. You had better tidy the place up before she comes."

"Oh, but we have just had a thumping good tidy up for you, Sister." Chummy was not offended, simply puzzled.

Trixie gave a shrill laugh and was about to speak, but Cynthia, the peacemaker, retorted, "We'll get out the Hoover, the polish and the dusters before the weekend, Sister."

Sister Evangelina snorted her disapproval and opened her workbox. Everyone did the same except Trixie and me. Neither of us owned a workbox; we did not sew or knit for recreation.

Sister Julienne was concerned. "Oh, my dears, perhaps you could each make a little tea cosy for the Christmas Fayre. Tea cosies always go down well. People buy them for Christmas presents."

Material, stuffing, scissors, needles and cotton were provided and conversation centred on the desirability of a large number of tea cosies to boost the convent's finances for the coming year. As well as everything else, the Sisters not only organised and ran a sale each year, but made a large number of the items to be sold. For many decades the finance for supporting the midwifery practice had, to some extent, depended on the monies collected at the Christmas Fayre.

The Sisters were making many small items considered to be useful or necessary in those days, such as handkerchief sachets, glove folders, pincushions, cushion covers, tray cloths, tablecloths, pillowcases and virtually anything else onto which a bird or a

Hackney Workhouse c.1911. *Photo courtesy of the Corporation of London, London Metropolitan Archives.*

BELOW The Poplar Tenements, known as the Canada Buildings. They were bug-infested and closed in the 1960s. Joseph Collett lived here. *Photo taken in the 1950s by midwife Jean Todd.*

ABOVE Typical domestic scene, c.1900: they are poor, but not destitute. When I look at this I think of Frank and little Peggy when their mother was alive. *Photo courtesy of Bancroft Library, the Cohen Collection 1900–1910.*

LEFT Poplar Workhouse c.1905.
Photo courtesy of Bancroft Library.

Women picking oakum c.1890. Oakum was pieces of old rope untwisted and pulled apart; the fibres were used to fill holes and cracks in wooden boats and ships. Women and children were forced to do this work, which tore the hands and nails. *Photo courtesy of the National Trust Photographic Library.*

Workhouse boys with their schoolmaster c.1870. The Education Act 1870 required children to be taught the three Rs. This is a very rare picture of workhouse boys with their schoolmaster. *Photo courtesy of the Local History Collection of Gravesend Library.*

ABOVE Flat barges with their distinctive red sails were a common feature of the Thames and were in use for at least 200 years. Joe Collett's first job was as a bargee. *Photo courtesy of the Island History Trust Collection.*

LEFT The gambling school, Shadwell, c.1910–20. Frank was an addicted gambler and groups like this could be found everywhere. It was illegal and the boys have a furtive air about them, on the look-out for the police. *Photo by F C Wright, the Highway Clubs in East London, Bancroft Library. Courtesy of Jeff Wright.*

LEFT Hackney Workhouse babies, c.1900. At least these babies went out! A Royal Commission Report 1909 revealed that in many urban workhouses the babies never left the premises and that 40% died in their first year in the workhouse. Jane would have been taken out in a pram like this. *Photo courtesy of the Hackney Archives.*

BELOW St Pancras Workhouse, London c.1906. *Photo courtesy of Camden Local Studies and Archives Centre.*

Hackney Workhouse children c.1900. *Photo courtesy of the Hackney Archives.*

daisy-chain could be embroidered. Conversation centred on the saleability of each item for the Christmas Fayre. The need for a large number of chair-back covers puzzled me and, even more, the name by which they were called – 'antimacassars' – until I learned that they were intended to protect the back of a chair from the grease on men's hair. Many men plastered their hair with Brylcreem in those days and the oil used in Victorian times was Macassar.

I looked around me with pleasure. It was all very genteel and sweet; it could have been a scene from any period in history when ladies had almost nothing else to do. Sister Julienne was making rag dolls with great speed and efficiency, creating tiny waistcoats and shoes, fixing button eyes and snipping wool hair. Sister Bernadette was an expert in golliwogs. Children are not allowed to have such toys today, nor even to use the word, but in those days they were all the fashion. Sister Evangelina was hemming handkerchiefs, and Novice Ruth – what on earth was she doing? Novice Ruth had a wooden object rather like a large cotton reel. Four nails, without heads, had been hammered into the top. The Novice was plying heavy linen thread round and round the nails with a small blunt instrument and pulling the thread over the nails at each turn. Through the centre of the wooden reel a woven band emerged. It was already a yard or two long, but still Novice Ruth continued plying the thread and weaving.

What on earth was it? I watched, fascinated. She must have read my mind because she laughed and said, "You wonder what I am doing. This will be my girdle. I am approaching the time of my first profession, when I shall take my first vows. A Sister wears a woven girdle wound three times around her waist and, at the end, we tie three knots. This is a constant reminder of our three vows of poverty, chastity and obedience."

She had such a beautiful face and such a radiant smile. Her vocation clearly filled her with joy.

Conversation continued about the Christmas Fayre and who should attend the stalls. Mrs B as usual, was in charge of the cake stall, and Fred, the boiler man, always managed a very good stall selling second-hand tools, which attracted men to the Fayre. It was Fred's proud boast that he could sell anything. Give him a bag of bent, rusty nails and he would sell them for you.

The doorbell rang.

"Now who can that be?" said Sister. "We're not expecting anyone. Would you answer it, please, Nurse Browne."

Chummy laid down her expert embroidery and left the room. We continued talking about the Christmas Fayre, speculating if the band from the SPY Club could be asked to provide some entertainment. Should they be paid and, if so, how much? "How about tea and cakes?" someone ventured. "Wouldn't that be sufficient payment?"

"What on earth has happened to Nurse Browne?" Sister Evangelina grunted. "She's been gone at least five minutes. It doesn't take that long to answer the door."

At that moment Chummy re-entered the room. She was bright red. She took a step forward and kicked a waste-paper basket, which shot into the air, spilling its contents as it flew. It hit Sister Evangelina on the side of the head, knocking her veil and wimple sideways. The shock caused her to prick her finger and blood spurted over the handkerchief she was hemming.

"You clumsy fool," she shouted. "Look what you have made me do." She sucked her finger and waved the ruined handkerchief at Chummy.

Sister Julienne took charge. "Never mind, Sister, use the handkerchief to bind the finger or we shall have blood all over the other work. Better to spoil one item than half a dozen? Now, Nurse Browne, what on earth is the matter?"

Chummy opened her mouth and her lips moved but no sound came. She tried again with no success.

The Sisters were seriously concerned. "My poor child, do sit down."

Chummy sat down and again tried to speak. Her vocal chords finally responded and the words came out in a rush. "Please,

Sister, the policeman is at the door and he wants to see you."

Trixie gave a scream of laughter. "Didn't I tell you! There, look, Chummy's sweet on the policeman!"

Cynthia kicked her hard.

Sister Julienne looked troubled. "Oh dear, oh bother. I'll go at once."

We all looked at one another. Sister Julienne would only use such an extreme expression as "oh bother" in an extreme situation.

The knowledge that the policeman was at the door again gave me a nasty jolt. I had managed to lay aside the awful dilemma of the jewels found in Sister Monica Joan's room. I looked anxiously at Cynthia, who was embroidering a cushion cover and who refused to look up. All the Sisters were silently bent over their work. Chummy took up her sewing again but her hands were shaking so much that she could not control the needle.

Only Trixie spoke. "Well, now for it. They've come to take her away. There'll be a right old rumpus."

Sister Evangelina turned on her. "Hold your tongue, you thoughtless, loud-mouthed girl. Just keep quiet for once."

"Sorry, I'm sure." Trixie didn't look at all sorry.

I managed to catch Cynthia's eye and we exchanged a look of alarm. Novice Ruth stifled a tear and worked furiously at the girdle she was making. Sister Bernadette was stuffing a golliwog, poking the stuffing down hard into the legs. The clock ticked and no one spoke except for the occasional "Pass the scissors, please", or "Have you got the light-blue thread over there?"

The soft footsteps of Sister Julienne were heard and we all looked up expectantly, but she passed the door and went upstairs. Glances of real anguish were exchanged between the Sisters.

All the muscles around my chest and stomach seemed to tighten at once and I felt hot all over. "Could we open a window, do you think?" I enquired.

"I was about to suggest the same thing," said Sister Bernadette, and Cynthia, who was nearest to the window, stood up and opened it. The clock ticked on and we continued sewing. No one spoke.

Again footsteps were heard – descending the stairs this time. We all looked up, each with the same thought in mind. What were they going to do with her?

The door burst open and Sister Julienne stood there, her features filled with joy. "They are dropping all charges and taking no further action! Oh, the relief, I can't tell you the relief. I have just been up to see Sister Monica Joan to convey the news, although I am not sure that she understood what I was saying because she just looked at me in complete silence."

"Praise the Lord," said Sister Evangelina, sniffing hard. She blew her nose loudly into the blood-stained handkerchief and wiped the corner of her eye. "Let us praise the Lord for his mercy."

We were all overjoyed at the news, but Sister Evangelina displayed more emotion and relief than anyone else in the room. Her reaction brought home to me the genuine goodness and charity of the woman who had suffered so much from Sister Monica Joan's verbal cruelty. The apparent dislike between the two women was not of her making, and a less loving soul might have been indifferent, if not secretly glad, to see her Sister's downfall.

Sister Julienne sat down. "This calls for a celebration so I have asked Mrs B to bring up an early tea and we will have jam with our scones today."

Mrs B came bouncing in with a large tray. "There, din' I tell yer? As innocen' as a new-born babe, she is. An' them police, they wants their bleedin' 'eads (beggin' yer pardon, Sisters) bangin' together, vey do. An' I'd like to ge' me 'ands on vat lyin' coster, I would."

Sister Julienne burst out laughing. "You'll do no such thing. We don't want you had up for assault. Perhaps you would pour the tea, Novice Ruth, and pass the scones."

Mrs B withdrew. The tea and scones were passed round, not

forgetting the jam. Everyone was in festive mood.

Sister Julienne continued her story. "Apparently the legal adviser to the police has suggested that, due to the age of the suspect and the triviality of the items found in her room, the police might find themselves in a position of ridicule if they were to proceed with prosecution. The costers involved have been informed that a charge will not be brought by the Public Prosecutor but they would be within their rights to bring a civil action. Due to the fact that a civil case costs so much money and that they would be unlikely to get compensation, damages or costs, the costers have decided not to proceed." Sister Julienne gave a huge sigh of relief, caressing her cup as she raised it to her lips.

We four girls could not share the happiness of the Sisters. We knew something of which they were completely unaware. The knowledge of the jewels in Sister Monica Joan's possession weighed heavily upon us. I was terrified that Trixie would blurt out something ill-considered that would give the game away. Cynthia and I exchanged glances and clearly the same thought was going through her mind also. She was sitting near Trixie so she nudged her and I was grateful to see her mouth the words, "We'll talk later." A plan was forming in my mind to remove the jewels from Sister Monica Joan's room, take them to Hatton Garden and just leave them somewhere. My mind was racing – yes, that would be the answer, or perhaps I could leave them outside a police station a long way away, so no one would suspect. But where would I find them? The beastly things had gone from Sister's bedside cabinet. Perhaps I could talk to her about it. Would she see reason? It would be good to talk to Cynthia later; she was always so sensible.

Sister Julienne said, "I knew our prayers would be answered. I do so believe in the power of prayer. No need for a lawyer now, eh?" and she giggled, happily. I squirmed – if only she knew – and my resolve to find the wretched jewels and dispose of them grew firmer.

Tea was being cleared away, the sewing brought out again, and we all settled down to work.

The door opened. Sister Monica Joan stood at the threshold. She did not enter the room immediately but stood quite still, one hand resting on the door. She was wearing her full outdoor habit, with the long black veil, perfectly adjusted over the white wimple. She looked magnificent. Everyone stopped talking, laid down their sewing and looked up at her. Yet she did not move, her hand remained motionless on the door handle, her hooded eyes were half-closed, her eyebrows raised, and a slightly supercilious smile played around the corners of her mouth. She had a magnetic quality about her that forbade speech.

Then she moved for the first time; slowly and deliberately she turned her head, beautifully poised on its long neck, and scrutinised each person in the room with a level and unfaltering gaze. She looked each of us straight in the eye for a few seconds, then turned her head very slightly and looked at the next person. No one dared to speak or move. I have never seen a more riveting performance in my life.

It was Sister Monica Joan herself who broke the silence. She tilted her head slightly to one side and raised an eyebrow. A naughty little grin lit her features. "Greetings all. Did I ever tell you about the Thief of Baghdad? They boiled him in oil, don't you know; or perhaps they drowned him in a butt of Malmsey wine. One or the other, I'm not sure which; but they did him in, I'm sure of that."

Sister Julienne rose, both arms outstretched. "Oh my dear, say no more about that dreadful business. Not another word. It was all a misunderstanding and we have put it behind us. But come in and join our happy circle. I see you have your knitting bag with you."

Sister Monica Joan graciously consented to be led into the room. Sister Evangelina rose from her seat. "Have this chair, my dear; it is the most comfortable." Sister Monica Joan sat down.

The jewels! They flashed and glistened into my mind. They

had to be disposed of and now was the perfect time. Sister Monica Joan was knitting quietly and everyone else was sewing and chatting. There might never be such an opportunity again.

I excused myself and left the room. At the bottom of the stairs I removed my shoes, so that no one would hear footsteps. It was the work of a moment to reach Sister Monica Joan's room. Quietly I entered and wedged a chair under the handle, in case anyone tried to enter. The search started. I scrutinised every inch of that room, every drawer, every shelf, every cupboard; I felt all over the mattress, the pillows, the cushions; the tops and the hems of the curtains. I rummaged through her underwear and her habits – it wasn't seemly to pry into a nun's private things, but it had to be done. Nothing! Nowhere! My earlier thought about the lavatory cistern returned, and I raced along the corridor to the bathroom. Still nothing. I began to feel panic grip me; recreation hour must surely be drawing to a close. If one of the Sisters found me on their private landing or in their bathroom, there would be a lot of explaining to do. Running downstairs and replacing my shoes took only a few seconds, and I was back in the sitting room just as the ladies began to fold up their sewing and talk about the evening visits.

I muttered my excuses: "I'm sorry, Sister, I don't seem to have got on very well with the tea cosy. I don't think I'm much good at sewing."

Sister Julienne smiled. "That's perfectly all right, we can't all be good at the same things."

She turned to Sister Monica Joan. "Can I help you, dear? That is a lovely baby's shawl you are knitting. Can I help you put it away?"

She took the handle of the knitting bag. Sister Monica Joan grabbed the bag back. "Don't touch it, leave it to me." She pulled the side nearest to her, but the handle on the other side was caught over Sister Julienne's wrist. The seam burst and a shower of rings, watches, gold chains and bracelets was flung across the floor.

THE TRIAL

Total silence followed. The two halves of the torn knitting bag were held by Sister Julienne and Sister Monica Joan, who looked at each other for what seemed an eternity.

Sister Monica Joan was the first to speak. "Inanimate objects have a life of their own, independent of the creature, have you not noticed?" She glanced at each of us in turn. "And whenever an atom gets excited it creates magnetic fields."

"Are you suggesting, Sister, that these inanimate objects were somehow magnetised into your knitting bag, independent of human activity?" Sister Julienne's voice was sarcastic.

"Most certainly. 'There are stranger things in heaven and earth than are dreamed of in your philosophy, Horatio.'"

"Don't call me Horatio."

"Poof, hoity-toity." Sister Monica Joan was aloof. "The difficulty of comparative study is the incomprehension of lesser minds. But keep the trinkets. Use them well. In the latter days they will be interpreted in a mystery play, a drama, an allegory. Use them well, I say; they have their own life, their own force, their own destiny." And with that she floated out of the room.

Trixie's suppressed giggles exploded. She turned to me. "I believe you now. I thought your fevered imagination was working overtime. The cunning old . . . Sorry, Sister."

Sister Julienne looked at me. "How long have you known about this?"

"About two weeks." I was feeling very uncomfortable.

"And you said nothing to me?"

I could only mutter a feeble: "I'm sorry, Sister."

"Come to my office after supper and before Compline. We

must gather up these things." She bent down and started picking up the jewels. We all helped in silence.

It was difficult to concentrate on my evening round, and babies that would not feed seemed perverse and irritating. Part of me was glad that the secret, which had oppressed me for days, was at last out in the open. On the other hand I was furious with myself for not having managed to dispose of the jewels before Sister Julienne found them. The knowledge that she required me in her office later gave me an uneasy feeling, and my legs turned the pedals reluctantly as I cycled back to Nonnatus House.

As soon as I entered the clinical room I knew, from the atmosphere, that the police were in the house. Usually, after a day's work, a group of young girls would make quite a lot of noise, chattering and giggling as they packed their bags and cleared up; but not on this occasion.

Novice Ruth looked up. Her eyes were red and her voice seemed subdued. "You are to go to Sister Julienne's office at once," she said.

A sick feeling grabbed at my stomach. Cynthia said: "I'll do your bag. Leave it here, and don't worry."

I knocked on the office door and entered. The same sergeant and constable who had been assigned to the case earlier were present. The jewels were spread out on the desk.

Sister Julienne spoke. "Here is the nurse who has known of the existence of this —" She hesitated — "this ... little haul, for more than fortnight."

My face was burning and I felt like a criminal.

The sergeant spoke to me, the constable taking notes all the while. They required my name, my age, home address, next of kin, father's occupation and many more details besides.

"When did you first see these jewels?"

"On a Monday afternoon, two weeks ago."

"Can you identify them?"

"Not really, I did not look closely enough."

"But are they substantially the same?"

"Yes."

"Where did you find them?"

"In the third drawer down of the bedside cabinet."

The constable looked back through his notebook. "We looked in the bedside cabinet, sir, and there was nothing there. They must have been placed there after our search."

"Just what I was thinking. And what did you do, nurse?"

"Nothing."

"Were you aware that these jewels are of considerable value?"

"I guessed they might be, but I didn't know."

Sister Julienne intervened. "Why did you not tell me?"

"I promised I wouldn't."

Sister Julienne was about to speak, but the sergeant silenced her.

"Who did you promise?"

"Sister Monica Joan."

"So she knew you had seen them?"

"Yes."

"And she made you promise not to tell?"

"Yes – no. She didn't make me promise. I just did."

"Why?"

"Because she was so upset."

"What was she upset about?"

"The jewels."

"Upset that you had found them?"

"I suppose so."

"Upset that she had been found out?"

"I don't know."

"Was she upset before you found them?"

"No. She was happy."

"And she was happy when you left her?"

"Yes."

"Why?"

I didn't want to answer. But he repeated: "Why?"

"I suppose she was happy because I had promised not to tell."

The sergeant looked at the constable. "Sister Monica Joan obviously knows what she has been doing. First she moves the jewels around to avoid detection and then when they are found, she is clearly relieved when a promise of secrecy is made."

He turned to me again. "At the time of finding the jewels, nurse, did you know that the police were investigating a charge of shoplifting brought by local costers?"

"Yes."

"And did it not occur to you that the jewels might be relevant to police investigations?"

"I don't know."

"Nurse, I won't insult you by suggesting you are stupid!"

"Well, yes, I did think they were relevant."

"Were you aware that withholding evidence during a police investigation is a criminal offence?"

My mouth went dry and my head began to spin. It is one thing to engage in underhand behaviour, but quite another to be told by a police sergeant that you have been guilty of a criminal offence. My voice was barely audible.

"I didn't know until a few days ago that it was a criminal offence."

"And what happened a few days ago?"

"I told the girls."

Sister Julienne exploded. "You told the girls and you didn't tell me. This is outrageous!"

"Why did you tell the girls and not the Sister-in-Charge?"

"Because I knew that Sister Julienne would have to tell the police, but the girls wouldn't."

"And what did the girls say?"

"I can't quite remember. We had a couple of bottles of sherry and I'm not sure what we said. It all got a bit confused."

The constable taking notes gave a chortle, that was quickly smothered when the sergeant stared at him.

Sister Julienne's blood pressure was rising fast. "This gets worse and worse. You girls had a couple of bottles of sherry when you were on duty! We will talk about this later."

I groaned in despair. Now I had got my friends into trouble too.

The sergeant interrupted. "Let's get back to the jewels. You decided to conceal the information from the police, but what did you intend to do?"

"I thought I could take the jewels from Sister Monica Joan's room and just leave them somewhere, in Hatton Garden, or outside a police station."

The sergeant and the constable exchanged glances.

"But I couldn't find them, so I couldn't do it."

"She had moved them from the bedside cabinet?"

"Yes."

"It's a very good thing for you, nurse, that you could not find the jewels. If you had done as you have suggested and been apprehended with the jewels on your person, you would have been in serious trouble."

I went cold. Theft, prison. The end of my nursing career. The end of everything.

The sergeant was watching me carefully. Then he spoke. "We are not going to take any further action, nurse. This is a caution, and will be recorded as such. You have been very foolish. I hesitate to call you a silly young girl, but that is what you are, and I hope this will be a lesson to you. You can go now."

I crept out of Sister's office numb with shock. To be called a "silly young girl" by a police sergeant when you think you are so mature and responsible is not a pleasant experience.

The girls pressed me for information. We sat round the kitchen table eating cheese-and-pickle sandwiches and home-made cake and I told them all about it. Narrowly missing prison was foremost in my mind.

"Not a chance, old scout. We'd have stood by you," said Chummy staunchly. Her loyalty reminded me of my own dis-loyalty – I had let the cat out of the bag about the sherry party. I was contrite in my apologies. Cynthia, as always, was soothing, pointing out that we were all in it together and no harm had come of it. She advised cocoa all round and an early night.

The jewels were taken by the police for identification and Hatton Garden jewellers who had reported losses over several years were asked to examine them. One man, Samuelson by name, positively identified a rope of antique pearls and a diamond ring as having been stolen from his stock a few years previously. He produced record books verifying his statement.

The testimony of costers who had seen Sister Monica Joan take small items from their stalls was also required. With their evidence, combined with that of Mr Samuelson, the police decided that, on a variety of counts, there was now a case against Sister Monica Joan. However, her mental fitness was in doubt, so a medical assessment was required.

The general practitioner who had known Sister Monica Joan for many years and who had attended her through her recent bout of pneumonia was consulted. He said that he was baffled and quite unable to decide whether or not she was senile, and advised obtaining the report of a psychiatrist.

The psychiatrist was a lady, a senior consultant in psychiatry at the London Hospital, who examined Sister Monica Joan twice at Nonnatus House. Her report stated that, in spite of her age, Sister's mind was remarkably clear. All her responses were swift and accurate; she was astute, observant and cryptic in her conversation; her understanding of past and present events was impressive; and she had a clear understanding of the difference between right and wrong. No evidence of mental deterioration could be found and the psychiatrist considered that Sister Monica Joan could be held responsible for her actions.

Having considered the two medical reports, the police decided to prosecute and they referred the evidence to Old Street Magistrates' Court for a preliminary hearing.

Three magistrates agreed unanimously that there was a prima

facie case of larceny, for which a younger person would undoubtedly have stood trial at the London Quarter Sessions. However, the presiding magistrate was exceedingly doubtful, considering the age of the accused. He had a grandmother of ninety-three who did not know the time of day nor even recognise her own daughter and he was very sympathetic towards extreme old age.

Whilst the charges were being read by the police superintendent, Sister Monica Joan sat between her solicitor and Sister Julienne, who was scarlet with embarrassment and kept her eyes lowered. In contrast, Sister Monica Joan sat upright and looked around her with haughty grandeur, every now and then exclaiming something-like "poof" or "tosh" or "fiddlesticks".

When the superintendent had finished, the presiding magistrate said, "You have heard the charges?"

"I most certainly have."

"And do you understand them?"

"Don't be impertinent, my man. Do you think I am stupid?"

"No, Sister, I don't. But I must be quite sure that you understand the charges brought against you by the police."

Sister Monica Joan did not answer. She looked towards the clock on the wall and raised her veined hand towards her chin like an actress posing for a photograph.

"I am not sure that she does, sir," said Sister Julienne quietly to the solicitor who stood up to speak.

But, before he could do so, Sister Monica Joan turned on them with quiet rage. "Do not presume to speak for me. Speak for yourselves. Bear witness to your own imperfections. We stand, each of us, alone and naked before the Judgement Throne, where none but the silent dead can testify."

The presiding magistrate was having second thoughts. This was very different from a grandmother whose conversation was confined to: "I'm ninety-three, you know, think of that, ninety-three." He addressed Sister Monica Joan very seriously. "Have you understood the charges brought against you?"

"I have."

"Do you plead 'guilty' or 'not guilty'?"

"Guilty! Guilty? Do you imagine, my good fellow, that I accept a charge of guilt from the hoi-polloi I see before me?" She sniffed scornfully and drew out a laced handkerchief from beneath her scapular, which she applied to her nose with an affected gesture, as though an unpleasant smell had assailed her. "Guilty indeed – huh? 'Let he who is without sin cast the first stone.' Does your small mind understand the hidden meaning of 'guilt'? Before you use the word again, it behoves you to find out, if perchance you are capable of such intellectual exercise, which I very much doubt."

Such rudeness to the presiding magistrate was Sister Monica Joan's undoing. Had she shown a little more humility, a little more uncertainty or even contrition, it is likely that, in their discretionary powers, the magistrates would have taken the matter no further. As it was, after a brief consultation, the decision was made to accept a plea of not guilty and to refer the case to the London Quarter Sessions for trial by judge and jury.

Sister Julienne was devastated by Sister Monica Joan's performance in the Magistrates' Court. She had hoped that the matter would end quietly there, but now the full publicity of the Quarter Sessions would have to be faced. But Sister Julienne was not a woman easily beaten. She prayed about the matter. The inspiration granted to her from a heavenly source was that the defence of mental deterioration should be strengthened. She consulted the solicitor and it was decided to obtain a third medical opinion.

Sir Lorimer Elliott-Bartram had an enviable reputation as a psychologist. He was well known in London, having given medical evidence in several legal cases. Sir Lorimer was getting on in years but not so far on that he could not maintain a thriving practice in Harley Street. In fact, the further on he got, the more patients came flocking to his doors and therefore the more money he made. It was all very satisfactory.

Sir Lorimer had qualified as a surgeon in 1912, and had had a distinguished record as an army doctor in the First World War – distinguished, according to the military commanders, as a first-rate officer and doctor; and distinguished, according to the men in the ranks, as a butcher.

Although Sir Lorimer had never qualified, nor attempted to qualify, as a psychiatrist, he had made a fortune in Harley Street by dabbling in psychotherapy, memory loss, personality change, mental block, hypomania, dypsomania, kleptomania and related subjects. He was a tall, handsome man with a deep, resonant voice that could easily adopt a silky tone. The majority of his patients were women.

There is an old saying in medical circles that if you want to make a study of invective, you should listen to two doctors talking about a third. In psychiatric circles Sir Lorimer, a mere psychologist, was regarded as a pompous old windbag and a chancer, who fuelled the tank of his Rolls-Royce with the blood of rich old ladies.

Oozing opulence, Sir Lorimer entered Nonnatus House and was taken to Sister Monica Joan's room. He kissed her hand and called her "dear reverend lady".

She murmured, "What a relief to meet a mature gentleman of experience and understanding."

He kissed her hand a second time, whispering: "I understand everything, dear lady, everything."

She sighed and smiled: "I am sure you do, Sir Lorimer, quite sure."

Later that day, just before Compline, I asked Sister Monica Joan if she liked Sir Lorimer.

She was sitting comfortably by the window knitting. Her face assumed a bright, plastic smile as she cooed, "He is charming, my dear, perfectly charming –" the smile vanished, and a hard edge entered her voice – "and determined to be so."

Sir Lorimer's report was very long and technically complex. For the benefit of the lay reader who is unfamiliar with medical terminology, I have attempted to summarise and simplify it. The report stated:

> Sister Monica Joan is a lady of the Leptosomatic type with a nervous affinity to the Cyclothymic make-up on the one hand and a tendency to Catatonic excitement on the other. Neologism and Disconnection, though slight, could not be discounted. Whereas elucidation of the former may throw light upon the latter, comprehension of the latter seldom throws light upon the former, from which it may be deduced that individual psychological symptomatology must be sought in personal biography. The Korsakaw Psychosis of Registration, Retention and Recall is important. A link between Retrograde Amnesia is consistent with the facility, richness and rapidity of association. Whilst Depersonalisation is not a factor, Derealisation is and Catatonic symptoms are not evidence of Catatonia, though significant to the trained mind. Kleptomania is consistent in Cyclothymic behaviour, but inconsistent with Leptosomatic tendencies.

Although they could not understand it, Counsel for the Defence and the Sisters were very impressed by this report.

The trial of Sister Monica Joan at the London Quarter Sessions attracted much attention. The public gallery was full. Many costers, and several jewellers from Hatton Garden, were present. Several older women, who remembered the accused as a young midwife and who owed their lives to her, had come out of sympathy. The press gallery was full. A shoplifting nun was good news to a hard-bitten reporter.

Sister Monica Joan sat in the dock. She was knitting quietly and seemed completely unconcerned with what was going on around her. Sister Julienne sat beside her, and attended throughout.

The usher entered.

"Silence in Court," he shouted. "Be upstanding for His Lordship."

Everyone rose to their feet – everyone, that is, except Sister Monica Joan, who remained seated. "Stand for His Lordship," shouted the usher.

There was no movement from Sister Monica Joan. The usher moved towards her, banged the floor with his staff and shouted louder.

Sister Monica Joan gave a surprised little squeak. "Are you addressing me, young man?"

"I am."

"Then let it be known that I will not be addressed in this rude fashion."

"Be upstanding for His Lordship," shouted the usher.

"Did your mother never teach you to say, 'please', young man?"

The usher swallowed hard and banged his staff down on the floor a second time. Sister Monica Joan sat immobile, her beautiful eyes half-closed, her lips pursed in disdain.

"Please stand up, madam." whispered the usher.

"That's better. That is much better. Courtesy is a virtue and costs nothing. I am sure your mother would be proud of you." Sister Monica Joan leaned forward, patted him kindly on the shoulder and rose to her feet.

Cheers from the public gallery.

"Be silent for His Lordship," screamed the usher, striving to restore his authority.

The judge entered, mumbled, "Please be seated," and everyone sat down, including Sister Monica Joan.

Counsel for the Prosecution addressed the jury. He outlined the facts as they were known and said that he would call as witnesses three jewellers from Hatton Garden who had lost jewellery, and eight costers who had lost sundry items from their stalls. He would also call a psychiatrist, who had examined the accused and considered her to be of sound mind and therefore responsible for her actions.

The three jewellers were all reliable witnesses. The first, a Mr Samuelson, stated that he had inherited the business with its stock from his father. A rope of antique pearls and a diamond ring had disappeared from the stock four years previously. The police had been informed. The stolen jewels had never been recovered until the police had contacted him recently saying that a cache of jewellery had been found, and asking him to examine the jewels. With the help of his record books, Mr Samuelson had been able to identify the pearls and the diamond ring.

The second jeweller stated that Sister Monica Joan had entered his shop three years previously and asked to see a tray of small items of little value, such as charms and trinkets. He had been called away to attend to another customer and left her alone with the tray, confident that, as the lady was a nun, it would be safe to do so. However, an assistant had seen the nun take a small item from the tray and slip it into her pocket. He had warned his employer, and together they had escorted Sister Monica Joan into a back room and challenged her. She had produced a small trinket, valued about two shillings, from the folds of her dress. The jeweller said that he had taken the item back and told Sister that he would not call the police on this occasion, but that she would not be admitted to his shop again.

The assistant was called to the witness box. He verified everything his employer had said and identified Sister Monica Joan as the nun referred to. He said that he had not seen her in the shop since that day but had noticed her wandering around other shops in Hatton Garden. He concluded that she must have remembered that she was barred from entering his employer's premises and therefore he rejected any suggestion that she was suffering from memory loss or senile dementia.

Sister Monica Joan continued to knit and displayed no interest in what was being said about her. Sister Julienne, on the other hand, seemed to be on the verge of tears.

The costers were called to give evidence. They were a colourful group of seven men and one woman. The first stepped confidently into the witness box to be sworn in, giving his name as Cakey Crumb.

"Could you give your first name please?"

"Well, I've allus bin known as Cakey. Wiv a name like Crumb, wha' would you expec'?"

"With what name were you christened?"

"Cuthbert."

Shrieks of laughter from the costers, which were silenced by the judge.

Counsel for the Prosecution continued: "Could you please describe your occupation?"

Cakey stuck his thumbs into the armholes of his colourful waistcoat and drummed his fingers on his chest. "I'm a business man. Managin' director of me own company. Bin a' i' since I was four'een, wiv a break for the war, when I was in the merchan' navy; 'orrible, va' was, real 'orrible. Never did like wa'er, I never. We was torpedoed an' 'undreds of men was frown in ve wa'er. 'Alf of 'em drowned. 'Orrible i' was to 'ear 'em cry for 'elp, poor sods. An' then another time we was . . . "

"Yes, Mr Crumb. I am sure the court would like to hear your reminiscences, but we must confine ourselves to the case against Sister Monica Joan. You are a business man, you say?"

"Yerst. Costermonger. I 'as me own cock sparrer, an' sells in ve park its."

The judge interrupted. "Did you say you sell cock sparrows in the park its?"

"No, no, m'lud. Cock sparrer is wha' we calls ve barrer an' park it is ve market."

"I see." The judge made a note. "Please go on."

"I sells ladies fings, and vis nun, she comes up to me stall an' afore you can blink an eye, she picks up a couple of bread an' cheeses, tucks 'em in 'er petticoats, an' is off round the Jack Horner, dahn ve frog an' toad, quick as shit off a stick. I couldn't

Adam an' Eve it, bu' vats wot she done. When I tells me carvin' knife wot I seen, she calls me an 'oly friar, an' says she'll land me one on me north and south if I calls Sister Monica Joan a tea-leaf. Very fond of Sister, she is. So I never says nuffink to no one, like."

The judge had laid down his pen long before Cakey had finished giving his evidence. "I think I am going to need an interpreter," he said.

The usher spoke. "I think I can help you, My Lord. My mother was a cockney and I was brought up with the rhyming slang. Mr Crumb has testified that he saw Sister Monica Joan take a couple of handkerchiefs – bread and cheese is the usual expression for handkerchiefs – off his sparrow, or barrow, and set off round the Jack Horner – corner, My Lord – down the frog and toad – meaning road – as quick as – I need not go on, my Lord, a harmless vulgarity implying no disrespect to Your Lordship – quick, stick – the rhyme is obvious my Lord."

"'I am beginning to understand. Ingenious, very. But what was all that about Adam and Eve? We are not talking about the Garden of Eden, you know."

"'To Adam and Eve it' is a very common expression my Lord. It means 'to believe it', or the negative. Mr Crumb could not Adam and Eve the evidence of his own eyes."

"You are very knowledgeable, usher, and I am indebted to you. But that was not all the evidence Mr Crumb gave the court, and it has to be written down for the record."

The usher was standing up stiff and straight and feeling very important. All eyes were upon him. "Mr Crumb said that he told his wife what had happened. There are several expressions for wife – carving knife, trouble and strife, Duchess of Fife spring readily to mind – and she called him a liar – holy friar, My Lord, and said she would hit him in the north and south – mouth – if he called Sister Monica Joan a thief – tea-leaf was the rhyming slang used by Mr Crumb."

"I understand now. Thank you, usher." The judge turned

towards Cakey. "Would you say that that interpretation is sub-stantially correct, Mr Crumb?"

"Oh yerst, yers. That's Isle of White."

"I suppose I am correct in understanding that it is . . . right?"

The judge looked pleased with himself and smiled at Cakey. He motioned for the Counsel for the Prosecution to continue.

"When did this all occur?"

"Abaht a year ago, I reckons."

"And you never told no one – ahem, I mean, anyone?"

"Nah, nah. I'm no' daft. There'd 'ave bin a righ' 'ole bull and cow if I 'ad. I don't want me jackdaw broke, do I?"

The judge sighed and looked towards the usher.

"Mr Crumb did not tell anyone, My Lord, because he was anxious to avert a row with his wife, whom he felt was capable of breaking his jaw."

"Is this correct, Mr Crumb?"

"Gor, not 'alf, an' all. Got an Oliver Twist like a piston, she 'as. Knock yer 'ampstead 'eafs out soon as look at yer, she would."

"Mr Crumb, I was referring to the accuracy of the usher's translation, not to your wife's skill as a pugilist."

"Oh, I see. Well yers, 'e's got ve lingo taped an' all."

"Thank you, Mr Crumb. Usher, I should be grateful if you would attend closely to what the witness says and interpret for me, should it be necessary."

"Certainly, My Lord."

Counsel for the Prosecution continued. "Having said nothing for a year, why have you come forward now?"

"Because I earwigged some of me mates 'ad seen ve same sort of fing; vis ole blackbird goin' round ve markets, lookin' all 'oly like, bu' pinchin' fings off stalls and then scarperin'. So we goes to ve grasshoppers, an vey took it to ve garden gate."

"I understand your evidence as far as the grasshoppers, Mr Crumb," the judge interrupted. "Usher, perhaps you could enlighten me as to the meaning of the last sentence?"

"Grasshopper, My Lord, is rhyming slang for copper, which

Your Lordship may know is a colloquialism for the police. And the police referred the case to the magistrate – the garden gate."

"I understand." The Judge turned to Mr Crumb. "If the police are grasshoppers and magistrates are garden gates, what, may I enquire, is a judge?" he asked politely.

"Barnaby Rudge, m'lud."

"Hmm. Not too bad. Could have been worse, I suppose. We might have gone down in local terminology as a pile of sludge, or something equally unsavoury. All things considered, I think we have been let off quite lightly. Counsel, do you have any further questions?"

"No, My Lord."

Cakey Crumb stepped down from the witness box, and a costerwoman took his place. She stated that she had seen Sister Monica Joan take three skeins of embroidery silk from her stall and hide them under her scapular. She continued: "I didn't do nuffink abaht it because ve Sisters are well respected arahnd vese parts, an' in fact saved my life when I was younger. The silks only cost a shillin', an' it just didn't seem worthwhile to make a fuss. I jus' thought to meself – poor olc girl, she's goin' off 'er rocker – an left it; but when I heard from the other costers that she'd been pinchin' things left, right and centre, I decided to go in wiv them an' go to the police. After all, we got a livin' to earn, an' thievin' is thievin' whoever 's doin' it. We can't afford 'a be sentimental."

Five other costers told similar stories reporting the thefts of sundry items they had seen Sister Monica Joan take. Lastly, the coster who had instigated the proceedings in the first place was called. He told the court that he had seen Sister Monica Joan take a child's bangle from his stall and hide it under her scapular. When he had challenged her, she had flung the bangle across the stall and stalked off. Five people were called to the witness box, each one declaring under oath that he or she had witnessed this scene.

Things looked black for Sister Monica Joan, but she appeared completely unconcerned, as though the proceedings had nothing to do with her. She was knitting quietly, occasionally counting her stitches and noting them down on her knitting card. She would smile serenely at Sister Julienne who, in contrast, was in a state of real anguish.

The day's proceedings ended and the judge adjourned the court until ten o'clock the following morning.

On the second day, Counsel for the Prosecution called the psychiatrist to the witness box. She stated that she had examined Sister Monica Joan and could find nothing suggestive of senility or mental deterioration. On the contrary, she found Sister to be exceedingly quick and accurate in her responses. Her memory was good and she had a clear perception of right and wrong. In conclusion, the psychiatrist stated that, on the balance of medical evidence, Sister Monica Joan knew what she was doing and was responsible for her actions.

The general practitioner was less positive. He agreed with everything that his colleague had said but nevertheless had a feeling that something was amiss. He doubted if Sister Monica Joan could really be held responsible for her actions although he was unable to say exactly why. In conclusion, he said that the court should prefer the evidence of the specialists. He sat down next to the psychiatrist.

Sir Lorimer Elliott-Bartram was called to the witness box. Sister Monica Joan looked up from her knitting, caught his eye and gave him one of her ravishing smiles, then lowered her eyes demurely.

Counsel for the Defence asked the first question. "From your examination of Sister Monica Joan, would you say she is of sound mind?"

Sir Lorimer paused for a long time before speaking. His pause was calculated for maximum effect. The jury was impressed and leaned forward attentively.

"That is an interesting question and one to which I have given much thought over the years. On mature reflection, and after a lifetime of experience, with reference to Smellingworthy and Schmitzelburg on the subject and not forgetting the work of Crakenbaker, Corensky and Kokenbul as published in *The Lancet*, I have come to the conclusion that the sound mind is a figment of the imagination."

"What on earth is he on about?" whispered the general practitioner.

"He is making, it up as he goes along," the psychiatrist murmured.

"Silence in court!" warned the judge. "For the benefit of the jury, Sir Lorimer, please elucidate. A figment of the imagination, you say."

"Indeed I do. Which of us can contemplate his friend and say: 'He is of sound mind,' gentlemen of the jury? Which of us can gaze upon the wife of his bosom and say: 'Her mind is sound'?"

The jury took notes and shook their heads.

Counsel for the Defence continued. "Perhaps then you would say that the accused suffers from senile dementia?"

"Most certainly not," said Sir Lorimer indignantly. He was old himself and senility or senile dementia were words that he never used.

"I have heard the evidence of the psychiatrist and would point out that normal sensory perception is far from being an objective picture of reality, but is conditioned and modified by many personal factors both sensory and extrasensory. In my opinion, psychiatrists make the problems that are to be solved."

"Could you enlarge upon that, Sir Lorimer?"

"Certainly. Psychiatrists need to earn a living like everyone else. A similar syndrome can be observed in the fields of sociology and counselling. Left to themselves, most people will sort out their own problems. If it is suspected that someone else will sort them out, the problems multiply exponentially."

"The insufferable old hypocrite," whispered the psychiatrist.

Counsel for the Defence continued. "I have read your most erudite report, Sir Lorimer, and I am impressed by your reference to the Korsakaw Psychosis of Registration, Retention and Recall. Could you please enlighten the jury?"

"Certainly. A prominent feature of Korsakaw's Psychosis is that Registration may be interposed by Deregistration, preventing the proper interpretation of happenings. Retention for shorter or longer periods may differ markedly, and Recall may be either voluntary or involuntary."

"That rubbish goes back to 1910," hissed the lady psychiatrist. "He ought to be struck off. I wonder if the General Medical Council knows about him?"

"Silence in court," said the judge. "Please continue, Sir Lorimer."

"Not infrequently psychological experiences are important as regards the origin of psychological symptoms. It is possible to ascribe to the psychological experiences that determine the genesis of the psychological symptoms aetiological importance in the production of the whole."

"This is an example of the three Bs," mouthed the lady psychiatrist.

"The three whats?" replied her colleague.

"Three Bs – Bullshit Baffles Brains," she hissed.

Counsel for the Prosecution stood up. "May I enquire what all this has to do with the theft of valuable jewellery from shops in Hatton Garden?"

"Here, here!" chorused the jewellers in the gallery.

"Silence in court!" said the judge. "Sir Lorimer, with respect to your eminent position in the field of mental health, I was wondering the same thing."

Sir Lorimer continued. "Sister Monica Joan is a lady of great intelligence and fertile imagination. She was brought up in wealth and luxury. Association with her childhood is strong. If valuable jewellery was found in her possession, I have not the slightest doubt that, by the Korsakaw Psychosis, the lady thought that the jewels belonged to her mother."

"Her mother!"

"That is what I said."

"I don't believe a word of it," whispered the lady psychiatrist. "She put him up to it. I told you she is as sharp as they come."

"If it is true, it is a sign of senile dementia," her colleague muttered.

"Rubbish. The old girl's up to every trick."

Counsel for the Prosecution continued. "A remarkable theory, Sir Lorimer. 'Fanciful' would perhaps be a better description. But it does not get us any nearer to answering the question about how the jewels came to be in Sister Monica Joan's possession. Have you any theories, fanciful or otherwise, on that score?"

"No, I have not."

"No further questions, My Lord."

Sister Monica Joan had continued knitting placidly all afternoon, occasionally muttering to herself as she made notes on her knitting chart. Sir Lorimer stepped down from the witness box and she smiled at him again. The time had reached 4.30 p.m. and the judge adjourned the court for the day to reassemble at ten o'clock the following morning.

The court was crowded again on the third morning, when Sister Monica Joan was due to appear in the witness box. She was waiting in the dock, calmly knitting as before, and occasionally speaking to Sister Julienne, who was sitting beside her.

The usher entered and, before doing anything else, he went over to the nun and whispered, "When I call: 'Be upstanding for His Lordship,' would you be kind enough to stand up, madam, please?"

Sister Monica Joan smiled sweetly. "Of course I will," she said, and she stood with everyone else.

Counsel for the Prosecution opened the morning's proceedings. "I wish to call Sister Monica Joan of the Order of St Raymund Nonnatus to the witness box."

A buzz of excitement ran through the courtroom and the jury leaned forward expectantly.

Sister Monica Joan stood up. She wound up her ball of wool, stuck it on the end of the needles and placed it in her knitting bag, which she handed to Sister Julienne. "Would you make a note, dear. The next row will be row fifty-six. Slip one, knit two together, purl four, slip one, purl three, knit two together, pass slip stitch over, repeat to end."

"Yes, dear, of course I will." Sister Julienne marked the knitting card.

"Did I say purl four, slip one, purl three, knit two together, pass the slip stitch over?"

"Yes, you did, dear."

"That's wrong; it should be purl three *after* slipping the slip stitch over, not before."

"Oh yes, of course, that makes sense."

The judge leaned forward. "Have you ladies sorted out your knitting?"

"Yes, My Lord."

"Then perhaps we can start the morning's proceedings."

Sister Monica Joan made her way to the witness box. She looked completely composed; in fact she looked beautiful in her full black habit with the halo of white linen around her face. A small smile lightened her features and her eyes sparkled mischievously. Naughty Sister Monica Joan always enjoyed the limelight.

Counsel for the Prosecution opened. "The police report states that certain jewels were found in your knitting bag. Is this a true statement?"

Sister Monica Joan looked towards the jury, then to the visitors' gallery. She turned towards the judge and raised one eyebrow quizzically. Her composure held everyone captive as they waited for her reply.

Her voice, always clear, had a ringing quality. "Truth. The eternal mystery. 'What is truth?' asked Pilate. Mankind has been seeking the answer to that question for thousands of years. What would be your definition of truth, young man?"

"I am here to ask you the questions, Sister – not the other way round."

"But it is a perfectly fair question. Before we can establish the truth, we must have a definition of it."

Counsel decided to humour her: "Truth, I would say, is an accurate record of fact. Would you accept that, Sister."

"You have studied Aristotle?"

"A little," replied Counsel modestly.

"Truth. Truth is a movement of inexhaustible power, containing within itself divine truth. In the depths of space, matter is forever being formed into the heavenly bodies and transformed into the speed of light and disappears from our ken. Would you say that this is an accurate record of fact when it has disappeared from our ken?"

"I am not a scientist, Sister, but a lawyer, and I am enquiring about jewels found in your possession."

"Ah, yes, the jewels. The stars are the jewels of heaven. But are they fact? Are they truth or are they a chimera? Do we see the stars? We think we see them, but we do not; we see what they were light years ago. Would you say that the stars are an accurate record of fact, young man?"

"You see, she *is* confused," whispered the general practitioner.

"She's clever. She is deliberately trying to confuse the issue. That's what she's doing," the psychiatrist replied in hushed tones.

The judge interrupted. "Silence in court! Sister, this court is here to consider stolen jewellery. It is not here to discuss metaphysics. Please confine your answers to the matter in hand."

Sister Monica Joan turned her shapely head towards the judge. "Matter, and what is matter? Einstein says that matter is energy. Are these jewels matter? Are they energy, moving at the speed of light into cosmic forces beyond the limits of our consciousness? Are these jewels living matter, living energy, circling the earth in the full moon of April, or are they mere clods of clay, dull and lifeless, as postulated by the police?"

Although Sister Monica Joan was speaking to the judge, her

clear voice rang through the courtroom. An eloquent hand reached towards the jury, who sat spellbound although they did not understand a word she was talking about.

Counsel for the Prosecution continued. "But how did the jewels come to be in your possession, Sister?"

She turned on him angrily. "I do not know, young man. I am not a seer; I am but a humble seeker of eternal truths. These jewels, which seem to excite so much interest, have their own life, their own consciousness and their own energy force. When an atom gets excited it creates magnetic fields independent of human activity. Did they not teach you that at school, young man?"

Counsel, who was close on fifty, was beginning to look out of his depth. "No, madam, I was not taught that at school."

"Were you not taught that all matter is subject to the laws of gravity?"

Counsel refused to answer. "Sister, I am enquiring into stolen jewellery. Are you trying to say that jewels were magnetised or gravitated from jewellers in Hatton Garden into your knitting bag by their own volition?"

"I do not know. I am not a seer. Only God knows the whole truth. Questions, foolish questions all the time. You wear me out with your questions, young man. Can I not expect a little repose in my old age?"

Sister Monica Joan raised her hand to her face and tottered slightly in the dock. A gasp of anxiety was heard in the courtroom. She murmured: "May I sit down, My Lord?" and the usher ran forward with a chair. She smiled weakly. "So kind, so very kind; my poor heart." She raised her eyes appealingly to the judge and said softly, "Thank you, My Lord. Are there any more questions'?"

"No further questions," said Counsel for the Prosecution.

Sister Monica Joan had created a good impression in the witness box. Even though most of the jury did not know what she was talking about, her sincerity and conviction were compelling. Her age and frailty were appealing and their sympathy was with her. A verdict of not guilty seemed likely.

The Judge adjourned the court until 2 p.m.

Counsel for the Defence opened the afternoon's proceedings. "Are you sitting comfortably, Sister?"

"Most comfortably, thank you."

"I will try not to fatigue you with my questions."

"You are most kind."

"The jury has heard you say that you do not know how the jewels came into your possession."

"I do not."

"But were they really in your possession?"

"I possess nothing."

"Nothing?"

"No, nothing. I renounced all worldly possessions with my profession. Poverty is one of the vows of the monastic life."

"So you do not and cannot possess anything?"

"No."

"And you have never possessed the jewels in question?"

"Never."

Counsel for the Prosecution stood up. "Then what were they doing in your knitting bag?"

Counsel for the Defence was furious. "My Lord, I really must protest at this interruption, which is designed to intimidate the witness. I was coming to that point myself later, but without the bullying tactics adopted by my learned friend."

The judge allowed the protest, but nonetheless he leaned forward and said kindly, "Sister, if as a professed nun you cannot own or possess anything, can you account for the fact that a quantity of jewels were found in your knitting bag?"

"No, I cannot."

"Did you put them there?"

"I don't know."

"Well, if you did not put them there, who did?"

Sister Monica Joan looked vague and tired. "I don't know, My Lord. I suppose I must have."

"And where did they come from?"

Sister Monica Joan was crumbling fast. The day had been too long. Her sparkle and confidence were fading leaving a tired old lady who did not really know what she was saying. "I suppose they came from Hatton Garden, like everyone says they did." She leaned her forehead on her hand and sighed deeply. "I don't know why respectable elderly women do this sort of thing, but they do. Oh, they do, they do. Is it a sickness? Is it a madness? I do not know. I do not know myself."

A ripple of shocked sympathy spread through the courtroom. To incriminate oneself is sad, but for Sister Monica Joan to have done so was tragic. If a pin had dropped it would have been heard in the silent courtroom. The judge leaned back in his chair and sighed.

"'I adjourn the court for today. I will make my summing-up tomorrow. The court will reassemble at ten o'clock.

The atmosphere in the courtroom was tense the following morning. A verdict of guilty was a foregone conclusion in the minds of the jury. Could it be prison for a lady of such advanced years? Perhaps the judge would order confinement to a mental asylum. A recommendation for clemency was everyone's hope.

Sister Julienne was seated in court, her face white with shock and sorrow. On the other hand, Sister Monica Joan once more looked completely relaxed and unconcerned, knitting contentedly and smiling at people she recognised. She stood when the usher gave the order.

The judge opened the morning's proceedings. "Last evening, at seven o'clock, I was informed of new evidence which throws a different light on this case. The witness arrived in London this morning and is at present waiting outside. Call the Reverend Mother Jesu Emanuel, please, usher."

A murmur of surprise spread through the court. Sister Julienne gave a gasp and stood up when her Superior entered. The latter was a good-looking lady of about fifty with calm grey eyes. She walked purposefully to the witness box to be sworn in.

Counsel for the Defence spoke: "You are the Reverend Mother Jesu Emanuel, the Mother Superior of the Order of the Sisters of St Raymund Nonnatus?"

"I am."

"And you have been in Africa recently."

"I have been with our mission in Africa for the past year. I returned yesterday."

"Would you please tell the court what you have told me."

"On my return to our mother house in Chichester I learned that Sister Monica Joan had been accused of the theft of jewellery. I knew at once that this was a mistake. The jewels have not been stolen. The jewels belong to Sister Monica Joan."

Everyone started talking at once.

The judge ordered silence. "Please continue," he said.

"When a Sister takes her final vows, all her property is given to the order. In some orders this is irrevocable, but not so in ours. We hold the property in trust during the Sister's lifetime. If the Sister leaves the order, or has need of the property for any reason, the property reverts to her. Sister Monica Joan made her final vows in 1904. She had inherited great wealth from her mother, including a quantity of jewellery, which has been kept in the security vaults of the convent's financiers ever since. Sister Monica Joan is now a very old lady. It is the policy of our order to give special privileges to our retired Sisters, who have given a lifetime of service to our work. Knowing that Sister Monica Joan likes pretty things and that she would enjoy having her mother's jewels to play with, I gave them to her the last time I visited Nonnatus House."

"Have you any confirmation of this?"

"I have the certificate of withdrawal from the bank with me for Your Lordship's inspection."

Counsel for the Defence spoke. "The jewels have been checked against the certificate, My Lord, and they can all be accounted for."

The judge was handed the certificate, which he examined; then he said: "Did you not tell anyone about this, Reverend Mother?"

"No, My Lord, I did not, and in this respect I am entirely culpable. Sister Julienne was away on retreat at the time of my visit to Nonnatus House, or I would probably have mentioned it to her. Immediately after that, preparations were made for my visit to Africa and it slipped my mind. I am devastated that my action should have caused so much trouble. But frankly, it was not something that I regarded as important. I looked upon the jewels not as objects of monetary value but as pretty things that would give innocent happiness to a very old lady, bringing back memories of her childhood and her mother."

The Judge adjourned the court until two o'clock that afternoon to allow time for full consultation. The jeweller, Mr Samuelson, who had earlier identified the pearls and the diamond, was called, and he acknowledged that he might have been mistaken. It was agreed by all parties that if Sister Monica Joan had forgotten how she came to be in possession of the jewels, she could not be held responsible for her actions, whatever the psychiatrist might have said, and the charges of petty theft made by the costers was dropped.

After lunch the judge informed the court that the Prosecution had withdrawn all charges. There was wild cheering and hat-throwing in the public gallery.

The judge motioned to the usher to call for silence. Then he addressed the court. "I think I speak for the popular voice of this courtroom when I say how pleasing is the outcome of this case. Much needless strain and anxiety has been caused to the Sisters of St Raymund Nonnatus. However, I say to the Sisters, as I say to the police, the Prosecution, the doctors and everyone involved in this case, including the press and the wider readership beyond these walls: it is folly to jump to conclusions."

Part III

THE OLD SOLDIER

MR JOSEPH COLLETT

Sister Julienne and I left Nonnatus House and cycled towards the tenements, known as the Canada Buildings. We made our way to Alberta House, to a patient I had not met before – a man with leg ulcers that required daily dressing. Sister had told me the ulcers were severe, and warned that dressing such wounds in the patient's home was very different from doing so in a surgically equipped and sterile hospital. The man was a Mr Joseph Collett, aged over eighty, and he lived alone in one of the ground-floor flats.

We knocked at the door. There was no immediate response, but we heard movement inside. The door was opened by a very old and rather dirty man. He peered at us through thick-lensed glasses, and it was obvious from the way he was looking and trying to adjust his focus that he could not see at all well. Nonetheless, he must have recognised us, for he opened the door wide, drew himself up very straight, and bowed slightly, saying: "Mornin', Sister. I've been expecting you. Good of you to come. Who have you got with you today? Someone new?"

"This is Nurse Lee, and when I have shown her the routine, she will be looking after you."

He turned towards me, and put out a hand to touch my coat sleeve, as the partially sighted do. He couldn't quite see me, but he was obviously assessing my height and general contours, by which he would recognise me. "It's nice to have you here, young lady, and I am sure we are going to get on famous. Allow me, Sister."

He said this with old world courtesy, took her bag, and slowly walked with it to place it on the table.

"I've got the boiling water ready for you, and the flavine, and lint. I think you'll find everything's there."

Sister Julienne started unpacking her bag, and I looked around the room. The smell was none too pleasant, but I had got used to that in the tenements. The walls were a dirty beige, with wallpaper peeling off. The paint was dark brown, blistered and cracking. A small gas stove sat in one corner, by the stone sink. Next to the sink was a lavatory, which was an obvious addition to the room and not part of the original structure. The windows were so dirty that very little light could penetrate, and there were no curtains. An open doorway revealed the bedroom, with a brass bedstead. The whole area – living room, bedroom, kitchen area and lavatory – could not have been more than about fifteen to eighteen feet square, and there was no separate bathroom. It was quite adequate for an old man living alone, but I knew that many such tenement flats housed whole families. How did they manage, and stay sane?

A fire was burning merrily in the hearth and a hod of coal stood beside it. I noticed a tin bath full of coal under the sink. A very beautiful grandfather clock stood proudly against the opposite wall, next to a large wooden crate full of sticks and old newspapers. A heavy wooden table – the sort antique dealers would fight over today – filled the centre of the room, and some grimy plates and mugs were spread out on a newspaper. The room was full of old military photographs, prints and maps, and what looked like medals and trophies, yellowed with age and dirt. I concluded that Mr Collett had been a soldier.

Our patient sat down in a high wooden chair next to the fire, took his slippers off and placed his right foot on a low stool. He pulled up his trouser leg, revealing horrible blood-and-pus-soaked bandages. Sister Julienne told me to do the dressing, whilst she watched me. I knew everything had to be disposed of in the patient's house, so I placed newspapers on the wooden floor. I kneeled down and started to undo the bandages with forceps. The stench was revolting, and I felt nausea rising as I struggled to peel off the layers of bandage, which were stuck to each other with slimy fluid. I let them fall onto the newspaper, to be burned on the fire. The ulcer was the worst I had ever seen, extending upwards from the ankle for about six to eight inches. It was deep and suppurating badly. I cleaned it with saline, packed the cavities with gauze soaked in flavine, and rebandaged. Then the other leg had to be treated.

Mr Collett didn't complain whilst I was attending to his legs, but sat back sucking an old pipe with no tobacco in it, talking now and then to Sister Julienne. The grandfather clock ticked loudly, and the fire crackled and blazed. The siren of a cargo boat echoed through the room as I completed the second dressing and bandaged up the leg, with the quiet satisfaction of knowing that I had made this dignified old soldier more comfortable.

I cleaned up, saw that everything was burned, packed my bag, and Sister and I prepared to leave.

"Won't you stay for a cup of tea, Sister?" he asked. "It won't take me a minute."

"No, but thank you; we have other work to do."

I thought he looked crestfallen, but he said quickly, "Then I won't keep you, marm."

This old-fashioned use of the royal "marm" surprised me, but strangely it didn't sound out of place.

"Nurse Lee will come to you each morning from now on."

He laid his pipe on the mantelpiece and stood up. He was very tall, more than six feet, and stood very straight. He walked slowly over to the door and opened it for us, then bowed again slightly as we left.

Out in the courtyard the air smelled sweet and fresh. A horse-drawn coal cart entered, and a huge man jumped out, lifting a tiny child of about two or three onto the cobbles. The man strode through the courtyard calling in a distinctive and penetrating yodel: "Co-al, co-al," the second syllables rising a perfect fifth from the first. The long strides of the man took him swiftly through the court and the little boy, running as fast as he could to keep up, tumbled and fell. As he picked himself up, he lifted his fluffy blond head, and in a tiny, piping voice called out: "Co-al, co-al." A perfect fifth!

Women came out of many doors and hailed the coal man, who carried a bag, or half a bag, up the stone steps to the balcony where it was required. No one had a real bunker or space to store coal, so small amounts of half a hundredweight had to be bought frequently. Coal fires were to become obsolete due to the 1960s Clean Air legislation, but in the middle fifties they were the only form of heating for most people.

Inevitably, if you see a person daily in his own home over several months, you will cease to regard him as a patient and come to know him as a person. Treating Mr Collett's leg ulcers took about half an hour, during which time we talked and, as old people can always remember the distant past more easily than they can remember yesterday, we talked about his early life.

Mr Collett was not a typical Cockney in appearance, speech or manner. He was much taller than average, and had a slow, thoughtful way about him. His quiet dignity and formal way of speaking commanded respect and I never presumed to call him 'Joe'. He was a Londoner, first generation, and spoke with a London accent, but it was not heavy Cockney, typified by an idiosyncratic use of grammar and idiom. He told me his parents were country people from Sussex who had been tenant farmers. The family had been displaced by the Enclosure Acts of the nineteenth century and, unable to sustain themselves even at a subsistence level, they had drifted towards the city in search of work. They had settled in Croydon, where Mr Collett had been born in the 1870s, the oldest of eight children. His father had been a painter and decorator, and an unskilled builder's labourer. He was often out of work, because in the nineteenth century painting was a trade at the mercy of the weather. Paints had no chemical quick-drying components in them and would take about four days to dry, so in wet weather no painting could be done externally, and the men were laid off. The building trade was in the same position, because cement would not dry in less than three days.

"But my father was a good man," said Mr Collett. "He would not see his wife and children go without. There was always stone-breaking to be done for road-building and railway construction, and he would go to the yards and break stones all day. He would come home at night wet through, aching all over, with a few pence in his pocket that he had earned, and my mother would rub his back and chest with liniment and apply flannel soaked in hot mustard water to keep out the cold. He was a good man. He wouldn't go to the pub and drink away his money, like many we came to see."

Mr Collett shook his head in disapproval, and cut off a chunk of tobacco, which he proceeded to shred finely in the palm of his gnarled hand and stuff into a leather pouch, in which he kept a piece of apple peel "to keep the tobacco moist", he told me. I was fascinated by this tobacco, called shag or twist, which was sold in lengths. Shag was the tobacco my grandfather smoked, and the smell of it filled me with happy childhood memories. Tobacconists kept long coils of it, perhaps two or three feet long, like a curled, black sausage, and a few inches would be sawn off and sold to a customer. I thought the smell was lovely as Mr Collett shredded it in his hand (or perhaps it was just an improvement on the usual fusty smell of the room), and I encouraged him to cut it up and smoke the stuff, which produced clouds of thick, grey smoke when a match was applied. Incidentally, shag was the same tobacco that men often chewed. You would see a lot of old men chewing away with toothless gums, sucking the last drachm of juice from the tobacco, after which they would spit it out.

Mr Collett always asked me to join him in a cup of tea, and I always refused, for two reasons: I had never been able to drink strong tea, the unvarying brew of East Londoners; but, more importantly, the thought of drinking anything from the filthy mugs that I saw on the table made me feel sick. Neither of these reasons could I tell him, so I always said that I was too busy. He accepted this, but he always looked sad, and once he just nodded his head quietly and swallowed hard, as though there was a lump in his throat. I could see him, of course, better than he could see me, and if he had known that I was studying his face, trying to read his thoughts, he would have stood up quickly and turned away; but I was packing up my bag and watching him at the same time. There was a patient weariness and sorrow written all over his strong features, which made me think he was lonely, and that my visit was the bright spot of his day. I didn't like to leave him, even though it was always a relief to quit the all-pervading smell of the place.

Then I had a brilliant idea. Boiling water poured into those filthy mugs would melt the grease and accumulated dirt, which would then float to the top. If I asked for a cold drink, the dirt would remain stuck to the sides of the mug. It was foolproof. So I said that I didn't like hot drinks, but would enjoy something cold. I was thinking of orange juice.

His face burst into smiles, like the sun coming out on a grey day. "That's what you shall have, my maiden."

He stood up, and went to a small cupboard near the sink. He fumbled about, feeling for the things that he could not see clearly, and came out with two hand-cut crystal glasses and a bottle of sherry.

"Oh no, no," I protested, "I can't drink alcohol, not when I'm on duty. I meant orange squash, or something."

His face fell. The sun went behind the clouds. I realised how much it meant to him, and how little it meant to me. The scales are unevenly balanced, I thought. I laughed and said: "All right, I'll just have half a glass. But don't you dare tell the Sisters, or I shall get the sack. No nurse is ever allowed to drink on duty."

I sat down on the wooden kitchen chair by the big mahogany table, and we drank a glass of sherry together, sharing the secret of my disobeying orders. The light was dim, because of the dirty windows, but the fire glowed red, transforming the squalor into cosiness. Mr Collett's eyes gleamed with pleasure, and I had the impression that he was so happy he could hardly speak. Two or three times he dabbed his eyes with a filthy old handkerchief, and muttered something about having a cold in the eye.

That moment was significant in my life, because I understood that he had wanted to give me something, but had not known how. A cup of tea was all he could think of. My refusal had been a rebuff. By joining him in a clandestine glass of sherry, we had shared more than just the drink: we had shared a conspiracy of silence. It obviously meant more to him than I could have imagined, and I felt all my youthful pride and arrogance crumbling to dust beside his humble, unaffected joy in my company.

That day was the beginning of a friendship that was to last until his death.

As I left and stepped out into the court, a woman with a shopping basket was entering the flat next to Mr Collett's. She was old, but brisk and spritely. She looked up at me, challenge written all over her features.

"You seein' vat dirty old man agen – phew!" She spat out the sound, with a hiss.

"Nasty old bugger, I says. I'm tellin' yer, you Sisters oughta have somefink better to do than run around after him all the time. Phew!"

She spat on the cobbles again.

"Him, who is he, any road up? He's not nobody, he's not. He's not one of us, he ain't. Where's he come from? – that's what I wants 'a know. And look at 'ow he keeps 'is place. Filthy. It's disgustin', I says. He ain't not got no right 'a be livin' there among God-fearing folks as likes to keep themselves respeckable."

She nodded her head emphatically. The curlers under her scarf stuck out at angles, making her look particularly vicious. She smacked her gums together, and repeated "disgustin'" as though she were stating the ultimate in moral depravity, and disappeared through her doorway before I could say a word.

I was seething with fury. What right had this woman to speak to me, or anyone else, in that way about her neighbour? I felt deeply protective of Mr Collett, as obviously she would not hesitate to spread such venom about him to anyone who cared to listen. It was insufferable. He was dirty, admittedly, but no worse than many. And anyway, he was partially sighted. The sherry had left me with a warm glow inside, and this gratuitous attack on a gentle old man whom I respected sent my blood racing. No wonder he was lonely, if he had this woman as a neighbour.

I mentioned the incident over lunch at Nonnatus House, with great indignation.

Sister Julienne tried to calm me down. "We meet a lot of that sort of thing among the older people of Poplar. They are deeply suspicious of anyone from the next area of the Docklands, even the next street, sometimes. If we believed everything they tell us, we would believe everyone to be a murderer and villain, or a wife-beater and granny-basher. I cannot be quite sure, but I believe Mr Collett had two sons who died in the First World War. If this is the case, our deepest sympathy is due to him." She smiled at me quietly, and said no more.

The next day, a bottle of orange juice was standing on Mr Collett's table. Bless him, I thought, he must have made a special shopping trip on my account. I wanted to ask him about his sons, but decided it would be better not to. He could tell me if he so wished. I asked him to tell me more about his early life in Croydon, and about his family.

"It was a good life for children. Back then Croydon was a small place in the countryside. There were fields and farmhouses, and streams where the children played. We were poor, but not as poor as many, and my mother was always a good manager. She could make a meal out of a bone, she could, and my father kept an allotment, so we always had fresh vegetables. But it all came to a tragic end." He paused, cut off another chunk of tobacco, and filled his pipe.

I bandaged up his first leg, and started the second. "What happened?" I asked.

"My father died. The scaffolding on the building where he was working collapsed. Five men were killed. It was due to slipshod workmanship on the part of the scaffold-builders. There was no compensation for the wives and children of the dead men. My mother could not pay the rent, and we had to get out of the house. It was a nice house," he added, reflectively, and sucked his pipe. Clouds of smoke filled the room.

"I don't rightly remember where we moved to, but it was smaller and cheaper. We kept on moving to smaller and smaller places. I was thirteen, and the eldest of the children. I left school at once, and tried to get work, but in 1890 there was no work." He told me how he had tramped for miles trying to find anything: on the land, on building sites, with horses, on the railways. But there was nothing. "The only job I could get was in the yard where my father used to break stones in the bad weather. But it was piecework, and I wasn't really old enough or strong enough to break the granite boulders. I hardly got a thing for a day's hard labour. I remember my mother cried when she saw me at the end of the day. She said, 'You are not going to do this, my son. I'm not going to have you die as well.' The men were rough, you know, really rough, and they were all swinging fifteen-pound sledgehammers. Most of them were drunk. You can imagine the accident if a lad of thirteen had been hit instead of a stone."

I undid the second bandage. "So what did the family do?" I asked.

"We came up to London. I don't know why; perhaps my mother was told there was more chance of work for her, or for me. We came here, to Alberta Buildings. I can still see the old flat from here – that one on the fifth floor, second from the end, by the stairway. It was just one room, like this one, but with no water or lavatory, of course. I think there was gaslight, when we could afford to use it. It was cheap, but even at three-and-sixpence a week my mother had to work day and night to keep a roof over our heads. From the day my father died, my mother never stopped working." With the childhood memories flooding back to him, Mr Collett described how his mother did cleaning by day, portering, and took in washing and ironing. There were good wash-houses at Alberta Buildings in those days, he said. On top of that she took in mending for the second-hand-clothes dealers, did umbrella stitching in the winter and parasol-making in summer.

He went on to tell me that she had applied to the Poor Board for relief, but was told she was not of the Parish, and to go back where she came from. As a special concession, the chairman had offered to take three of her children, saying that she would then be relieved of the burden of having to feed them, and would have only five children left. The three children would be put in the workhouse. When his mother refused, they had called her ungrateful and improvident, and told her that she need not trouble herself to come back to them, because the offer would not be repeated. They sent her away, saying she would have to manage as best she could.

"She did manage, but I don't know how. She kept a roof over our heads, and provided enough food to keep us from starving. But we seldom had a fire, even in the coldest weather. We never had shoes, and our clothes were thin, and mostly in rags. All the families around us were just as poor, and it was made far worse by drunkenness. Most of the men drank, and that meant a lot of violence in some of the homes. Many women were in such despair they drowned themselves. Every week the cry would go up: 'A body in the Cuts,' and it was always a woman. You can imagine how the children felt ... always scared their mother might be next ..."

He sat thinking for a while, puffing his pipe, then chuckled. "It's a funny thing, you know, but children can accept almost anything when they feel loved and secure. In spite of being cold and hungry, my brothers and sisters were always laughing, always playing out in the court, always inventing new games. I never heard any of them complain. But I was different. I was thirteen when my father died; I remembered the old life and hated our new one. I hated seeing my dear mother working eighteen or twenty hours a day for a pittance. She would sit late into the night, sewing shirts by candlelight, in a freezing room, with no food inside her, all for sixpence. I resented the injustice of it. Of course, I was out each day looking for work, but times were hard and the best I could find were odd jobs, like holding a horse, or running errands, or sweeping out a yard.

"I tried to get work in the docks. You would think there was plenty of work in London's Docklands, wouldn't you? Well, there was, but there were thousands and thousands of men after the same work. I reckon there were ten men for every job – no chance for a young boy like me."

In those days such jobs as there were went mostly to the boys whose fathers and grandfathers had been dockers, Mr Collett explained. There were frightening scenes at the dock gates: hundreds of half-starved labourers, clad in rags, crazed and desperate, fighting for the chance of a few hours' work. Perhaps fifty would be taken on for the day while five hundred would be turned away to idle their time away in the streets. No wonder men were violent.

"At low tide there was always scavenging to be done in the mud. Some lads found things of value, but I never did. The best thing I found was bits of coal, washed off the barges, and driftwood. At least that made a fire for the evening.

"The worst thing was the way the gentry was so suspicious all the time. I was looking for honest work, but I was called "ragamuffin", "varmin", "lout", "thieving dog". Just because I was thin and ill-clothed and looked hungry, they assumed I was a thief."

Mr Collett's mouth tightened. His proud face stiffened at the memory of the insults. I had finished his second leg and sat back on my heels looking up at him, thinking that the accumulated experience of old age was much more interesting than the chatter of the young.

I had a glass of orange juice, whilst he drank a cup of tea. It was a good compromise, because he gave me a glass, which was dusty, but not filthy.

I was enjoying his company and conversation and didn't want to leave him, as he seemed so happy. On impulse I said: "I must go now, but it's my evening off tonight. Can I come and have a glass of sherry with you, and you can continue your stories?"

The joy on his face answered my question. "Can you come, my maiden? Can you come? I'll say you can come, and a thousand times welcome."

YOUNG JOE

Cycling back to Nonnatus House, I had misgivings about my quixotic suggestion of returning that evening. Medical people are warned about the difficulties that can develop when friendships with patients are formed. It is not something that is forbidden, but it is discouraged, and for very good reasons. So, after lunch, I spoke to Sister Julienne in private. She didn't look disapproving, or even particularly concerned.

"Well, having said you will go this evening, you cannot possibly fail him. That would be needlessly cruel. I think he is a lonely old gentleman and your visit will give him pleasure. Enjoy yourself. He is a very interesting old man, I have found."

With Sister Julienne's blessing, my misgivings vanished, and I cycled round to Alberta Buildings at about 8 p.m. with a light heart.

Mr Collett was so obviously overjoyed to see me that he seemed nervous. He had gone to some trouble, and put on a clean shirt and waistcoat and a pair of highly polished boots. Like all old soldiers, he had never got out of the habit of buffing and rubbing his boots to perfection and the whole room smelled strongly of boot polish. The dirty plates and mugs and newspapers had been removed from the table, and two fine crystal glasses and half a bottle of sherry had been put out in readiness. The fire burned brightly, casting flickering shadows over the dingy walls.

He said, "I was so afraid you wouldn't come, but here you are."

He walked slowly and carefully over to his chair. "It's good to have you here. Sit down. It's so nice to see you."

I was overwhelmed and a bit embarrassed by all this, and sat down awkwardly, not knowing quite what to say.

"You've come. You are here," he repeated. "Ah, this is so lovely." Obviously I had to say something. "Yes, I've come. Of course I have. I'm not going to run away, so let's have a glass of sherry, and we can talk about old times."

He laughed with delight, went over to the table and lifted the bottle. He felt around for the glasses and I moved to help him, but he said, "No, no, I can do it. I have to all the time, you know."

He poured out two glasses. His hands shook a little and he spilled a considerable quantity on the table, of which he was unaware. I realised that spilled food and liquid would probably account for much of the smell in the room. The rest was likely to be an uncleaned lavatory, unwashed clothes and the bugs that infested Alberta Buildings. I wondered if he had a home help.

But I wasn't going to think about that sort of thing. If he was unaware of, and quite content with his dirt, why should I criticise? Sister Julienne had told me to enjoy myself, and that I was going to do.

I took a sip of the sherry, and said, "Lovely. This is a cosy room, and you know how to make a nice fire. You were telling me about your childhood. I'd love to hear more."

He settled down comfortably in his wooden chair, and put his feet on the stool (ulcerated legs have to be kept raised as much as possible). He pulled out his shag and his penknife, and started cutting it up. I inhaled a sniff of the strong tobacco. He took a sip of his sherry.

"This is luxury. When I was young I would never have dreamed of such luxury. A fire every day! A warm bed at night! Enough food to eat . . . A welfare state that pays my rent because I am too old to work, and pays me a pension of ten shillings and sixpence a week, to buy all that I need, including a bottle of sherry when I want it. This is luxury my poor, dear mother never knew in all her life."

He was cutting up his shag slowly and carefully, holding it in the palm of his left hand and drawing the knife downwards. It looked alarming, as though he was going to cut his hand, because the tobacco was clearly tough and needed a lot of pressure. But from long practice he knew just when to ease the pressure, and he never cut himself. He worked by feel, not by sight. He slowly unravelled strands of the villainous-looking stuff with which he filled the bowl of his pipe. Next, he took a wooden spill, about eight inches long, from a pot at his side and stuck it into the fire. It burned up brightly, the flame leaping high into the air. He brought it towards him, sucking hard on the pipe, and the flame dipped downwards into the tobacco. He sucked and puffed contentedly, and smoke filled the air. Then he blew the flame out, and returned the half-burned spill to the pot, in much the same way that my grandfather used to do.

"Sheer luxury," he said, smiling contentedly. "I was telling you about our first years in Poplar, after my father died; how my poor mother had to work day and night; and how I couldn't find work, except odd jobs, to help her. Well, there was one job I got that was good fun for a lad who's looking for adventure.

"I was down the Blackwall Steps, waiting for the tide to go out, so that I could go scavenging. A man came along and said to me: 'Here, boy, can you cook a stew?'

"'Yes, sir,' I said (I would have said 'yes' to anything).

"'Can you skin a rabbit?'

"'Yes, sir.'

"'Bone a fish?'

"'Yessir.'

"'Make tea and cocoa?'

"'Yessir.

"'Clean a wick and fill a lamp?'

"'Yessir.'

"'You're the boy I want. My cabin boy's done a bunk. Can you sail today?'

"'Anywhere, sir.'

"'Be here at high tide. The *British Lion*'s the barge you want. A florin a week all found.'

"It was all so quick I hadn't time to draw breath. I raced back to Alberta Buildings, round to the washhouse where my mother was toiling away, and told her I had been hired as cabin boy on a Thames barge. My mother didn't look as thrilled as I had expected. In fact, she was dead against it. We had words, and I shouted at her: 'Look, I'm off, whatever you say, and I'll come back a rich man. You'll see.'

"So I ran back to the Steps, no extra clothes, nothing like that. Sure enough, at high tide, the *British Lion* came along, and I jumped aboard. It was the most wonderful time I had in my life, and I reckon every boy's dream. I was on the river for six months. The barge carried flints, coal, wood, bricks, sand, slates – anything. We would take a load of coal down to Kent, and pick up a cargo of bricks to bring back to Limehouse. In those days hundreds of trading vessels plied the river, huge ocean-going cargo boats down to one-man skiffs. You could always tell a barge by the red sail, and often the sail and the cabin were all that could be seen. The barges were so low that, with a full load, the whole deck would be under water. It's true."

He heard my incredulous gasp and roared with laughter, and sucked his pipe.

"People would stare from the banks, because honestly, all they could see was a red sail, and men paddling about knee-deep in water, with apparently nothing beneath them.

"I was as happy as a boy could be," he continued with another laugh. "I made the stews, trimmed the lamps, learned boat-handling, and didn't mind I wasn't paid. The skipper always said he would pay me after the next trip. After a bit, the mate whispered to me, 'That bloody monkey's not goin' 'a pay you. He never does. All the cabin boys do a bunk in the end.'

"That was a shock to me, that was. I had been counting up the florins in my mind, and had reckoned on one pound after working ten weeks, and two pounds after twenty weeks. I thought I was rich – except that I hadn't got the money. So I asked the skipper and he said, 'After the next trip, lad. When I'm in funds.'

"Well, the next trip came and went, and no money. Three or four more trips – no money. I got cross and resentful and told him if he didn't pay me, I'd do a bunk. He just smiled pleasantly, and said, 'After the next trip, Joe, the next trip, trust me.'

"Well, of course, I knew he wouldn't pay me, and the next time we reached Limehouse, I left the barge and didn't go back."

He paused, and sucked on his pipe, but it had gone out, so he scratched around in the bowl with a sharp implement that he pulled from his penknife, and lit another spill from the fire. The flame leaped upwards again, narrowly missing his eyebrows. I thought with alarm that he might one day set himself, and the whole building, on fire. His eyesight was not good, and his hands shook. I wondered how many old men in a similar state of infirmity were playing with fire in Alberta Buildings.

"If I had known what I was doing, I don't think I would have left the barge, pay or no pay. You see, I was happy and busy, which is what a boy needs. The skipper and his mate were nice men. We got on all right. I had enough food to eat, and a bunk to sleep on. What more can you ask in life? What does money matter? The trouble was, the skipper had hired me for a florin a week, so I was expecting it. If he'd asked me in the first place to join him to learn boatmanship and navigation, with no pay while I was learning, I would have accepted, and my mother would have been pleased. But he lied to me, and that was his mistake, and my misfortune."

Joe had left, fully expecting to find a similar job on another barge. But there were no jobs. The other barges supported just a skipper and a mate, but no cabin boy because the skippers could not afford to pay a boy. The *British Lion* only had the luxury of a boy because he was never paid. Joe hung around the water's edge and haunted the wharfs and jetties every day, begging to be taken on, but in vain.

After six months on the river, he was tanned and strong from long hours of work in the fresh air. He had trapped rabbits and caught fish, or pinched carrots and turnips from fields at the water's edge. He had grown taller and filled out, with good food inside him. The dense population of Poplar, the stuffy buildings and crowded streets suffocated him, and the lack of fresh air and sunlight nearly drove him to despair. Food was scarce, and he grew pale and thin again. On the barge, he had held himself upright, and his eyes had sparkled with the pride of his position as cabin boy. Returning to the streets of Poplar, he slouched and dragged his feet, his eyes dull and downcast. Worst of all was his state of mind as it dawned upon him that he was one of the myriad flotsam drifting around the Docklands, unwashed, underfed, ill-clothed, barely educated, with no realistic hope of anything better. He was fifteen.

Of all the jobs that a boy could aspire to, casual dock labour was one of the least viable and most depressing. Joe could, and no doubt should, have looked further afield, but after a taste of life on the river and the thrill of handling cargo, he saw himself as a river man. Most days, he would linger round the dock gates with a crowd of seedy, hungry, ignorant men, waiting for the chance of a job. Violence could explode at any time.

His poor mother worried about him, naturally. It had been a joy to see him fit, taller, stronger, after six months on the barge. When she learned that he had been cheated of his pay, she was justifiably furious. But there was nothing anyone could do, so she wisely said little and was thankful to have her son back, looking so well. But as the months passed, and she saw the degrading effects of poverty and unemployment biting deep, her worries increased. Furthermore, she now had to feed him. She earned her money mainly from washing. The two eldest girls had left school and worked in a shirt-making factory. Joe knew that he was fed on sweated female labour, and his proud young heart rebelled at the knowledge. At thirteen he had seen himself taking his father's role and supporting the family. Now, two years later, he had to acknowledge not only that had he provided nothing but also that he was a burden on the female wage-earners.

"It was when I was at my lowest that I met the recruiting

sergeant," he said. "But what time is it? I've been sitting here, talking nineteen to the dozen, and you, bless your heart, listening, as though an old boy rambling on is interesting to you. You mustn't mind me. I don't often get the chance to talk. I hope I haven't bored you."

At that moment the grandfather clock, solemn and stately, sounded the quarter hour.

"What time is that? Quarter past ten?"

"No. Quarter past eleven."

"Eleven! It can't be. Oh, how time flies when you are enjoying yourself. I've talked far too much, and you must go, my maid. You've got a day's work to do tomorrow, and you need your beauty sleep."

I had to assure him that he hadn't talked too much, that he couldn't possibly be a bore, that I was fascinated by his story and that I hadn't enjoyed myself so much in ages. Nonetheless, I had to go, but would certainly have another sherry with him, for the pleasure of his company, and in anticipation of hearing about the recruiting sergeant.

As I stood up, I glanced above the fireplace. I was surprised to see that a large area of the chimney breast was black – about two feet in an irregular circular shape. In addition, it seemed to be moving slightly, or shimmering, like oil on a damp surface. I had not noticed this earlier, and curiosity compelled me to take a couple of steps nearer to see what it was.

I saw, and I recoiled with horror, my hand over my mouth to prevent a scream escaping. The moving mass was thousands of bugs. I had heard that Alberta Buildings were infested with house bugs, but had not seen them before. They were behind the plaster of the walls and ceilings, where they crept along, infesting every level and every flat. They came out at night, attracted by the heat, and it was impossible to get rid of them. Only with the demolition of the Canada Buildings, a few years later, were the bugs destroyed.

I stood there, rooted to the spot, my eyes darting around me to other areas of the room, feeling these vile creatures were everywhere. I imagined I was itching. My mind flitted to a horrible incident during my training when an old gypsy woman had been admitted to the ward on which I worked. She was gnarled and weather-beaten, and her long grey-black hair was matted and unwashed. On the third morning after her admission, the white pillow was entirely black, and we found it to be literally covered with fleas. Thousands of them had hatched from the eggs in her hair, due to the warmth of the hospital ward. I was one of the young nurses who was told to clean her up. She was aggressively resistant, and the fleas were hopping everywhere. It took days to get rid of them, and to rid ourselves of fleas. No wonder I began itching all over when I saw the bugs!

Mr Collett could see neither the bugs on the wall nor the expression on my face, which was just as well. He rose, smiling, and held out his hand to say goodbye. With great difficulty I controlled myself and said goodbye, with renewed thanks for a lovely evening.

Outside, I shuddered, as much from shock as from the cold air after the warm room. I got on my bike and rode back to Nonnatus House. A hot bath was the only thing on my mind.

THE RECRUITING SERGEANT

Bugs crept and crawled through my dreams during half the night and seriously disturbed my sleep. I dreamed of a huge scaly creature that got bigger and bigger. It was poised to jump on me. It opened its horrible jaws and let out a ferocious "Aaaarrrgh". I awoke with a scream. It was the alarm clock. Shaken and trembling, I looked fearfully around the walls. No bugs. I pulled back the curtains and examined the whole room. None. "I can't go back there," I thought, "it's too horrible."

At breakfast, pale and heavy-eyed, I picked at my cornflakes in the big kitchen where we ate our breakfast at the large pine table.

"What the hell's the matter with you?" said Trixie, sharply. "I thought you had been to see an old man of nearly eighty last night. Or did we get it wrong? Is he nearly eighteen?"

"Oh shut up, you cynical cat," I muttered crossly, and told the girls about the bugs. They gasped with horror and Trixie, being the most affected, threatened to strangle me if I said another word. Cynthia gazed at me in sympathy, and Chummy said: "Great Jehosaphat! How perfectly ghastly. What did you do, actually?"

A suppressed sound came from somewhere in the region of the boiler. It was a kind of gurgling, a spluttering, like a valve leaking. We had forgotten Fred, the boiler man and odd-job man for the convent, who was crouched on the floor among the ashes. The splutterings became louder and more frequent, ending in a long-drawn-out wheeze. I could see that Fred understood and sympathised with my experience. But did he? He took a deep breath, threw back his head, and bellowed with laughter. His eyes watered. He coughed, and the fag shot off his lower lip to a distance of three or four feet. His skinny body fell forward onto his knees, and he shook with laughter. He took a grimy handkerchief from his pocket, wiped his eyes and blew his nose.

"You girls'll be the death of me, you will. Cor bli'! I'll shi' me breeks if you goes on like vis. You wai' till I tells ve ol' girl. She'll pee 'er drawers, she will. Likes a good laugh, she do, bu' can never 'old 'er water, poor soul."

I was deeply offended. This was not a suitable reaction to my experience.

Fred saw my expression, and went off into another paroxysm of wheezing and coughing. "Who' a lo' o' fuss abou' a few bugs!" he exclaimed when he could speak.

"There weren't a few, there were thousands," I said indignantly.

"Great Jehosaphat! How perfectly *ghastly*. Tell me, what did you do, actually?" he said wickedly, mimicking Chummy's plummy accent. She coloured deeply, and looked uncomfortable. Most of the Cockneys made fun of Chummy's accent, but Fred had not done so before. She was hurt, and I was cross with Fred on her account.

"I didn't do anything," I said sharply. "It's none of your business anyway, and I assure you it was perfectly ghastly, so there."

He curled up again in another paroxysm of laughter. "All righ', all righ', Miss Perfic'ly Ghastly, keep yer wig on, but don' ask me 'a git worked up. I've seen them bugs too offen 'a gi' excited."

At that moment the Sisters entered the kitchen, and wanted to know what was going on. I gave a graphic account, dwelling on the vast numbers of bugs, and my sleepless night, perhaps just exaggerating a little.

If I had expected cries of sympathy and horror, I was to be disappointed.

Sister Evangelina humphed. "Well there are bugs in all the tenements and in many of the houses. I'm surprised you haven't seen them before. Don't make a fuss. They won't hurt you."

Sister Bernadette added, "I was delivering a baby one night, by gaslight. I looked up and the gas mantle, which was fixed to the wall, had a circle of black around it, just as you have described. This was on the wall over the woman's bed!

Sister Julienne, who had kept her hand firmly over her mouth, to prevent herself from laughing, I suspected, especially after Fred winked at her, said: "It's a bit of a shock to us all, when we first see them. You have to understand that they live in buildings, and do not infest human beings. The real danger is that they are suspected of carrying typhoid, but as there has not been an outbreak of typhoid since the nineteen-thirties, I think you are quite safe. As for your never going back there, I'm afraid that is out of the question. You are going back this morning, to treat Mr Collett's legs." With that she left the kitchen to start her morning's work.

I dug my nails into the palm of my hand and clenched my teeth. I had hoped to be relieved of treating Mr Collett. If he had been told that another nurse would be taking my place, he would have had to accept it, and not see me again. What could I do? Nothing. But Sister Julienne was as firm as she was saintly and I had no choice but to go back. I realised I would have to take a grip of myself.

Cynthia whispered to me, "Come on. Let's go to the clinical room, away from Fred."

Her soft voice was reassuring, but her first words unexpected. "Now come off it. It isn't like you to get so worked up. If bugs are in all the tenements, we must work with them all the time, only we don't see them. Out of sight, out of mind. Now forget about it. You will probably never see them again."

I knew she was right. Her slow, gentle grin put everything into perspective, and we laughed together as we got our bikes out and pumped up the tyres. District work tends to blow the cobwebs away.

Mr Collett was smiling and happy when he opened the door. "Welcome, my lassie, and I hope you had a good night's sleep. Yesterday evening was the happiest time I've had for ages."

I didn't tell him that I had been awake half the night, but

wondered what his thoughts would have been if I had never come back. He would have suspected something, and supposed that he was to blame. I didn't like to think of the hurt he would have suffered.

As I undid the bandage, I remarked: "These ulcers are improving – why did you not have regular treatment before?"

"Well, I didn't like to bother anyone. I've had them for years, and always bandaged them myself. I had to see the doctor about my eyes, and he saw I was limping a bit and asked to see my legs. Then he arranged for you Sisters to come. I didn't ask for treatment. I never thought they were bad enough."

They were the worst leg ulcers I had seen, and he didn't think they were bad enough to justify a nurse's treatment! I asked him how they had started.

"It was gun wounds during the war. They healed up all right, but there was always a weakness. As I got older, little patches started, and then spread. But I can't grumble. My legs have been good to me most of my life. You expect these little things as you get old."

Little things, I thought, I wouldn't call these ulcers "little"!

The mention of gun wounds made me think of the recruiting sergeant, who had been driven from my mind by the bugs. "Last night, before I left, you said you would tell me how you met the recruiting sergeant."

He settled back comfortably in his big wooden chair. That morning he began a story that he continued in subsequent visits, often over sherry in the evening.

"Well, I was fifteen, going on sixteen, and I reckon if I hadn't met him, it would have been a life of crime for me. There was no work, and I'd met a lad who was into everything. He always seemed to have money. He was younger than me, but quicker and smarter. We palled up together. I'm not going to tell you what we did, because I'm not proud of it, but one day he suggested going up the West End, where the pickings would be better. I'd never been up West before. I remember feeling dazzled by the great buildings, the fine open streets, all the carriages, and ladies and gentlemen in their fine clothes. We went to Trafalgar Square and hung around. My eyes were popping out, especially at the sight of the soldiers in their crimson jackets and black trousers. One of them came over to where we were standing by a fountain. I was so flattered; I couldn't believe he wanted to talk to us."

He chuckled and blew a cloud of smoke across the room.

"I thought it was a special honour. No one had told me they were at it every day, on the look out for lads like me.

"'Nah then, nah then, my fine young man' (he was talking to me, not to my mate), 'aint a fine young man like you got nothing to do on a day like this?'

"I must have shrugged and grinned sheepishly.

"'Well then, did you ever see a soldier with nothing to do?'

"I hadn't, but then I had never seen soldiers before, and I was struck dumb with the honour of having this splendid figure of a man single me out for conversation.

"Then he asked me what I'd had for breakfast.

"Nothing," I said.

"'Nothing!' he roared, 'nothing! I've never heard nothing like it. Did you say *nothing*?'

"I nodded.

"'No wonder you're looking a bit skinny, begging your pardon for the liberty, squire, but one can't help noticing these things. Look at me, now.'

"He patted a well-filled stomach with appreciation.

"'Bacon and liver, and brawn and kidneys, with fresh farm eggs and field mushrooms. As much bread-and-dripping as a man can eat, with beer if your taste runs to beer at breakfast, or tea and coffee, with fresh cream and sugar from Barbados. That's the sort of breakfast a man needs to line his stomach for the day. And did you tell me you had *nothing*? That is unbelievable. *Unbelievable*.'

"He shook his head as though he honestly had never heard anything like it before.

"'Well now, young man, you come along with me. A special friend of mine runs an alehouse over there. As a great favour to me, I'm sure he can find you something to fill your stomach with. He's got a kind heart, he has, and when I tells him that my friend – if I can make so bold as to call you my friend – has had no breakfast, it will fair melt his tender old heart, it will . . . No, not you,' he said to my mate, who had edged forward at the mention of breakfast. He put his hand on my shoulder and led me to the alehouse.

"It was dark and smoky inside and, after the sunlight, I couldn't see anything, but the soldier led me to a table and sat me down.

"'Bill,' he roared, 'Bill. Does a man have to wait all day for a pint of porter? Look lively, man.'

"The fat, well-fed figure of the landlord emerged from the gloom.

"'A pint of your best for me, and for my friend – er – why, bless my soul, can you believe it, I don't even know your name. I've felt so comfortable with you, like I've known you all my life, but I don't even know your name.'

"I'm Joe Collett.

"'Joe! What a coincidence. My young brother's called Joe. And a tall, handsome young man he is, just like you. Oh, what a lad he is, my brother Joe. Such larks! Remember the larks we've had in here with Joe, eh, Bill? Those were the days. My young brother Joe joined the Dragoons, and now he's a commanding officer, with a servant and a carriage, and as much money as he knows how to spend. But I was forgetting. Now, Bill, my old mate, my young friend Joe has had a bit of a night of it, and has unfortunately missed his breakfast.'

"The landlord sounded astonished.

"'Missed his breakfuss? A man can't get through the day without a good breakfuss 'a warm him. That's terrible, that is.' He patted his large belly, and looked at me with a sympathetic face.

"The sergeant winked suggestively. 'There! I knew as how

you'd see the gravity of the sitivation, Bill. I says to young Joe over by the fountain there, I'll take you over to my mate Bill, I said, and he'll see you right. Now what have you got out the back there you've got a bit of spare of, that would satisfy young Joe? Not nothing too flash, like, because he ain't got much money on him at present.'

"I was alarmed. I hadn't got *any* money. But before I could speak, the landlord said, 'Call it on the 'ouse, sarj, on the 'ouse. It's an honour to entertain a Guardsman any time. And any friend of yours is a friend of mine. Now, young sir, would tripe and faggots, and a good chunk of last night's pease pudding fried up crispy-like, suit you?'

"I couldn't believe my luck. It sounded like a meal fit for a king.

"'Oh, an' do you like bread-and-drippin', young sir?'

"I loved bread and dripping!

"The meal arrived, and it was enough for two kings. I just ate and ate. The sergeant didn't say anything. He just smoked his pipe and drank his porter, and looked out of the window at the pigeons squabbling on the window sill.

"When I had finished, he said, 'You were hungry, squire.'

"I nodded, and thanked him warmly.

"'Don't thank me, lad. You heard what the landlord said: it's an honour to entertain a Guardsman. We gets that all the time, we do. We gets used to it. Treated like royalty, we are, wherever we go. No one can do enough for us. Did you ever see a soldier go hungry? Course not.'

"He puffed his pipe, and called for another pint of porter, saying, confidentially, 'Between ourselves, the ale in this house is real special. Old Bill brews it himself. If you are a konosser of good ales, young squire – and I am sure you are – I don't think you will be disappointed. Unless, of course, you prefer coffee after breakfast.' What a suggestion to a fifteen-year-old, going on sixteen!

"Bill brought two pints of porter, and I began to confide in the sergeant. I told him my father was dead.

"'Oh, your poor mother,' the sergeant said huskily, pulling out a handkerchief. 'My father died when I was a young lad – much younger than you, of course. I was sixteen when my father died, and my poor mother had a life of hard, hard work in order to keep us.' He blew his nose and dabbed his eyes. 'What would a man do without his mother? She sacrifices everything to bring up her family, and does without herself. A man can't do enough to repay his mother, he can't. My mother's settled comfortably in a nice little cottage in the country, which me and my brother John got her with our army pay.'

"'I thought your brother was Joe.'

"'I mean Joe. John's the other brother I haven't told you about. Here, Bill, more ale, and look lively.'

"'Did you say a cottage in the country?'

"He nodded.

"'Yerse. It was the least we could do for our poor old mum. My brother Joe and me – he's a good lad, he is – we saves up our army pay, and now she lives like a princess, our old mother does. Wants for nothing.'

"I thought of my mother, sitting up half the night, mending for a rascally second-hand-clothes dealer, going out at five in the morning to clean offices, and then toiling all day over the wash tub. I said, 'How do you get into the army?'

"He looked surprised, and raised his eyebrows.

"'Oh, was you thinking of an army career, then?'

"I nodded. 'But how do you get in?'

"He drew his chair closer to mine, and lowered his voice. 'It's not easy. I can tell you that for a start. You needs hinfluence. It's not what you knows, but who you knows, as the saying goes. It's a lucky day for you, squire, that you met me, because I've taken a real fancy to you, seeing as you are like my young brother Joe. How old are you, Joe? Seventeen, eighteen, eh?'

"'Seventeen,' I said. It was a lie, I was fifteen.

"'I thought as much. A good judge of age, I am. It's lucky for you you are seventeen, because you couldn't get into the army if you was only sixteen.'

"He leaned closer, and muttered out of the side of his mouth: 'Is your health good? No nasties, nothing like that, I take it?'

"I said my health was good.

"'Are you a Christian? The army won't have none of them heathens and hatheists.'

"I said I was Church of England.

"'Now, you're an intelligent lad, I can see that. Can you write your name?'

"I said I had been at school full-time until I was thirteen.

"'A scholar, my word. With your edifaction, sir, you will rise to the rank of brigadier general, you will.'

"He stretched out his hand, took my porter from me, and drank it himself.

"'If you are going to put pen to paper, young sir, you will need a steady hand. All the edification in the world aint going to help if your hand is shaking, on account of too much strong porter before lunch. Where was you planning lunch, by the way? Perhaps I can join you?'

"I said I hadn't any plans, but I was thinking about joining the army, and how could I do it?

"He leaned closer, and tapped his nose. He looked all around, before whispering, 'It's your lucky day, lad. I reckons as how I can help. I knows where the recruiting office is sitivated, and if I recommends you to the company's commanding officer – I'm very well thought of in higher command, I am – I reckons you would be in with a chance. Without me you haven't a hope. They'd turn you away as soon as look at you, they would. Come on, let's go.'

"Out in the sunlight, I blinked, and lowered my head from the glare, but the sergeant turned to me.

"'Right now, Guardsman Joe – what did you say your name was? Collett I must remember that – Collett. Guardsman Collett, stand up straight. Throw your head and shoulders back. Breathe deep, chest out. The soldiers of the Queen don't slouch around the place. Now, pick your feet up. Left, right, left, right. Eyes straight ahead. Left, right.'

"We marched across the square at a cracking speed. People fell aside. Everyone looked at us. I felt so proud. We passed my mate, who just gawped. I didn't turn my head to look at him.

"We entered the recruiting office, and the sergeant snapped his heels together with a crack like a whip, and shot his right arm up in salute to the officer who stepped forward.

"'Sah. Mr Joseph Collett, sah. Aged seventeen. Good health. Good education. Father dead, sah. Wants to be a soldier, sah. Highly recommended, sah.'

"There was a lot of saluting and 'sah-ing', and heel snapping, and the sergeant said, 'Right, young Joe. I'll leave you with the commanding officer. I'll be off now. Good luck, lad.'

"And I never saw him again."

With bewildering speed Joe had been hustled into the medical room, and asked to stick his tongue out and drop his trousers. A doctor gave him a quick look over, and passed him as fit. He was taken to a desk and told to write his name and address at the top of a printed form, then to sign his name at the end of the page. Confused but confident, Joe did so.

"Guardsman Collett, you are now a soldier in Her Majesty's Scots Guards. You will receive full uniform, full rations, full billeting, and a shilling a day. Here is a travel warrant to take you from Waterloo to Aldershot, which will be your first camp. You may go home now to tell your mother and collect your personal belongings. The last train from Waterloo goes at 10 p.m. If you are not on it, remember: you are now a fully enlisted guardsman, and failure to report at barracks will be counted as desertion, which is punishable by a flogging and six months in prison on bread and water. Here is your first day's pay of one shilling. Now follow the uniform sergeant downstairs, where you will be fitted with boots and uniform. Stand to attention, Guardsman Collett, and salute when you are leaving a superior officer."

In the wardrobe room Joe had been fitted up with full uniform and boots. He looked exceedingly handsome in the scarlet jacket and black trousers, and he gazed at his reflection with barely suppressed joy. He put the shilling and his travel warrant in his pocket, and was given a brown-paper parcel containing his old clothes. He was given directions to Waterloo Station and, with dire warnings about prison and flogging if he failed to turn up, was sent on his way.

Joe marched all the way back to Poplar, his newly acquired military swagger getting stronger with every step. His buttons gleamed, his boots shone, his red tunic dazzled the eye. People stood aside. Older men touched their caps. Small boys marched beside him, imitating his step. Best of all, young girls giggled and whispered and tried to attract his attention. But "eyes straight ahead", as ordered by the recruiting sergeant, was Joe's rule, and never once did he glance back, however enticing the female attentions. Girls had never looked at him before. "A soldier's life is the life for me" – and his young heart sang in tune to his step.

He marched into the court of Alberta Buildings, round to the washhouse, and flung open the door. The chatter stopped and a gasp of admiration went up from the women at the wash tubs. But his mother had her back to him. Turning round, she gazed uncomprehendingly at the figure in the doorway for a few seconds, as though she didn't recognise him. Then a low moan escaped her lips, rising to a terrible scream, and she fainted.

Joe rushed forward in alarm. Women crowded round. Water was splashed over her face and neck, and she opened her eyes, which, seeing Joe in his scarlet tunic, flooded with tears. She sobbed uncontrollably, unable to speak. A woman said, "You best get her back to your place an' all, Joe. Poor soul. She's that took she can't hardly stand, poor lamb. Oh Joe, you didn't never oughta've done it, you never."

Alarmed and bewildered, Joe helped his mother across the cobbled court and up the stone stairway to their flat. Doors opened, and women came out onto the balconies to witness the drama.

A neighbour brought in a cup of tea, and handed it to her with the words, "I've laced it with a drop o' somethin' soothin', Mrs Collett, to keep yer strength up. Lor' knows, yer goin' 'a need it," and she gave Joe a reproachful stare.

His mother drank the tea, and the sobs diminished. When she could speak, Joe asked her why she was crying.

She clung to him, and rubbed her swollen face on his sleeve. "A soldier, Joe! My eldest son, my comfort, my hope, a soldier. They draw them in, young men, thousands of them, every year. Cannon-fodder, they calls them, 'the scum of the earth'. They draws them in to die." Tears again flooded her eyes, and she wiped them away with her shawl.

"Go and ask Mrs Willoughby three doors down if I could have another cup of that tea, will you, dear? She's a kind soul, and won't mind, I know that. She feels for me. She's lost sons in the army."

Joe was not merely deflated. He was shattered. He had expected a hero's welcome. He took his jacket off, not wanting to step onto the balcony in scarlet, and fetched another cup of tea, laced with a drop of rum, which many good Poplar housewives kept for moments of crisis.

While gratefully sipping the tea, his mother said: "I 'ad four older brothers, and they all died in the Crimean War. I was only a little girl, and 'ardly remember them, but I remember my mother crying, an' 'ow she never recovered. The grief seemed to cling to 'er for the rest of 'er life. My older sister was engaged to be married to a young man who died at Sebastapol. The suffering was terrible, by all accounts – just terrible."

"But the Crimean War was ages ago," Joe protested; "it's all over and done with. The Empire's strong. There are no wars now. No one would dare attack the British Empire. And I'm a soldier of the Queen Empress, and proud of it."

She forced a smile. "You're a good lad, my son, and your

mother's a silly old fusspot. She's not going to spoil your last afternoon with tears. When do you have to report to barracks?"

He remembered the travel warrant and the shilling in his tunic pocket. He pulled it out and laid it proudly on the table beside her. "I'm paid a shilling a day and it's all for you. I get my billet and my food and my uniform, so I don't need money. I'll bring it all to you, and you won't want no more."

Poor woman! She had cried all over again. What mother wouldn't?

"You must keep some for yourself, my son."

"Nope. Not a penny. I done it for you, and you shall get the pay."

"My boy! Oh, my lad!" She kissed his hands and wiped her tears on his sleeve. "My dear boy. But I fear for you. My heart is heavy. I fear for you."

She finished the tea, and pulled herself together. The rum helped. The children would soon be in from school, and later the girls from the factory. She couldn't present a tearful face to them.

"You start getting your things together in a bundle, while I go down to the yard to wash my face. Then we'll use your shilling to buy some whelks and a loaf, and some real butter and a saucer of jam for the little ones. We'll have a real feast your last evening at home."

And that is exactly what they did. The younger boys were over the moon about their big brother's uniform. Each of them tried on the jacket, and the six-year-old pranced around the room with the jacket trailing on the floor and the sleeves flapping wildly. The sisters were agog with admiration. Suddenly Joe had become a man in their eyes. Only their mother was silent, but she kept a brave smile on her face.

Time passed all too quickly. The laughter, the cheers, the songs, had to come to an end. Joe had a train to catch from Waterloo at ten o'clock that night. He dared not miss it.

ARMY LIFE

Guardsman Joe Collett arrived at Waterloo Station at 9.30 p.m., along with about sixty other young men recruited that day. Each of them thought that he had been singled out for special consideration by a recruiting sergeant. They were all very poor boys and were surprised to see each other. None of them knew that the army was obliged to recruit twelve thousand men each year to make up the numbers, mostly lost through death.

Also at Waterloo Station were around a hundred girls, dressed to kill. Oh, the skirts, the ribbons, the laces, the tucks, the frills and flounces! Oh, the boots with dainty buttons, and the wide-brimmed hats, heavy with fruit and flowers and feathers! And what was that Joe saw? Could it be paint? Joe had never seen rouged lips and cheeks before, and he was enchanted.

The girls clung to the soldiers, two or three to each. Some of them carried a phial of gin or rum in their garters, and these were brought out with much skirt-rustling and mock modesty. There was only half an hour before the train was due to leave, but the girls knew how to use the time to advantage. Much can happen in half an hour, and each girl knew that the recruits had been paid a shilling that day.

Most of the new recruits had gone alone to the station, but some were accompanied by mothers, aunts or sisters. These young men were put to great embarrassment by the girls, who openly sneered at them, and cast bold, contemptuous eyes on their womenfolk. These good women were scandalised by the wanton behaviour of the girls, and tried to protect and warn their sons, which only made matters worse.

Joe, being alone, taller than average, and undoubtedly good-looking, was mobbed. He was offered a phial of rum which, laughing, he swallowed in one gulp. It went straight to his head. He clung to a brunette, who cuddled him, and led him round the station, singing. Joe felt he had never been so happy in his life. Two more girls joined them and led him out of the station into the little lanes. It was a quarter to ten. In the lanes the girls cuddled and kissed him, and fondled him all over. In his intoxicated state Joe felt that more than his blood was rising. It was then that the girls discovered that Joe did not have his shilling on him. They screamed with rage. They kicked him and pushed him and he fell against a wall, hitting his head. They tore his jacket off him, frantically going through the pockets, threw it on the ground – Joe's beautiful red tunic – and trampled it in the mud. He cried out, but could not stop them. They pulled his hair and scratched his face until the blood ran. They spat on him and then rushed off, with a flick of skirts, around the corner.

Dazed, bewildered and bleeding, Joe leaned against the wall. He tried to gather his senses, but couldn't think what had happened. His head hurt from the blow. He was sliding comfortably down the wall when a sharp noise penetrated his fuddled hearing. What was it? It was repeated. Dear heaven, it was the train whistle. Aldershot ... the last train ... must catch it ... desertion ... flogging ... prison. He snatched up his jacket, nearly falling flat on his face as he did so, staggered towards the station, hurtled towards the moving train, was pushed onto it by a porter and fell into a seat.

"Blimey, mate, you look as if you've had a good time," said his companion, with a sardonic grin.

The train gathered speed, and Joe fell asleep. He was awakened by a rough hand shaking him. "Wakey, wakey, Sleeping Beauty. You're a soldier now, and we're at Aldershot. You can dream of her another time."

Aldershot? What was that? Joe woke to see half a dozen grinning faces above scarlet tunics staring at him, and it all came back. He was a soldier now ... the recruiting sergeant, that was it. Head up, shoulders back, chest out, breathe deeply, no slouching now. He jerked himself upright, and pain split his head from ear to ear. He groaned.

The men roared with laughter. "He's only a kid, leave 'im be. He'll learn. Here, mate, give us yer arm."

Joe staggered off the train on the arm of his unknown companion, and a staff sergeant stepped forward. "Right men. In line. Roll call. Look sharpish."

The motley group of raw recruits shuffled backwards and forwards, sideways and hitherways, trying to make a line. The staff sergeant bellowed and swore and brandished his regimental swagger cane, trying to get them into military line. He was not successful, but had to make do with second best.

"Right, you horrible men. You wait till I get you on the parade ground. You'll damned soon learn how to form a line. Roll call."

An old duty sergeant stepped forward with two sheets of paper in his hand containing lists of names, which he proceeded to read out. His reading was not very good. No doubt the process would have been quicker if a duty sergeant who could read properly had been sent, but the ability to read was not an accomplishment that was rated very highly in the army.

He got through several simple names without mishap – Brown, Smith, Cole, Bragg – but then was stuck.

"Warrarramb . . . " he shouted.

No one answered.

"Warrarrnad" Louder.

No response.

"What you say?" yelled the staff sergeant.

The duty sergeant tried to look confident, and shouted "Warrarrandy"

No response.

The staff sergeant strode over to him, his cane swishing, his boots clicking, and snatched the paper. In the flickering gaslight of the station he squinted at the page. "Warrenden," he shouted.

A man stepped forward. Roll call proceeded in this manner. The duty sergeant did his best, but got stuck on Ashcroft, shouting

"Askafoot". Bengerfield, Willowby, Waterton set him stuttering, until everyone thought roll call would never be finished.

One man was missing. The name was shouted backwards and forwards several times, but no one stepped forward. The staff sergeant struck the calf of his leg with his swagger cane and, with great deliberation, pulled out a stub of pencil and underlined the name.

"It will be the worse for him," he said menacingly. "Right men, form a column, four abreast, quick march."

Forming a column for untrained men is as difficult as forming a line. The staff sergeant swore and cursed and used his cane liberally, eventually getting some sort of ragged column together. With a "left, right, left, right" they marched off.

It was four miles to the camp, which did Joe good. By the time he got there, his head had cleared from the effects of the rum, and ached only a little from the crack on the wall. The night air refreshed him, and the men surrounding him gave him a feeling of security.

The sentries at Aldershot Barracks leaped swiftly to attention when they heard the column approaching. An incomprehensible word was barked out by the staff sergeant, sounding something like "Awt". No one in the column thought it meant anything and continued marching. The four at the front were confronted by a menacing row of guards, each with a bayonet raised at forty-five degrees, and pointed directly at their stomachs. Another step, and they would have been skewered. They halted. The men behind carried on marching, straight into the backs of the men in front. About half the column fell on each other in this way. Being fresh from a sane world where this sort of thing is considered funny, they fell about laughing, but the staff sergeant failed to see the joke. He swore and raged at their imbecility.

The column re-assembled inside the gates and marched another quarter-mile to the billet, a grey rectangular building, four storeys high.

A short way off from this building the staff sergeant shouted.

"In a minute, I am going to say 'halt', and that means 'stop', and when I say 'halt' I want you to stop. Got it?" They continued marching.

"Awt." Half the men stopped, the other half didn't. The result was exactly the same as at the gate. The staff sergeant nearly went berserk. Somehow he managed to re-assemble them, marched them another fifty yards and shouted, "Halt."

This time everyone stopped.

"Right. In line."

This was no easier than it had been at the station. In fact it was harder, because it was pitch-dark. Men stumbled and fell over each other, muttering and laughing.

"Silence!" roared the staff sergeant.

"Silence yerself, yer bloody windbag," shouted a voice.

"Who said that?" roared the sergeant.

"Father Christmas," said the voice.

"Corporal, open the door," roared the sergeant.

The corporal on duty opened the door of the billet.

"Forward. Quick march," roared the sergeant, leading the way up four flights of stone steps. At the top, the corporal in charge of the billet opened the door, and the disorderly line of men entered.

"New recruits, Corporal, and a bigger bunch of stupid bastards I've never met." The staff sergeant turned to go. He turned to the men. "You wait. You just bloody wait. You'll wish you'd never been bloody born, you will." And with those pleasant words, he departed.

I roared with laughter at this story. We both laughed, Mr Collett and I. Nothing binds people more strongly than the same sense of humour, and the ability to laugh together. I was thoroughly enjoying my evenings of sherry and an old soldier's reminiscences. The British Army of the 1890s was not something I would have expected to find interesting, but in the firelight, with a good storyteller like my companion, the years came alive.

I was also aware that Mr Collett had become deeply fond of me, which was touching. One of the pictures on his walls was of a pretty young girl in 1920s dress. I understood that this was his only daughter, who had been killed in the bombing in the Second World War. Perhaps I was becoming a substitute granddaughter to him. I didn't mind. I liked him. He was a dear old man, and reminded me of my own grandfather, whom I had loved and admired deeply, and who had been more of a father to me than my own father. He had died a couple of years previously at the age of eighty-four, and I still felt the loss. If Mr Collett and I were both substituting another person into our growing affection, it was all right by me.

He refilled my glass. "Do you like chocolates, my dear? I bought a box of Milk Tray this morning, with you in mind."

He reached up to the mantelshelf, and felt for them. I was still a bit chary about eating anything, because of all the filth around the place, and once, when he had produced a grubby plate of biscuits, which I had seen him drop on the dirty floor and pick up, I had said that I didn't like biscuits. But an unopened box of chocolates was a different matter. Anyway, I loved them. After that, it was always sherry and chocolates. Incidentally, I never saw the bugs again, and after a while I ceased to look for them.

"So you got to your billet, and your head wasn't too bad. What happened then?"

"We were told to make up our cots. A soldier sleeps in a cot, not a bed. They are constructed in two halves, the bottom half of which pushes into the upper half. This allows for more space during the day in the centre of the billet. The corporal showed us how to do it. The biscuit, which is a soldier's straw-filled mattress, and two rough blankets, were folded on the top part of the shortened bed. We had no pillows, no sheets. Nothing fancy like that. The corporal told us the sip-but was on the landing."

"What on earth is a sip-but?" I interrupted.

"Oh, that's back slang for a piss-tub. There's a lot of rhyming slang and back slang in the army. At least there was in my day. It may have been dropped by now.

"I remember my first night very well. It was so new, so exciting, that I couldn't sleep. Apart from which I still had a headache from the girls pushing me against the wall. My thoughts were racing – those girls, my mother, the recruiting sergeant, the staff sergeant, the station, the march through the night. I must have dozed off towards dawn and in my dreams I vaguely heard a bugle call. Seconds later the corporal burst into the billet, shouting: 'Show a leg now, get out of it. Open those blasted windows and let some fresh air in. It smells like a bloody farmyard in here. Get out of it now, do you hear me?'

"Perhaps I didn't move, but the next thing I knew was that my cot collapsed, and I landed on the floor. The corporal had pulled the bottom half away from the top half, which was a very effective way of rousing anyone who did not leap out of bed the instant reveille was blown. This sounded at 5 a.m., summer or winter.

"The corporal ordered us to dress and put away our cots and fold the biscuit and blankets. I was in a daze, but the roar of the corporal kept me on my toes. He kept bellowing on about the blankets not being folded straight, and how, he'd never seen such a useless, slovenly bunch of recruits, and how we would be licked into shape and no mistake. He ordered two men next to the door to carry the sip-but to empty it down the drains and clean it at the pump, where it would be left until the following evening.

"'Right now. Stand by your cots. This is only the reception centre, where you are treated gentle-like. Later you will learn what army life is, when you have been sorted into the regiments what you have enlisted for. Get me. You will have an hour's drill before breakfast. Then your breakfast, then an hour's parade, then present to the colour sergeants for sorting. Got it? Right. In line. Down to the parade ground.'

"We got into some sort of line and filed down the stone stairs. In the darkness outside we could hear voices rather like the staff sergeant's barking out orders. We were put to physical exercises –

press-ups, star-jumps, squatting with straight back, step-ups. Imagine all that with a headache and no sleep! But I kept thinking this was better than hanging around the dock gates looking for work, and it was. The last quarter of an hour consisted of the most exhausting exercise so far – running with your knees lifted high at each step. After this, we were starving for our breakfast. This consisted of dry bread and sweet tea. It tasted delicious. After that we were led to the parade ground for another hour of drill. At 9 a.m. a bugle sounded and the colour sergeants marched onto the square, each followed by a duty sergeant carrying a list of names, which they read out in turn. The recruits were sectioned into their colours, and marched off. This happened every day, because the recruiting sergeants were busy enlisting unsuspecting young lads like me every day of the week.

"There were only four Scots Guards recruits that day. It's a crack regiment." (Mr Collett said this with great pride, lifting his chin high.) "We were taken in marching order to the quartermaster's stores, where we were issued with top-coat, cape, leggings, one suit of scarlet, one of blue for drills, boots, shirts, socks, and numerous pieces of regimental dress. We were issued with a rifle, bayonet, and two white buff straps, with pouches that could hold fifty rounds apiece. We were also issued with a busby, the tall fur headdress reserved for Guards. Everyone in the regiment was very proud of these.

"We – the four of us, that is – were shown to a whitewashed barrack room overlooking the square. A corporal was in charge of each billet, and a couple of older duty-men also kept billet there. They showed us how to fix straps for drill purposes, how to roll the top-coat and fix it to the kitbag, how to fix leggings, what cleaning materials we would need, how to place our cape and scarlet top-coat, when not in use, on the racks above our cots – even how the straps of the kitbag should hang from pegs above the head of the cot."

The pettiness of it all, the meticulous attention to detail, reminded me of my nurse's training. I told Mr Collett about it.

We were issued with three fitted dresses, twelve aprons, five caps and a cape. We were given precise instructions on how they must be worn at all times. The hem of our dresses had to be fifteen inches from the floor, no more, no less. Caps, which were flat pieces of starched linen, had to be folded and pinned to an exact shape and size. Aprons had to be pinned at an exact point above the bosom, and adjusted to the precise length of the dress. Shoes had to be black lace-ups, of a specific style, with rubber soles for quietness. Stockings were black, with seams. Belts and epaulettes were of differing colours, distinguishing the different years of training a student nurse underwent. Full uniform had to be worn at all times when on duty. I recall, in my first year of training, being ordered out of the dining room by a third-year nurse, because I had forgotten to put on my cap. Later, when I became a ward sister, I forgot my cuffs on one occasion when I went to the matron's office, and was sent back to the ward to get them before I could address her!

We discussed whether this sort of discipline was necessary. Mr Collett said: "Well, it certainly is for men, because large numbers of men living together can easily become like wild animals. Men are brutes at heart, and without the civilising influence of women they quickly revert to savagery. The discipline of the armed forces is the only thing that keeps them under control. I wouldn't have thought it was necessary for women, though, would you? But I maintain that nurses always look lovely, and so I approve of the uniform."

I chuckled at this. There is no doubt in my mind that the nurses' uniform of the early and middle 1900s was just about the sexiest thing ever invented. Nothing has surpassed it for allure. I was not the only young nurse to be acutely conscious of a heightened sex appeal when in uniform. Ironically, the draconian old sisters and matrons who rigidly enforced the uniform seemed to be unaware of the effect it had on the male sex.

Those were the repressive days when student nurses had to live in barrack-like nurses' homes, and be in by 10 p.m. No men were allowed, and a nurse who smuggled one in would be dismissed if she was caught. Student nurses could not marry. All this was to repress our sexuality, yet we were dressed up like sex kittens. With exquisite irony, in today's permissive society, when anything goes and nurses can do whatever they like sexually, the uniform has changed beyond all recognition, and the average nurse now looks like a sack of potatoes tied in the middle, often wearing trousers rather than sexy black stockings.

I asked Mr Collett how he coped with all the regulation of army life. Was he as bad as I had been in my early nurses' training? I must have driven the ward sisters mad. He laughed, and said he didn't believe it.

"But I had a hard time at first. We all did. The Scots Guards prided themselves on being a crack regiment, so we had more hours of drill, rifle and bayonet training, longer marches, and heavier pack-weights than other regiments. Also we had less time off. We were so exhausted in the evening that we seldom went to the wet canteen. Often I just made up my cot at 8 p.m and went fast asleep until reveille.

"I had more money than I'd ever had. On a shilling a day I was able to send four shillings a week home to my mother. I knew that would pay the rent, and I swore to myself that I would always pay the rent, so that she need never again fear the workhouse. And I kept that up for years and years, even when I was married."

I asked him about his marriage.

"Well, after three months at Aldershot, I was given forty-eight hours' leave to go to see my family, before being posted to Plymouth. Across the court of Alberta Buildings lived a girl I had known for years, but she seemed so much more grown up than I had remembered her, and I reckon she must have thought the same about me. She was the prettiest little thing I had ever seen." He chuckled fondly, and slowly refilled his pipe. He rubbed it in his hands, and stroked his cheek with the warm bowl.

"We were only sixteen apiece, and forty-eight hours isn't long, but I knew she was the only girl in the world for me. We reached an understanding that she would wait for me until I was in a position to marry her. Long engagements were common in those days, and couples thought nothing of waiting ten or fifteen years before they could get married. As it happened we had to wait only three years." He lit a spill from the fire, applied it to the tobacco, and sucked hard. He looked thoughtful.

"It's a damned good thing I did meet my Sally during that forty-eight hours, because the promises we had made kept me clean while I was at Plymouth. It was a lively town, and ten or twelve regiments were garrisoned there, as well as sailors and marines. There were pubs and bawdy houses in every street, and prostitutes in every bar. I learned fast. You do in the army, and it didn't take long to figure out that if I went with one of them girls I was likely to pick up VD. That would have been the end of my army career, the end of my hopes for winning Sally and the end of the rent for my mother. So I kept myself clean. All the other chaps said I was mad, and I should enjoy myself while I could. But I saw enough of them go into the venereal wards of the sick bay to know they were the ones who were mad." He looked severe.

"But hadn't you better go, young lady? Are you going to be locked out at ten o'clock? I don't want to be getting you into trouble."

"I will go, but I want to hear about your marriage first," I said eagerly. "It sounds so romantic. Anyway, there are no restrictions with the nuns. They are much too sensible for that. Now tell me about how you got married."

He patted my hand fondly. "After Plymouth, I was posted to Windsor Castle, as one of Queen Victoria's foot guards. It was the best posting I had, and I loved it. There wasn't really a lot to do. It was all marching and square drill. There were several hours of sentry duty, day and night, but we relieved each other every two hours, and then we had two hours off, until the next relief. At Windsor Castle I started reading. I knew I was not properly educated, and wanted to do something about it. There was a library in the barracks, and I just read anything I could get hold of. It became a passion with me. The more I read, the more I realised how ignorant I was. I devoured history like other chaps devoured booze. I spent all my spare time reading, and it was a habit that never left me, until my eyes began to go, and it became impossible."

He looked sad, but perked up. "But I can listen to the wireless. There's nothing wrong with my hearing.

"Anyway, what with one thing and another, I loved it at Windsor Castle. Now, it's a funny thing, but in the army, I've noticed, the less work you have to do the more you get paid. We were paid ninepence extra per day for Royal Duties. I was now earning good money, and was able to apply to my colonel for permission to marry. He said I was too young, but when I told him that I had known the girl since I was thirteen, he relented. Married quarters were sometimes available to soldiers and their wives, and that was what I was after. I wasn't going to get married and have my Sal living in a room in the town, and me in barracks. The colonel said we would have to wait until a cottage became available, which we did, and within two years Sally and I were married at All Saints' Church, Poplar, just over the way there. I took her down to Windsor soon after. Our twins were born at Windsor Castle, and I was the proudest young father in the regiment. But our happiness was too good to last. News from South Africa was bad. Infantrymen were being sent out every week. I had a feeling, though I didn't say it to Sal, that my turn would come, and it did. On the first of November 1899 I sailed for South Africa."

SOUTH AFRICA
1899–1902

Mr Collett's legs were greatly improved with daily treatment. The ulcers were reduced from about eight inches in diameter to two inches. They were more superficial and were also drying out. Consequently, the smell in the room was improving. It was still dirty, with a faint whiff of urine hanging in the air, but the sickly-sweet stench had definitely gone. I realised that the smell must have been due to the suppuration of the wounds. If only he had sought treatment earlier, and not tried "do-it-yourself" remedies, the ulcers would never have got into such a state in the first place. I reduced the visits to alternate days, and then every third day, and the improvement was maintained.

Our sherry evenings continued as a regular feature, and I knew how much he loved my visits. He made no pretence about his joy at seeing me. I began to think that I was the only person who visited him and wondered about his family and friends. It was unusual, if not unknown, to see a Poplar man without either. Family life was close, and old people were valued. Neighbours lived on top of each other and were always in and out of each others' doors, especially in the tenements. Yet I never saw nor heard of anyone popping in on Mr Collett to see if he was all right, to ask if he needed anything, or just to pass the time of day. I wondered why.

He said to me once, regarding his neighbours: "I'm not one of them, you know. I was not born and bred in Alberta Buildings, so they will never accept me."

I asked him about his family. He said, simply and sadly, "I have outlived them all. It is God's will that I should be left. One day we will be reunited." He wouldn't say any more, but I hoped that as time went on he might.

One evening, I asked him to tell me more about the Boer War.

"I was drafted in the autumn of 1899. My poor Sally was heartbroken. We were so happy at Windsor. We had a nice little army cottage. She did washing and mending for the officers and earned some money that way. She was happy, and as pretty as a picture. What's that jingle now, let me think:

> The Colonel's wife looks like a horse
> The captain's wife is not much worse
> The sergeant's wife looks a bit slicker
> But the private knows how to pick 'er.

"Or something like that. Anyway, my Sal was the prettiest girl in the regiment. Our twins were born, and they were on their feet and running around, when the postings came. We knew it would be for a long time. Sally and the boys couldn't stay at Windsor, so they went back home to live with her mother. The flat is just above where we are sitting now. That's why I like living here. I can sit of an evening, and think of Sally and the twins, when she was so young, living right above me.

"We sailed from Plymouth. There were crowds on the quay-side, cheering, waving, singing. Some of the lads were happy and excited at going, but my heart was heavy, and a lot of others felt the same. I reckon that single men make the best soldiers, because they have few regrets about what they leave behind."

He went on to describe the troopship, crowded with men and horses, carts and wagons, guns and munitions, food and supplies. The journey took five weeks. Discipline had to be very strict, because of living in such a close, crowded space. The men did hours of drill on deck. But they were in good spirits, because it all seemed like an adventure. "We were going to knock hell out of those Boer farmers who dared to defy the British Empire," he said.

They landed at Durban and were ordered to form ranks and

march. They weren't told where they were going, just told to march. They marched for eight days in full winter uniform in the boiling heat, carrying 150 lb packs. The sun burned down relentlessly, and flies and mosquitoes followed them all the way. There were no roads, so they marched through open scrubland, and along rough tracks. The countryside was beautiful, and wild, nothing like home, but they were too tired and too hot to take it in.

"I was in a Highland Regiment, as you know – the Scots Guards – and I'll tell you something: there is nothing in the world like the sound of the bagpipes to raise a man's morale, to lift his spirits, and give him strength. However tired and thirsty we were, the bagpipes at the front of the column only had to strike up and within seconds you felt your feet lift off the ground, your step lighten, your spirits rise, and every man-Jack was marching strong, in rhythm to the pipes." Mr Collett chuckled, straightened his shoulders, threw back his head, and swung his arms as though he were marching.

"There's a photograph of my regiment hanging on the wall over there, if you'd like to have a look."

I peered at the grey-and-yellow photo of a column of soldiers, which didn't really mean a lot to me, but I said it looked impressive.

"Yes, it was impressive, you're right. But, at the same time, it was insane."

I was surprised to hear him say that.

"Well, you imagine: going to war, and marching through open country, soldiers in scarlet, playing bagpipes! Talk about secrecy or surprise tactics! The enemy could see and hear us for God knows how many miles around. And we never saw them. All over South Africa columns like ours were marching, and being attacked by an unseen enemy. Yet the British generals still didn't learn. We carried on in our old swaggering ways, and lost count-less thousands of young men because of it."

He told me they were ordered to climb a hill one night. He

didn't know where, because none of them were told, but it was steep and treacherous, more like mountain terrain than a hill. They had no special climbing equipment. They wore their military uniforms with full pack, as well as rifle and bayonet, and were wearing boots made for marching, not for climbing. Nor were the men trained for mountaineering.

By dawn they had got to what they thought was the top, only to find that there were higher ridges all around that were invisible from below, and in which groups of armed men were hiding. When the whole brigade had gained the first ridge, fire opened up from all sides, from cannons, rifles and long-range muskets. They were completely unprepared. Hundreds of men were mown down before they could retaliate.

"I shall never forget the scene," said Mr Collett. "The cries and screams were terrible to hear. We formed ranks and fired back, but our position was hopeless. We were in full view of an enemy we could not see. It was a day of gunfire, under a baking sun. No shelter, no water. Just relentless gunfire."

By nightfall the barrage from the guns died away, and in the darkness all that could be heard were the cries and groans of the wounded. "We tried to help them, but we were stumbling over rocks and dead bodies. In any case, there were no doctors or medical orderlies, no bandages or morphine, no stretchers – nothing." The men were ordered to retreat, and to leave the dead. In the sun the injured would die of thirst the following day. "That was the moment when I realised the truth of my mother's words, that we were just 'cannon-fodder'. Young private soldiers were ordered, time and time again, to march directly into gunfire, and High Command didn't give a damn how many died, nor the cost in human suffering." Mr Collett was trembling and his voice was shaky.

He bit his lip to control himself.

"And would you believe it, it was all unnecessary. Of course, we didn't know it at the time – the ordinary soldier didn't – but there had been no reconnaissance. There were no maps of the terrain, and no scouts had been sent ahead to assess the area or the heights of the various hills. If we'd had a ground map, the whole incident would never have happened. The British lost two thousand men that day, the Boers two hundred – all because there was no reconnaissance.

"I've read a lot of history in my life, and bad leadership seems to crop up time after time in the British Army. Of course, we had some good colonels, and generals as well, but it was always a lottery."

Mr Collett spoke with some bitterness about the effect in those days of the class system when, as he put it, only the aristocracy and upper classes could hold a commission, and they bought their rank. Working-class men could not afford to buy a commission. This meant that a young man with money, however stupid he might be, however lazy, or indifferent to army life, could buy a rank and be put in charge of other men. The tradition of an easy life for the officers, with nothing but parties and races, was well entrenched, and any friendship between officers and other ranks was forbidden. "They did not think of us as human beings," said Mr Collett. "We meant nothing to them. We were just 'the scum of the earth', utterly disposable.

"I don't know how it was that I wasn't killed. In my regiment, more than three-quarters of the men who went out to South Africa died, either in battle or in the military hospitals. Yet somehow I was spared."

Another killer was disease. Mr Collett had suffered slight leg wounds in one skirmish, and had a short stay in hospital. While he was there he saw a constant stream of men being brought in with what was called dysentery. It was, in fact, typhoid fever, due to infected water, and it spread like wildfire. At one stage it seemed to be out of control. He commented: "I don't know if anyone who caught the disease recovered, but I know that I never saw a man walk out. I only saw the bodies carried out – ten or twenty a day from one ward – and they were quickly replaced by as many new patients with the same disease. The small hospital that I was in had been built for three hundred patients, and it was carrying two thousand. There were nowhere near enough doctors or nurses to treat all those men, so most of them died. Three times as many men died in the hospitals as died on the battlefields. I don't know how it was that I didn't catch typhoid. I was spared for something worse."

I wondered what could be worse, and imagined the heartache and frustration of trying to nurse sick and dying men under such impossible conditions.

"Somehow I survived and had to take part in what was called 'the bitter end'. After two and a half years of fighting we were no closer to victory than we had been at the beginning. We couldn't engage the enemy. They were always hiding and attacking our lines, our communications, our stores, always surprising us. So our generals decided to attack their food supplies. This meant attacking their farms. A 'scorched-earth' policy was approved and we private soldiers had to carry it out. We hated it. Most of us felt degraded and emasculated, attacking women and children. We turned them out of their homes and burned their farms and barns. We killed their animals and burned their fields. Nothing was left after we'd finished. They were turned out to wander the veldt with no water, no food, prey to wild animals. I remember one young Boer woman with two little children and a baby. She was sobbing, begging us to spare her. I wanted to, but refusal to obey military orders is unthinkable. It would have meant execution by firing squad if I had done so. Perhaps I would have risked it if I had been single. But my money was going to Sally and the boys, and to my mother for the rent. What could I do? And even if I had disobeyed orders, it would have done no good. Other men would have carried out the job." He looked very grim and bitter.

"It was humiliating to us, and to our commanding officers. We were sent out to fight men, not defenceless women and children. We should never have done it. Never." Mr Collett clenched his hands tightly.

"It was a black time for the British Empire. Thirty thousand women and children died, mostly young children, and we were disgraced in the eyes of the world. We outnumbered the Boer fighting men by twenty-five to one, yet even then we couldn't win without attacking their homes, their womenfolk and their children.

"In the spring of 1903 I sailed for home, and I was discharged from the army in 1906."

"Did you regret your army years, or do you look back on them with pleasure?" I asked.

"Mixed feelings. The army certainly educated me and broadened my mind. I mixed with men from other backgrounds and experienced other ideas and points of view. Without the army, I would have been a casual dock labourer, mostly unemployed, so I am grateful for the work. With my army record, I was able to get a good job as a postman. And a postman I remained for the rest of my life until I retired with a pension to keep me comfortably in my old age."

His ingenuous simplicity had always charmed me. He looked upon his squalid, bug-ridden flat as comfort, even luxury; he was grateful for a modest pension that enabled him to buy food and coal sufficient for his needs. He saw himself as a wealthy man, who could afford to buy a bottle of sherry and a box of chocolates with which to entertain a young nurse of whom he had grown fond. He was completely content.

I leaned forward and squeezed his hand with affection. "I think it's getting late and I must go, but next time you must tell me about re-adjusting to civvy life. I guess your twins didn't know you?"

He didn't reply, but looked dreamily into the fire. "You go, my maiden, you go," he said, softly. I left an old man to his memories, the consolation of loneliness.

My next visit to Mr Collett was a morning about three days later. His legs had improved beyond all recognition and the ulcers were now completely dry. It was very gratifying.

On the mantelpiece, amid all the dingy and faded old photographs, was a gleaming white card, with a gold border and an embossed crown on it, requesting the pleasure of the company of Mr Joseph Collett and lady at the Old Guards' reunion at Caterham Barracks on a Saturday in June. I remarked on the card. He told me that for several years he had enjoyed going to the Old Guards' Day, but had not been able to go in recent years, due to his deteriorating eyesight and bad legs.

Impulsively I said, "Look, your legs are so much better now. It won't be any trouble for you to get around. Let's go together. It looks like good fun. It's not every girl has an opportunity like this, and I don't want to miss it."

He positively lit up. He took my hands and kissed them. "You darling girl! What a wonderful idea. It hadn't even crossed my mind. We'll go, and we'll make a day of it. I can tell you, the Guards do us old soldiers proud. What a day we'll have! What a day!"

I requested the day off well in advance, telling Sister Julienne about the invitation, and the plans. The girls were most intrigued; what on earth would it be like? Trixie suggested that a Young Guards' reunion might be more exciting, but wished me pleasure with my old ones.

The day itself dawned bright and fair. I was round at Alberta Buildings shortly after eight o'clock. Mr Collett was excited and chatty. He was dressed for the occasion in a faded old suit. His shoes had been polished, and he carried a new trilby hat. Most important of all, and by far the most impressive, he was wearing a row of medals on his chest. It had not occurred to me that he had medals, and I looked at them closely. He was proud and happy, telling me what each of them was for.

We took the bus from Blackwall to Victoria Coach Station, and then a coach to Caterham, arriving at about ten o'clock. I was excited, having never been inside a barracks before. For a young, inexperienced girl it was a stupendous occasion, and my excitement communicated itself to Mr Collett. We stayed very close together, because of the crowds, and I held his arm all the time as he couldn't see clearly. I had expected a rather solemn occasion with a lot of old men talking about old times. But it was nothing like that. It was an Open Day, with full military honours and pageantry. The reunion itself was an evening event.

The day was exhilarating. The British Army really knows how to put on a show. The colour, the flags, the pipes and drums, the drills. The scarlet uniforms, black busbies, the marching, with the pipe major throwing his staff high into the air. I was thrilled. Mr Collett had seen it all before, and couldn't see it very well this time, but he heard my cheers and was delighted.

Towards evening, when the marching and the drilling had ceased, and the tired crowds were starting to leave, I thought we would be leaving also. But Mr Collett pulled me back. "Now it is time for the regimental dinner. Come on, my beauty. This way. They'll see 'the privates know how to pick 'em'."

We went to the great dining room by special invitation. We were a little late, because Mr Collett's walking was slow. We passed young soldiers, who clicked their heels and saluted. We entered, the doorman took our card, and called: "Mr Joseph Collett and Miss Jenny Lee." There were about two hundred men and women seated at the tables. Heads looked up, and then a voice called out: "Gentlemen, now here is a really old guardsman." And everyone in the room stood up and raised their glasses: "To an esteemed old soldier."

Tears of emotion sprang from Mr Collett's eyes. We were led to the Colonel's table, and placed at his side. The dinner was sumptuous, and the Colonel and his lady so gracious to the old man. They talked about the Boer War, and Africa, and army life sixty years earlier. He was treated with the respect and recognition that he deserved so well.

FRANCE
1914–1918

The joyous day at Caterham Barracks cemented our friendship and I knew then that, come what may, I was bound to Mr Collett for life. We chatted and laughed all the way home, and parted at the bus stop near Blackwall Tunnel. He insisted that he didn't need me to go back with him, as he was perfectly capable of finding his way in the dark. It gladdened my heart to remember the respect, even deference, with which he had been treated at the barracks by the Colonel. He would not forget that day in a hurry.

One day, whilst treating his legs, I asked him about his life after leaving the army. I knew that Sally and the twins were living in Alberta Buildings by that stage. Did they continue to live there when he came back?

"No. I got a job in the Post Office you see, and so we had to move near to the sorting office in Mile End." He went on to tell me about his new life. Postmen had to sort their own mail in those days, and had to be in the sorting house by four o'clock each morning to receive the night mail. Sorting took a couple of hours, then they would be out on the road delivering until about 1 p.m. After a couple of hours off, they went back to sort and deliver the evening mail, which finished about 7 p.m. Mr Collett thought it was a good life.

"The twins were getting bigger. Pete and Jack were about six or seven, and the spitting image of each other. No one except their mother could tell them apart and even she got it wrong sometimes. They were lovely boys."

He bit his lip and swallowed hard, choking down the emotion.

"You've heard, I suppose, that identical twins often seem to live for each other. Well, I can tell you how true that is. They were two people, but I often thought that neither of them could be quite sure where one ended and the other began. They were always together, you couldn't separate them. They didn't seem to need anyone else. They even spoke their own language. Yes, it's true! We would listen to them playing, Sally and me, and they used different words with each other than they used with everyone else. It was a mixture of ordinary English and their own language. They could understand it, but we couldn't. You can never be quite sure what's going on in a child's mind, and identical twins are more of a mystery than other children. Pete and Jack lived in a world created by their combined imaginations, filled with giants and dwarves, kings and queens, castles and caverns. They didn't really have any friends. They didn't need them. They had each other."

"Didn't their mother feel left out?"

"You're right there, she did. The boys weren't lacking in affection, or anything like that. They were just totally self-sufficient. In fact, Sally once said, 'I reckon you and me could die, Joe, and they wouldn't notice. But if one of the boys died, I reckon the other would just fade away.'"

Tears glistened in the corners of his eyes, and he murmured, "Perhaps it was best, all for the best. The Lord giveth, and the Lord taketh away." He fell completely silent, lost in thought.

I had heard of two sons being killed in France, and looked at the picture of two handsome little boys on the wall. I asked, "Did you have any more children?"

"Yes, we had a little girl, and Sally nearly died in childbirth. I don't know what went wrong, and the midwife didn't know either, but my Sal was near to death for weeks after the birth. Her sister took the baby and wet-nursed her for the first three months, and the boys went to my mother. It frightened the life out of me, so I never let her go through it again. That's one thing you learn about in the army, if nothing else: contraception. I never could understand these men who let their wives have ten or fifteen children, when they could prevent it.

"But Sally recovered, thank God, and the children came home. We called the little girl Shirley – don't you think that's a pretty name? She was the loveliest little thing in all the world and a blessing to us both."

I did not need to see Mr Collet professionally more than once a week, because his legs were nearly better, but our sherry evenings continued, and during one of them he told me the story of Pete and Jack.

Young girls are not usually interested in war and military tactics, but I was. Wartime had shaped my childhood, but really, I knew little about war itself. The First World War was a mystery to me, and we were taught nothing about it in our history lessons at school. I knew that vast numbers of soldiers had died in the trenches of France, but so great was my ignorance that I did not even know what "trenches" meant. Later I met people who had suffered in the Blitz, and heard their first-hand stories, so when Mr Collett mentioned his sons' experiences I encouraged him to talk.

Pete and Jack had been sixteen years old when the war started. They had left school at the age of fourteen, and for two years had been Post Office telegraph boys, racing around London on their bikes delivering telegrams. They were known as "the flying twins". They loved it, were proud of their work, proud of the uniform, and were both healthy from all the fresh air and exercise. But in 1914 war started, and a national recruitment campaign was launched. "It will all be over by Christmas" was the government's promise. Many of their friends joined up, lured by the thought of adventure, and the twins wanted to go too, but their father restrained the boys, saying that war was not all adventure and glory.

1915 saw the launch of the famous poster of Lord Kitchener, pointing darkly out of the frame and saying "Your country needs you". After that, young men who did *not* join up were made to feel that they were cowards. Hundreds of thousands of young men volunteered, Pete and Jack among them, and marched off to their graves.

The men were sent for three months' military training in how to handle a gun and a grenade. Also how to care for horses and sword fighting for hand-to-hand combat were part of their training. Mr Collett commented wryly: "That just shows you how little the military High Command knew about mechanised warfare with high explosives!"

Men, boys and horses were packed into a steamer that stank of human sweat and horse droppings, and were shipped across the Channel to France. They were sent straight to the front-line trenches.

I said, "I've heard about this, front lines and trenches and going over the top and the likes, but what does it all mean?"

He said, "Well I wasn't there – I was too old. I suppose I could have gone as a veteran, but the Post Office was vital work, because all communications were handled by the Post Office, so I don't think I would have been released. However, I have met several men who were there at the front and who survived, and they told me the realities we never heard about back home.'

"Tell me about them, will you?"

"If you really want me to I will. But are you sure you want to hear? It's not the sort of thing one should discuss with a young lady."

I assured him I really did want to hear.

"Then you had better get me another drink. No, not that sherry stuff. If you look in the bottom of that cupboard you will find half a bottle of brandy."

I filled his glass, and he took a gulp.

"That's better. It upsets me, talking about it. My two beautiful boys died in those trenches. I reckon I need a bit of brandy inside just to think about it."

He finished the glass, and handed it back to me for a refill, then continued his narrative.

The things he told me that evening were deeply disturbing.

The trenches, I learned, were a series of massive dugouts intended as *temporary* camouflage in flat countryside that offered no natural protection for an army. In the event, they were used for four years of continuous warfare, and provided living accommodation for soldiers.

For months on end men were camped underground in trenches that were always damp, and sometimes waterlogged. Conditions were so cramped, and the men so tightly packed side by side, that the only way to sleep was to stand with their heads and shoulders learning over the parapet. Trench-foot (rotting of the skin caused by a fungal infection), frost-bite and gangrene were rife. The men endured filthy clothes, unchanged for weeks, and lice, millions of lice, that spread from one man to another and were impossible to eliminate. There was no sanitation, and drinking water was contaminated by mud and sewage. Hot food was an infrequent luxury. The rats were everywhere, thriving on an unlimited supply of human flesh as men died in such numbers that the living were unable to bury them.

Both armies were entrenched in their dugouts, often in a line only a hundred yards apart, and both sides were ordered to blow the other to smithereens. Men were being blown to pieces all around; arms, legs, heads were blown off; men were disembowelled, faces torn open, eyes shot out. If the men were ordered to leave their trenches ("go over the top" as it was called) and advance on foot towards the enemy line they would be heading straight into the line of fire and as many as 100,000 men could die in a single day.

And all the time, the cold, the damp, the hunger, the lice, and the stench of decomposition as rats gnawed at the corpses of the dead, drove the men stark raving mad.

"It's worse than I had thought, far worse," I said. "I can't even imagine it. I think I would have gone out of my mind in such a situation."

"Many did. And there was precious little sympathy for them."

"It is surprising that men did not simply run away. What was to stop them?"

"Desertion was punishable by death by firing squad."

In that instant I remembered my Uncle Maurice. He was a strange, withdrawn man subject to violent passions and irrational behaviour. He was potentially dangerous, and I had always been very afraid of him. My aunt told me that he had spent four years, the entire war, in the trenches and somehow miraculously survived. "Don't provoke him dear," she would say, and I could see that her entire life was devoted to trying to ease his mind and bring tranquillity to his life. She was an angel, and I thought at the time that he did not deserve her – but without her he would have been a nervous wreck, and probably even certified as insane.

She said, "He hardly even talks about the war, he bottles it up. Occasionally I can get him to talk about it, and I think it helps. But he still even now, thirty years afterwards, has dreadful nightmares. He screams and thrashes around the bed, and shouts to people in his dreams."

Having heard Mr Collett's descriptions of trench warfare I began, for the first time, to understand my Uncle Maurice, and my aunt's saintly devotion.

One day she told me the most dreadful story of all. Her husband had been ordered to join a firing squad of ten men to shoot one of their companions who had deserted and been captured. The victim was a boy of nineteen who had been so terrified by the noise of guns and the death happening all around him that his mind had snapped and he had run away screaming. He was quickly arrested, for he had not managed to stumble more than half a mile, then was court-martialled, and sentenced to death for desertion. All the men knew the boy and each one hoped and prayed he would not be ordered to join the firing squad. Ten men were selected and ordered to shoot the boy in cold blood, and my uncle was one of them.

★

I told the story to Mr Collett. For several moments he said not a word, but was busy cleaning out his pipe with a murderous-looking weapon, scraping and gouging the nicotine and tar from the encrusted bowl of his old friend. Then he blew hard down the stem and bits of black stuff flew into the air.

"That's better," he muttered "no wonder it wouldn't draw." Then he said, "Fill my glass, will you dear?"

I sloshed more brandy in, not knowing how strong it was. He took a sip and rolled it on his tongue, then said: "That is a dreadful story. It will remain with your uncle for the rest of his life. War brutalises a man. It is not surprising he was moody and violent. But you must remember two things: running away from battle has always been punishable by death. Military discipline must be harsh, or every soldier would run away; and secondly in a firing squad of ten men only one held a rifle with live ammunition – nine held blanks. So every man had a nine out of ten chance of not being responsible for the death of his colleague.

"I don't know what to think. I suppose it's as you say – military discipline must be harsh – but it's dreadful all the same. I find it almost unfathomable."

"Of course you do, my dear, you are in a profession that is devoted to caring for life, not destroying it. 'War is hell' – General William Sherman said that about the American Civil War a hundred years ago. It always has been hell and it always will be."

"My grandfather told me that his uncles had been in the Crimean Wars and never came back. The family never knew what happened."

"No they wouldn't. The common soldier was completely expendable, not even named. Did you know that after the battle of Sebastopol the bones of the dead were collected up in sacks and shipped back to Britain to be ground down into fertilizers that was sold to farmers for a profit."

"That can't be true."

"It is true. Perfectly true."

"It's disgusting! I think I'll try a shot of your brandy."

"Be careful. It's strong stuff."

"I'm not worried, I can take it." I boasted.

I poured some, and took a gulp as I had seen him do. It didn't just take the roof off my mouth; it set fire to my throat and gullet and windpipe. I started coughing and choking violently. He laughed. "I warned you."

When I had recovered, I said, "But that was a hundred years ago. They can't have been so callous after the First World War."

"Beautiful cemeteries were built all over Northern France, the graveyards of millions of young men. They rest in peace."

"Have you been there to see the resting place of Pete and Jack? It would be a comfort to you."

"No, they are not buried there."

"Where then?"

He sighed, a sigh so deep that all the sorrow of the world seemed gathered into it.

"We don't know what happened to them. A telegram, "missing presumed dead", was the message from the War Office. This was at the end of war. They had lived through three and a half years at the front, only to go missing presumed dead during the last few months. My Sally's heart was broken. Little Shirley was the only thing that kept us going."

He sat silent and still for a couple of minutes, sipping his brandy and sucking on his pipe. I did not care to interrupt his thoughts. When he spoke his voice was dull and resigned.

"About a year later we were informed that their bodies had never been found. Thousands of families received the same letter. You see men were just blown to pieces and nothing identifiable could be found. Or a trench wall might have collapsed and buried them alive; or they could have fallen and sunk into the mud and been sucked down, and the mud closed over them. We don't know. Millions of boys, on both sides, died and were never found. And millions of families are grieving still."

LONDON
1939–1945

I saw more of Mr Collett after that, but we never again mentioned the twins. He told me that Shirley, the pride of his heart, had had a good education, and passed the School Certificate, an achievement attained by very few East End girls in those days. This enabled her to go into the Post Office to be trained in accountancy and bookkeeping, to work as one of the counter staff. She also studied telegraphy and Morse code.

"It was two years of study," Mr Collett said. "The system was based on long and short sounds, or flashes of light. We spent many hours, the three of us, tapping and flashing messages to each other. Sally and I picked up some of the code, enough to learn the alphabet, but Shirley became a real expert. She had to be a touch-typist as well and could sit blindfolded, listening to a message being tapped out and typing the words with never a mistake. Then we darkened the room, and I sat flashing the code to her with a torch while she typed the message. Still no mistakes. Her skills were greatly valued when the Second World War came. In 1939 she was put straight onto the reserve Special Occupation List."

I asked him about his memories of the war and his admiration for Winston Churchill shone through.

"From 1935 onwards you had to be blind not to see that something was going to happen. Hitler was re-arming and mobilizing his troops, casting fear and unrest all over Europe. Unfortunately, most of our leaders seemed to be both blind and deaf. Only Churchill could see clearly and he poured out warnings, but his words fell on deaf ears, and the government refused to re-arm. Consequently, when war came in 1939, we were completely unprepared. We had the minimum trained army and navy, and virtually no equipment.

"Now, Churchill is a man who has interested me all my life. He is a contemporary of mine, and was also in the South African war. The first I heard of him was his famous escape from Pretoria prison, which electrified the troops, and the whole of England, when the news got back to London. The funniest thing about it was the letter he left behind for the Boer Minister of Defence. Something like: 'Sir, I have the honour to inform you that I do not consider your government has any right to detain me as a prisoner. I have therefore decided to escape from your custody,' and ending up: 'I remain, sir, your humble and obedient servant, Winston Churchill.'

"In 1916 Churchill became a lieutenant colonel of the Royal Scots Fusiliers (I was a Scots Guardsman, you remember). He served in the front line alongside his men, which was more than most of the officers did. After the war he dabbled in politics, but was never very successful. He made a lot of mistakes – but whatever he did, he did it on a grand scale, and he was always fascinating, a magnetic personality.

"I tell you, I have never been more relieved in all my life than when he became Prime Minister and Minister of Defence in 1940. He had moral strength and a command of words that put fire in your belly. He united the people to stand up to Hitler and fascism, even though we had only broken bottles and carving knives to fight with. I honestly believe that without Churchill we would have lost the war, and Britain would be a Nazi state today."

It was a sobering thought. I had always taken freedom for granted. I had been a child during the war, and had seen things through a child's eyes. It was not until after the war, when I was about ten years old, that I saw on a cinema newsreel the ghastly pictures of Belsen, Auschwitz, Dachau, and the many other death camps dotted across Europe. This was when I began to understand the evil we had been fighting.

Also, being a country-born child, I had seen very little of the war itself. We lived only thirty miles from London, but life was peaceful and untroubled. My mother took in evacuees, which was good fun as far as I was concerned. Food was scarce and I didn't see a banana or an orange until I was ten, but apart from that there might not have been a war going on at all. Where, I wondered, had Mr Collett spent the war?

His response was firm. London was his home and it was where he had remained throughout the war years. Sally didn't want to leave London either – it was where she had been born and bred. They both felt there really was no other option. This attitude was fairly typical of Londoners. In 1939 large-scale evacuations of women and children occurred, but within six months most of them were back. They couldn't cope with the countryside and returned in droves, preferring the risks of London to the quiet of the countryside.

I had heard a similar story from the Sisters. About seventy Poplar women, all of them pregnant, had been evacuated with two of the midwifery Sisters to Cornwall. One by one these young women returned, always giving the same reason: the silence got on their nerves; they were frightened of the trees and the fields; they couldn't stand the wind moaning. At the end of six months there were only around a dozen left, so the Sisters themselves returned to the place where they were needed the most – the heart of Poplar.

In 1940 Mr Collett retired from the Post Office. Straight away he joined the ARP (Air Raid Precautions) and Sally joined with him. In the early months of 1940 the duties were to see that government directives were carried out. This mainly involved checking that people carried gas masks, that blackout regulations were being observed, that sandbags were filled and that air-raid shelters were suitably equipped. At first, ARP wardens were often called snoopers and laughed at, but in September 1940 the Blitz started and their work really began.

For three long months London was bombed every night,

and there were sometimes daylight raids as well. Bombing was concentrated mainly on the Docklands, but this was also the area with the highest civilian population and hundreds of thousands of Londoners died or lost their homes.

If one looks at a map of London, the horseshoe loop in the Thames going round the Isle of Dogs is fairly obvious. From the air it is a landmark, and the German bomber pilots could not fail to see it. Bombs only had to be dropped on that target, and they were sure to hit either the docks or the housing around them. Thousands of tons of high explosive fell in less than three months. Poplar, housing up to 50,000 people to the square mile, was indeed a sitting target.

There were never enough air-raid shelters for such large numbers of people. In other parts of London people went into the Underground stations, but Poplar had none. The nearest underground was Aldgate. The government provided corrugated iron for people to build Anderson shelters in their gardens, but most Poplar people did not have a garden. Fortunately, many houses did have cellars, where people slept. The crypts of churches provided shelter for hundreds of people, and whole communities lived day and night in the churches. More than one baby was born in All Saints' crypt, as I learned from the Sisters. The overcrowding was terrible. Each person had just enough room to lie down, and no more.

There was always the fear that plague or disease would sweep through the shelters. Water and sewage pipes were frequently hit, but somehow they were always repaired, at least enough to prevent the spread of disease. Gas and electricity supplies were often hit too, but they were always patched up as well.

Mr Collett said to me: "Looking back it seems impossible, but everyone worked day and night, with amazing good spirit.

"When you are living in such conditions, close to death, every day is a gift. You are happy every morning to see the dawn break, and to know that you are still alive. Also, death was no stranger to us. Poplar people were used to suffering. Poverty, hunger, cold, disease and death have been with us for generations, and we have just accepted them as normal, so a few bombs couldn't break us.

"We were used to overcrowding, so the shelters didn't seem too bad. The loss of a house or rooms was no worse than eviction, and most people didn't have much furniture to lose anyway. A family would just move in with neighbours who still had a roof over their heads.

"It was an extraordinary time. Suffering and anguish were all around us, but so too, in a strange way, was exhilaration. We were determined not to be beaten. Two fingers up to Hitler, that was the attitude. I remember one old woman we pulled out of the rubble. She wasn't hurt. She gripped my arm and said: 'That bugger Hitler. 'E's killed me old man, good riddance, 'e's killed me kids, more's the pity. 'E's bombed me 'ouse, so I got nowhere 'a live, bu' 'e ain't got me. An' I got sixpence in me pocket an' vat pub on ve corner, Master's Arms, ain't been bombed, so let's go an' 'ave a drink an' a sing-song.'"

There was even more devastation when the firebombs came, and it was these that were responsible for Sally's death. Both Mr Collett and his wife had had a premonition, sensing that one of them would be killed, but they didn't know who, or when. The firebombs were small, and burst into flames when they hit the ground. They were easy to put out – it could be done with a sandbag, or even a couple of blankets – but if the fire spread it could set whole buildings alight. The government appealed for volunteer fire-watchers who would go to the top of tall buildings to keep a watch on the area around them. They gave the alert when a firebomb fell, and the men with sandbags rushed to the spot at once to put out the fire. These fire-watchers had to know the area well, and were mostly old people who didn't have the physical strength to deal with all the digging and heavy lifting required in the streets. Sally volunteered. He said: "She and others went up the highest buildings with nothing but a tin hat to protect them from the explosives and firebombs. One night the building Sally was in got a direct hit. I never saw her again. Her body was never found."

After telling me this sad story he paused, and stared into the fire, for a few minutes, then said softly: "She knew the risk. We both did. I'm glad that she was taken first, and not left on her own. Death is kinder than life. There is no more suffering beyond the grave. We will meet again soon, I hope."

He said the words "soon, I hope" a second time, and I didn't know what to say, so I asked him about his daughter.

Shirley's skills in Morse code and telegraphy were classed as a "special occupation". She joined the WAAF (Women's Auxiliary Air Force) in 1940 and entered the Intelligence and Communications Corps of the RAF. Her father saw a little of her when she came home on leave, but mostly he didn't even know where she was stationed, because all her work was highly confidential, and secrecy was tight. She had never married, and had always been very close to her parents. After her mother's death she threw herself into her work.

Mr Collett, too, found that hard work was the only remedy for unhappiness. After Sally's death he worked day and night, not bothering much about food or sleep. As an ARP warden he did anything and everything that needed doing: helping ambulance men, digging away rubble, carrying water, filling sandbags, and mending burst pipes. He went out at night when bombs were dropping all around, not caring if he was killed. He helped people out of burning buildings, got them to shelters, carried babies, pushed prams. "It was a hard time, but satisfying," he told me, "and all the while I fancied Sal was looking down on me, and sharing the experience."

Many of his experiences from those days he could still vividly recall. He told me about one little boy, about six or seven years old, he said he would never forget. The wardens had dug him out of the rubble he had been buried under for several hours. He was underneath the body of his mother. She must have thrown herself over her son in order to protect him, when the bomb fell.

She was quite stiff and cold, but he was safe beneath her. One does not know the psychological damage that such an experience can inflict, however. He said the boy's name was Paul. Mr Collett mused: "He would be in his twenties now, and I often wonder how he has grown up, and if there has been any lasting mental damage."

He continued his tragic story. "During the next five years I saw Shirley occasionally. She was flourishing. War has that effect sometimes. The unusual circumstances bring out the best in some people. All her intelligence and leadership qualities placed her in positions of command, and she thrived on it. I was so proud of her.

"In 1944 it seemed that the war was ending and we dared to plan for her demob and picking up our life again. But it never does to plan ahead in wartime. The V1 and V2 rocket attacks started. At Christmas 1944 I was told by the RAF that a rocket had fallen on the staff headquarters where Shirley was stationed, and that she had been killed. I have been alone ever since."

THE SHADOW OF THE WORKHOUSE

Jenny kissed me when we met,
Jumping from the chair she sat in . . .
Say I'm weary, say I'm sad,
Say that health and wealth have missed me,
Say I'm growing old, but add,
Jenny kissed me.
Leigh Hunt

Poplar was destined for change. Town planners had a new broom with which to sweep clean, and they were so successful that they swept virtually everything away. Poplar had survived the war, the blitz, the doodlebugs and the V2 rockets. The people had picked themselves up, brushed off the debris, and formed themselves into a community again, almost indistinguishable from the communities of their parents and grandparents. What finally destroyed Poplar was the good intentions of bureaucracy and social planning.

The tenements were to be demolished. In 1958 and 1959 notice was served to thousands of tenants and alternative accommodation was offered. This could be as far away as Harlow, Bracknell, Basildon, Crawley or Hemel Hempstead, which might as well have been the North Pole, as far as most of the older people were concerned. Social workers and housing officers buzzed in and out of the tenements all day with sheaves of forms and good advice and forced good cheer. The residents were not taken in. Most were wary or apprehensive. Some were distraught.

This was the time, and the only time, when I felt sympathy for Mr Collett's neighbour. She came up to me one day as I entered the court of Alberta Buildings and said piteously, "Vey sez we go' 'a go. Go where? Somewhere we don' know, somewhere a long way off. Somewhere no one'll know me, an' I won' know no one. It ain't right, it ain't. I've always paid me ren', you can look a' me book. Never a day la'e. I keeps me flat clean, like me mum used 'a. You can see for yerself. Can' chew do somefink? Ve Sisters 'ave a lo' of say in fings round here."

All the Sisters experienced scenes like this. The idea amongst the older generation that the Sisters would somehow intervene and help them save their little homes was touchingly persistent, but quite erroneous, of course. We tried to comfort the people as best we could, but I doubt if it did much good. The community was doomed. The people who had seen off Hitler by sticking two fingers up and carrying on were themselves seen off the premises.

Then the demolition men took over. The land became valuable. Big business stepped in. The ordinary people didn't stand a chance. Tower blocks were built, which were supposed to be so much better than the tenements. In fact they were the same thing, only far worse, because interaction between neighbours had been stripped away. The courtyards had gone, the inward-facing balconies had gone, walkways and stairways had gone, and upstairs and downstairs neighbours were strangers, with no obvious points of contact. The communal life of the tenements, with all its fraternity and friendship, all its enmity and fighting, was replaced by locked doors and heads turned away. It was a disaster in social planning. A community that had knitted itself together over centuries to form the vital, vibrant people known as "the Cockneys" was virtually destroyed within a generation.

But this was all in the future. We did not know, in 1959, that the effects would be so catastrophic to the Poplar people. We only knew what was happening at the time – namely that the Canada Buildings were to go. We discussed it endlessly over the luncheon table, and one of the nuns said, "Well, if the tenements go, it won't be long before we have to go, because we won't be needed here."

We all looked at each other with sadness, but Sister Julienne said, without a trace of regret: "For more than eighty years we have served God in Poplar. If we are no longer needed here, He will give us other work to do. In the meantime, I suggest we stop speculating on the future and get on with the job in hand."

When I next visited Mr Collett, a social worker was just leaving. She looked harassed, poor soul, and was besieged by women as she stepped across the courtyard. I felt sorry for her. What a job! You are on a hiding to nothing, I thought as I watched her go.

Mr Collett's legs were almost better now, and as he was quite capable of dressing the superficial wounds himself, I called only once a fortnight to check that there was no deterioration. His walking was much better and he was able to get about easily, which was entirely due to simple, regular treatment. Nursing is one of the most satisfying jobs in the world.

He was silent and thoughtful as I undid the bandages. I think we were both wondering what the other was thinking.

He was the first to break the silence. "You've heard, I suppose, that the Buildings are being closed? Yes, Of course you know all about it. I don't understand why. These buildings are sound. They were still here after the Blitz, when thousands of terraces went down like packs of cards. The Canada Buildings will last for centuries, yet they want to pull them down. All my ghosts will be cleared away with the rubble. Will they be laid to rest, I wonder? Will I?" His words sounded like a premonition.

"What are they offering you?" I asked.

He started, as though I had interrupted a dream. "Offering me? Oh, I don't know. Several things: a flat in Harlow; another in somewhere called Hemel Hempstead. I've got to think about it. I must say, it's very good of them to offer me anything at all. When I was a boy, if a landlord gave notice to quit, he was not obliged to offer you anything else. So I'm grateful for that, and I told the lady social worker so."

I smiled at his generous disposition. There can't have been many social workers at that troubled time who heard an expression of gratitude. "How long have you got to decide?" I asked.

"A few weeks. Perhaps a month. No longer. It's all very sudden."

It was indeed sudden. The sound of children playing was the first thing to go. Flats were vacated, and removal men were in and out of the courtyards; windows were boarded up; the stairways were left dirty and increasingly derelict; dustbins rolled across the cobbles. The constant hum of human activity was replaced by empty echoes as the courts picked up the sound of a single voice and threw it backwards and forwards, till it fell silent in the still air.

I wondered how much more I would see of Mr Collett. If he was going miles away to the countryside of Hertfordshire or Essex, how often would I be able to visit him? Our cosy evenings of sherry and chocolates and chats seemed to be coming to an end.

I popped in on him about a week later to ask if he had come to a decision. He had.

"I'm going to St Mark's in Mile End," he said. "When I was young, it used to be a workhouse. But that was a long time ago. Now it is a residential home for old codgers like myself. I think it will be for the best. The lady social worker tells me I will be well looked after. I'm going next week."

I was shocked and alarmed by the news. The shadow of the workhouse had darkened the lives of countless people for more than a century. Although officially closed in 1930 by Acts of Parliament, workhouses had merely lingered on under another name. I feared for Mr Collett, but I did not like to express my doubts, or even to sound negative, so I simply said: "I'll come and see you, I promise."

Back at Nonnatus House, I poured out my misgivings to Sister Julienne. She was thoughtful and looked grave, but said: "You must understand that this is his decision. He is intelligent, and I think he probably realises that he will not be able to manage to look after himself, alone, in a new place."

I was young and passionate, and argued the case. "But he's so much better now. He can get around without any trouble. Although his eyesight is dim, he's not blind, and he can find everything he needs."

Sister Julienne smiled her sweet, beautiful smile. "Yes, my dear, I know, but that is only because he knows where everything is, and habit makes it possible for him to continue living alone. In other surroundings he would be lost. It is the same for most old people."

My unease persisted, but I knew there was nothing I could do.

A few days later, when I was in the area, I thought I would pop in to arrange a final evening with my old friend. To my astonishment, the flat was empty. I peered through the curtainless window. Everything was the same – but different. Inanimate objects have a life of their own, especially when they are the daily companions of a living soul. Without that life, they take on a bleak, desolate appearance, like furniture piled up in a warehouse. I knew he was gone, and didn't need anyone to confirm it, although the woman next door stepped out, or rather shuffled out. Gone was her self-righteous aggression; gone, her busy-body ways and manners. Instead she exuded a dull, helpless apathy and despair. Her voice was subdued. 'E's gorn. Vey took 'im vis mornin' wiv 'is case. Vey'll take me an' all, vey will." She shuffled back into her flat, and bolted the door. Poplar people never bolted their doors in daytime, unless they were afraid of someone.

At Nonnatus House, I felt a heavy sense of loss as I climbed the stairs. It had all been so sudden. My first thought was to go and see him at once, but then I dithered around, thinking that he needed time to settle in and get to know other people. Perhaps it was all for the best. If a thing has to be, it's best to do it quickly. He was a wise old man; he would not have agreed to go so soon if he had thought there was anything to be gained by delay.

It was about a fortnight later, after lunch, when I cycled up to Mile End to find St Mark's. I entered by the huge iron gate, and looked at the bleak grey buildings. I was accustomed to the old workhouse buildings, because most of them had been converted into hospitals or isolation units. I knew that they all had a particularly grim appearance, but I had never seen anything as forbidding as St Mark's. My heart sank as I looked around.

I enquired after Mr Collett. Perhaps I had imagined that some helpful, pretty young nurse in a natty little uniform would take me straight to him. Not so. The only person I saw was a rather dirty-looking porter pushing a trolley of bins. He spoke no English, but pointed to a door. Inside was a sort of office area with no one around. It was cold and high-ceilinged, with plaster cracking and crumbling off the walls. I called, and my voice echoed up the stairwell. Still no one came.

I wandered out, and through another door. A wide, empty corridor stretched ahead, with doors going off it. I opened one, and entered a large, square room, where a lot of old men were sitting around Formica-topped tables. For a room so full of humanity it was eerily quiet. Faces looked up at me, all blank and expressionless. I looked round, but could not see Mr Collett. Nor could I see anyone to ask about him. Some plates rattled, which indicated a kitchen, and I went towards the sound. Two young men were inside, but neither of them spoke English. They repeated the name "Collett" several times, but shook their heads. One of them indicated another building. I followed the advice, and was fortunate to meet a porter, who said, "You need Reception, dear, over there," pointing to the first door I had entered.

Back in the hall with the echoing stairwell I hung around, and "hello-ed" for about twenty minutes. Eventually a middle-aged man entered, carrying a sheaf of papers. I gave him my request.

He looked at me in astonishment. "You want to see a Mr Collett? Is that what you are saying?"

"Yes."

"Why? Are you a social worker?"

"No. I just want to see him. Have I come at the wrong time, then? Am I out of visiting hours?"

"No. We don't have any visiting hours. We generally don't get any visitors. I'll have to open the office and find out where this Mr Collett is."

In the office, he thumbed through piles of papers. "I think I've found him. Mr Joseph Collett. Is that the name you want? Block E, Fifth Floor. Go up that staircase you see opposite."

He pointed to a stone staircase. I climbed five flights and pushed open the heavy door, entering a room similar to the one I had seen on the ground floor. It was large, with about twenty Formica-topped tables and four hard-backed chairs at each table. Old men were sitting on most of the chairs, their arms on the table, staring at the man opposite. Some had their heads down, resting on their arms. No one spoke. The room smelt acrid with urine and body odour. The high windows let in light, but they were too high for anyone to see out.

I looked around until I saw Mr Collett at the far end of the room. He was looking down at the table at which he was sitting, and did not see me approach. I went straight up to him and kissed him.

He gasped, looked up, and tears filled his eyes. His lips trembled, and the tears fell. He whispered, "My maiden, my Jenny, you've come, then." He was too overwhelmed to say anything more.

The chair opposite was empty, so I sat down and we held hands across the table.

"I would have come sooner, only I thought you should have a chance to settle in, and get to know your companions. I'm so sorry if you thought I wasn't coming."

He muttered, "Yes ... no ... I mean, that's all right, my pet, that's all right. You're here, and I love you for it. I'm so grateful." He squeezed my hand.

I bit my lip, close to tears myself, and looked round at the cheerless room, filled with lethargic old men saying nothing. I didn't know what to say myself. We had never had any difficulty with conversation before; in fact, time had always seemed too short for all that we had to say. But now I was tongue-tied. I asked empty questions like: "Are you all right, then?" "What's the food like?" "Are you comfortable here?" to all of which he replied, bleakly, "Yes, I'm doing very nicely, thank you. You don't want to worry your head about me."

Minutes ticked by, and there were long silences. I knew I would have to go, because I had my evening visits to start at 4 p.m. It had taken me at least forty-five minutes to find him, and time was short. It had been only the briefest of visits, and I hated leaving him, as I tried, haltingly, to explain.

He said, simply, "You go, my maid, and don't mind me."

I kissed him again, and fled from the room. At the door, I turned. He was stroking the cheek where my lips had touched him, and his tears were falling fast onto the table.

I don't know how it was I didn't have an accident as I cycled back to Nonnatus House. I was filled with sorrow.

After supper, I spoke to Sister Julienne. She listened in silence to what I had to say, and didn't speak for a long time. Thinking she hadn't taken it in, I said. "You do understand what I'm saying, don't you? It is simply dreadful. He shouldn't be there."

"Oh yes, my dear, I understand all right. I was thinking of Our Lord's words to Peter, as recorded in St John's Gospel: 'When you are young, you go where you wish, but when you are old, others will take you where you do not wish to go.' This was taken to indicate the manner in which St Peter would die, but I have always thought that it is a general reflection about us all. For we all grow old, and very few of us retain our health and strength to the last. Most of us become helpless and completely dependent on others, whether we like it or not. Old age is a time when we learn the virtue of humility."

I didn't know what to say. I had often found myself in a similar position with Sister Julienne. She had a purity of thought and a simplicity of expression that were quite unanswerable.

She continued: "Mr Collett's tragedy is that all his family were killed in the wars. The tragedy is loneliness, not the surroundings, which I doubt he notices. What you see as intolerable living conditions may be all par for the course to him. If he were living in luxury in a palace, he would be just as lonely. You are his only friend, Jenny, and he loves you. You must stay with him."

I said that I had pledged myself to do that, and then I started to rail against the folly and inhumanity of turning him out of the flat where he had been comfortable and independent.

She stopped me in mid-sentence. "Yes, I know all that. But you must understand that the Canada Buildings have long been due for demolition. People are not going to put up with a bug-infested environment and insanitary conditions today. The Buildings must go, so the people must go. I am well aware of the fact that most of the old people who are being moved will not be able to adjust to new surroundings, and that many of them will die as a consequence. Which brings me back to the words of Jesus: 'When you are old, men will take you where you do not want to go.'"

She smiled at me, because I must have looked so sad, and said: "Now I must go and take Compline. Why not join us this evening?"

The beauty and timelessness of the monastic office of Compline eased my troubled soul.

"The Lord grant us a quiet night and a perfect end."

I thought of Mr Collett and all the other old men, isolated – even from each other – by loneliness.

"In thee, O Lord, have I put my trust. Let me never be put to confusion."

The candles lighting the altar were reflected on the windows, shutting the dark without, and enclosing the nuns within.

"Be thou my strong rock and house of defence."

Jews and Christians have drawn strength and wisdom from these psalms for two to three thousand years.

"Thou shalt not be afraid of any terror by night."

All those sad old men – were they afraid? Afraid of living, yet more afraid of dying?

"For He shall give his angels charge over thee."
Did they know any joy, in their joyless surroundings?
"Lighten our darkness, we beseech thee, O Lord."
Just hold them in your prayers, as Sister Julienne will in hers.
"Protect us through the silent hours of the night, so that we who are wearied by the changes and chances of this fleeting world may repose upon Thy eternal changelessness."
The Sisters left the chapel quietly. The Greater Silence had begun.

I saw Mr Collett as much as I could after that. I never stayed very long – half an hour perhaps, not more, and this was mainly because we both found it difficult to know what to say. The circumstances were just not right for cosy chats, and we were no good at small talk. Also the inertia, I think, was dulling the mind that had once been so alert. Knowing how much he used to enjoy radio documentary programmes and plays, I asked him if he listened to his wireless. He looked at me blankly, so I repeated the question.

"No, I haven't got my wireless. I don't know what they did with it. I don't think I could have it here, anyway, so it doesn't matter."

I asked what had happened to his things.

"I don't know. The lady social worker said she would look after all that. I suppose they were sold, and the money put into my account. I've got a bank account, you know. I gave her the number."

"Have you seen her since?"

"Oh yes, she came here. She is very pleasant. She gave me this."

He fumbled in the inside pocket of his waistcoat, and produced a bit of paper. It was a receipt for £96 14s. 6d. for the sale of furniture. I thought of the grandfather clock, the fine old table, and his high wooden armchair. Now all that was left was a piece of paper.

The big room with its high windows was oppressive, and the all-pervading smell of urine nauseating, but I doubt if the old men noticed this (after all, the sense of smell fades along with the other senses as age advances). The worst thing for them, I could see, was the boredom of having absolutely nothing to do, hour after hour, day after day. One or two got up and shuffled off to the lavatory, or to another room, which I was later to discover was the dormitory. But apart from that, they did nothing. A few played cards or dominoes, but the games never seemed to excite much interest. The *Daily Mirror* and the *Express* were passed around, and some of the men glanced at them but, from what I observed, most of them just sat at the tables, looking at each other. I never saw any other visitor, and I wondered how it was possible that so many old men could have no one at all who wanted to visit them. I saw only Block E, Fifth Floor, and I did not know how many other blocks and floors there were, filled with old men, seemingly abandoned, each day killing the time, until time killed them.

One day I asked Mr Collett where his pipe was and if he smoked it. He said, "We are only allowed to smoke on the balcony."

"Well, do you do so, then?"

"No, I don't know where the balcony is."

I felt very cross at such thoughtlessness on the part of the staff. They were not unkind, as far as I could see, but they were mostly Filipino or Indonesian young men, who spoke little or no English, and it obviously had not occurred to any of them to take a nearly blind man to the balcony and make sure that he knew how to find his way there and back.

"Well, let's go out to the balcony, then, and you can have a smoke, and we can get some fresh air at the same time. Have you got your pipe, your twist, and some matches?"

"Not on me. They are in my locker. I'll go and get them. You can come with me. I don't suppose anyone would mind."

He stood up, and felt his way along the tables to a short

corridor at the end of which was a wide double door leading into the dormitory. My experienced eye saw at once that it was the size of the average hospital ward, designed for twenty-eight or thirty beds. It held, at a rough guess, sixty or seventy. They lined each wall, and the far end wall also. They were small two-foot-six-inch iron bedsteads, with thin mattresses over sagging springs. Beside each was a tiny locker about twelve inches wide, and the beds touched the lockers on either side. I looked down towards the far end of the dormitory. There were no lockers, and the beds were so close to each other that, presumably, the only way the occupant could get in and out was by climbing over the end. Some were occupied by old men, who just lay there, sleeping or staring at the ceiling. My critical nurse's eye looked at the bed linen and blankets. All were filthy, and the stench of urine and faeces was evidence that fresh linen was a rarity. A ward sister would have had a team of cleaners in there in seconds. But I saw no staff at all that day.

Mr Collett felt his way along fourteen beds, and then went to the locker beside the fifteenth. I watched him, and noticed that he was walking with difficulty again. I thought, with alarm, about his leg ulcers – so much better, but only because of regular treatment. Was he still getting it? I looked around at the general neglect, and had misgivings. Perhaps he was treating the ulcers himself. I resolved to ask him before leaving that day.

He found his pipe and chuckled as he cradled his old friend in the palm of his hand. We made our way, first to the table where he had been sitting, and then to the balcony, counting the number of tables, and the direction he would have to take. I wanted to be sure he knew how to get there by himself. The door was big and heavy, with a metal safety bar, but he could manage to open it.

The fresh air was lovely, though cold, and the balcony was pleasant, but there was nowhere to sit down. I had to hold Mr Collett's pipe and matches whilst he cut up the tobacco. He filled the pipe and lit it, and, with a satisfied sigh, exhaled clouds of thick smoke. "Luxury," he murmured, "sheer luxury."

I noticed the way he was standing. It was not good. He was shuffling from one leg to the other, and taking a few steps backwards and forwards. I didn't like the signs. People with leg ulcers can usually walk, but standing still in one place is nearly impossible for them. I asked him how his legs were, and who was treating them.

"Well, I can do it myself."

"Yes, but do you?"

"Now and again, lass, now and again."

"How often? Every day?"

"Well, not quite every day; but enough, quite enough."

"Do the staff renew the dressings?"

"They looked at them when I first came here, but I don't recall since."

I was silent. Two months, no trained person dressing the ulcers or supervising his treatment. It was not good enough. I said, "I would like to have a look at them."

"Another time. Another time. I'm enjoying the fresh air, and the pipe, and, above all, your company. I know you'll have to go soon and I don't want to spoil it. You can look at my legs another day."

He was right. The time was drawing near to 4 p.m., and my evening visits. I could not linger, so I kissed him tenderly, and left him with his pipe, and a rare smile on his face.

THE LAST POST

Something told me that Mr Collett did not have long to live. I was anxious about his legs, but apart from that I could see that he would never adapt to the communal life of St Mark's. Sister Julienne had been quite right, I discovered. The unpleasant surroundings meant nothing to him at all. The tiny bed in a dormitory with about seventy other men was quite acceptable. In fact, he described himself as "Very comfortable. Doing nicely. They are very good to us here." So if he had no complaints about the conditions, I realised that I should not. His trouble was chronic loneliness, and the inability to adjust to change.

On two occasions when I visited I asked to see his legs, but he prevaricated, making different excuses each time, and I didn't think I could force the issue. The next occasion when I called he was not at his usual table. The man who generally sat opposite him pointed to the dormitory and said, "He ain't got up today."

I went to the dormitory, and in the fifteenth bed on the right Mr Collett lay motionless. I looked at him for a long time from the doorway, hating myself for hating the smell, and for not wanting to approach the bed. A sort of dread had entered my heart, and I wanted to turn and run.

He moved and coughed slightly, and this set me in action. I went up to his bed, kissed him, and whispered, "It's me. Are you all right? It's not like you to stop in bed."

He took my hands and kissed them, and murmured that he would be all right by and by.

I sat beside him, not talking, squeezing his hand from time to time, thinking, If he stays here, not moving, for several days he will get pneumonia, and that will be it. Pneumonia is the old man's friend, they say. A quiet and peaceful end. I hope he goes that way in his sleep. What greater blessing can we ask at the end of life?

Then it occurred to me that, whilst he was lying in bed, it would be easy to look at his legs, so I asked him if I could. He neither agreed nor disagreed, but seemed indifferent.

I pulled the blankets away from the foot of the bed, and the stench of decaying flesh rose to greet me. A rough, fluid-sodden bandage covered each leg, and I unwound them with difficulty. I had no surgical forceps, or scissors, and had to do it with my fingers. The bandages looked as though they had not been changed for a fortnight, and were stuck to the flesh underneath. As I tried to ease them away I thought I might be hurting him, but he did not move, nor show any sign of pain or distress.

At last the wounds were fully exposed. I had to grip the iron bedstead, and call upon all my nurse's training of discipline and self-control to avoid crying out. From the knee to the ankle there was no skin at all, just livid, suppurating flesh, oozing pus and blood. Daylight was fading fast, and the dim electric-light bulb hanging from the ceiling was no great help, but I thought I could see traces of black around the edge of the wound. I looked down at his feet. The toes looked greyish and swollen, one or two of them a darker colour than the others.

"Oh, my God, it can't be. Oh, please, no. Not him. It's not fair."

There was only one way to tell. I unfastened the brooch I was wearing and dug the pin deep into the centre of the wound on each leg. He didn't move. Then I dug it really hard into his toes. He didn't feel a thing. There could not be the slightest doubt: gangrene.

He said, "They are feeling better today. They've been giving me gyp the last few weeks, but they don't hurt now, and I guess they're getting better."

I had to control myself. Fortunately he could not see my face, but he was sensitive to my voice. "As long as you are comfortable, you just stay there. I'll go and get someone to put another dressing on, because I've taken the bandages off. I won't be long."

I raised the alarm, and later the superintendent and a doctor came to the dormitory, but in the meantime I had to leave for my evening work. After I had finished my visits, I cycled back to St Mark's and, for the last time, climbed the staircase to the Fifth Floor of Block E. Mr Collett had been transferred to Mile End Hospital.

I was relieved to hear it, and I cycled the half-mile down the road to the hospital in order to find out which ward he had been admitted to. It was too late to see him, but I was told that he was comfortable and sleeping.

Immediately after lunch the next day, I cycled up to the hospital and went straight to the ward. The ward sister told me that Mr Collett had been operated on that morning, and had not yet come round from the anaesthetic. The operation had been a mid-thigh amputation of both legs.

I was taken to the side room where he lay. The calm cleanliness and efficiency of the hospital was reassuring after the shambolic dirt of St Mark's. Mr Collett lay on spotless white sheets, his face calm and relaxed. A nasal tube was *in situ*, and a nurse was sucking the mucus from his throat with an aspirator. She then counted his pulse and checked the flow rate of the blood drip that was running into his arm. She smiled at me as she turned to go. Hospital protocol and discipline had the upper hand, and Mr Collett was now a part of it.

I sat with him for a little while, but he was fast asleep, and looked quite peaceful, so I left, resolving to come back after my evening visits, by which time he might have come round from the anaesthetic and would recognise me.

It was about 7.30 p.m. when I approached the ward, and the screams assailed me long before I pushed open the door. A harassed-looking staff nurse was on duty, and as I ran towards the side ward a frightened nurse whispered: "I think he's gone mad."

Mr Collett was sitting bolt upright in bed, his blind eyes staring, wide with terror. He was waving his arms and screaming: "Watch out, to your left, a grenade exploding." He screamed and ducked to escape an invisible missile flying over his head.

I ran to him, and took him in my arms. "It's me, Jenny. Me, I'm here."

He grabbed me with superhuman strength and pushed me down to the floor. "Get down, keep your head down. They'll blow you to bits. A bloke over there had his head blown off a minute ago. That one over there has lost both his legs. It's a terrible place to be. Gunfire all around. Down. GET DOWN!" He screamed with all his strength and hurled himself forward. The stumps of his legs twitched violently and he fell out of bed. He seemed impervious to the fall, and grabbed me, pulling me under the bed with him.

"Stay here. You'll be safe here, in the shelter. I'll keep a lookout for any other poor soul. Look out!" He screamed and looked up. "That plane, see, it's just dropped its load of bombs, they're coming for us. It'll be a direct hit." He screamed louder than ever, "KEEP DOWN!"

A doctor and two male orderlies rushed into the ward. The staff nurse had a syringe filled and ready. The orderlies crawled under the bed and held Mr Collett, who was fighting and screaming. The doctor injected a powerful anaesthetic and a few minutes later, Mr Collett rolled over onto his side, asleep, but the stumps of his legs twitched violently with involuntary nervous spasms.

We were all shaken and trembling. The two orderlies picked the old man up and put him back into bed. He looked peaceful again. The hospital staff left, but I sat by his bedside for a long time, crying quietly.

At nine thirty the night sister asked me to leave, saying he would be kept sedated all night, and telling me to ring in the morning.

Before breakfast, I rang the hospital, and was told that Mr Collett had died peacefully at 3.30 a.m.

★

There was no last post for the old soldier; no solemn drum roll; no final salute; no lowering of the colours. There was just a contract funeral, arranged by the hospital, leaving from a hidden area next to the morgue. A priest and one mourner followed the coffin, and we travelled in the hearse, next to the driver. I had not thought of flowers until nearly at the hospital gate, so I had bought a bunch of Michaelmas daisies from a street flower-seller. We were driven to a cemetery somewhere in North London. I don't remember where it was. I only remember a cold, bleak November day, as we stood on either side of the open grave, the priest and I, reciting the office for the burial of the dead: "Dust to dust, ashes to ashes." The men shovelled the soil over the coffin, and I laid the purple daisies on the rich brown earth.

CODA

It was many years later – perhaps fifteen or twenty years – when Mr Collett visited me. I was happily married, my daughters growing up, my life in full flow. I had not thought of Mr Collett for years.

I woke in the middle of the night, and he was standing at the side of my bed. He was as real as my husband sleeping beside me. He was tall, and upright, but looked younger than when I had known him, like a handsome man of about sixty or sixty-five. He was smiling, and then he said, "You know the secret of life, my dear, because you know how to love."

And then he disappeared.

Epilogue

In 1930 the workhouses were closed by Act of Parliament – officially, that is. But in practice it was impossible to close them. They housed thousands of people who had nowhere else to live. Such people could not be turned out into the streets. Apart from that, many of them had been in the workhouses for so long, subject to the discipline and routine, that they were completely institutionalised, and could not have adjusted to the outside world. Also, the 1930s were the decade of economic depression, with massive unemployment nationwide. Thousands of workhouse inmates suddenly thrown onto the labour market would only have made matters worse.

So the workhouses were officially designated "Public Assistance Institutions" and, in order to make them more acceptable, would be locally referred to by such names as "Glebe House", "Rose House", and so on. But in practice they carried on much the same as before. The label "pauper" was replaced by "inmate", and the uniform was scrapped. Comforts, such as heating, a sitting room, easy chairs and better food were introduced. Inmates were allowed out. The inhumane practice of splitting families was stopped. But still it was institutional life. The staff were the same, and the attitudes and mindset of the master and officers were stuck firmly in the nineteenth century. Discipline remained strict, sometimes inflexible, depending on the character of the master, but punishments for transgression of the rules were relaxed, and life was certainly easier for the inmates of the Institution than it had been for the paupers of the workhouse.

The buildings continued in use for many decades for a variety of purposes. Some were used as mental hospitals right up until the 1980s, when they were finally closed by the Prime Minister, Margaret Thatcher. Many were used as old people's homes, and my description of Mr Collett's last weeks in such a place in the late 1950s is by no means unique. I was giving a talk to the East London History Society about this book when it was first published, and a lady in the audience stood up and said, "Your description is not exaggerated. In the 1980s I was with a group of people taken round an old people's home which had formerly been a workhouse and the conditions you describe were exactly the same. This was, as far as I remember, in 1985 or 1986."

The infirmaries continued as general hospitals for many decades. But the stigma of the old association with the work-houses was never eradicated. During my nursing career I saw many times the fear in a patient's eyes who thought they'd been put in a workhouse, even though they were in a modern hospital. In 2005 I was giving a radio talk and I mentioned this. The interviewer said, "I know exactly what you mean. Only a few years ago, in 1998, my granny was taken to the infirmary. She begged and pleaded not to go because she thought she was being put in the workhouse. She was terrified, and I swear it was that which killed her." The stigma lingered and most of the old infirmaries in the country have now been demolished, or con-verted into commercial or residential buildings

We who live comfortable, affluent lives in the twenty-first century cannot begin to imagine what it must have been like to be a pauper in a workhouse. We cannot picture relentless cold with little heating, no adequate clothing or warm bedding, and insufficient food. We cannot imagine our children being taken away from us because we are too poor to feed them, nor our liberty being curtailed for the simple crime of being poor. There are very few records left to tell us what the lives of workhouse paupers were like. Every workhouse kept meticulous records – but these were official records written by administrators; the paupers themselves kept no records. Similarly there are very few photographs of the paupers. Thousands of archive photographs of the buildings, the guardians, the masters, their wives and officers can be found in council records; but there are virtually none of the paupers themselves. The few that we do have are tragic to behold. There is a blank, hopeless look on all the faces, the same dull eyes, the same death-like despair.

But before we condemn the workhouses as an example of nineteenth-century exploitation and hypocrisy we must remember that the mores of the time were completely different from the standards of today. For the working class, life was nasty, brutish and short. Hunger and hardship were expected. Men were old at forty, women worn out at thirty-five. The death of children was taken for granted. Poverty was frankly regarded as a moral defect. Social Darwinism (the strong adapt and survive, the weak are crushed) was borrowed and distorted from the *Origin of Species* (1858) and applied to human organisation. These were the standards of society, accepted by rich and poor alike, and the workhouses merely reflected this.

Is there anything good that can be said about the old workhouse system? I think there is. Thousands of children who would have died of starvation on the streets were housed and reared – brutally, perhaps, by modern standards, but they survived, and after the 1870 Education Act, they were also educated. Mass illiteracy became history, and within a couple of generations the population of Great Britain could read and write.

I recall one woman who was over eighty when I met her in the year 2000. She was an illegitimate child of a servant girl and her master. His wife discovered the girl's pregnancy and dismissed her. The girl went to the workhouse – that was in 1915. The old lady said to me, "I am grateful to the workhouse. I learned the value of discipline and good behaviour. I learned to read and write. No, I never knew my mother, but none of us did. When I was fourteen I went into service. But I bettered myself, and learned secretarial work in night classes, and became a secretary. I am very proud of what I have achieved. I don't like to think what might have happened to me had it not been for the workhouse."

Further Reading

Mayhew's London, by Henry Mayhew, edited by Peter Quennell. (Hamlyn Publishing Group, 1969)

The Scandal of the Andover Workhouse, by Ian Anstruther (Alan Sutton, 1984)

The Workhouse System 1834–1929, by M. A. Crowther (Batsford, 1981)

The People of the Abyss, by Jack London (London, 1903)

The Poor Law, by S. Styles (Macmillan, 1985)

Outcast London, by G. Jones, edited by G. Steadman (Oxford, 1971)

In Darkest London, by William Booth (London, 1890)

The Life and Labour of the Poor (nine vols.), by Charles Booth (London, 1880–1892)

Pauper Palaces, by Ann Digby (Routledge, 1978)

The Workhouse, by Norman Longmate (Maurice Temple-Smith, 1974)

Down and Out in Paris and London, by George Orwell

The Victorian Workhouse, by Trevor May (Shire Publication, 1997)

The English Poor Law 1780–1930, by Michael Rose (David and Charles, 1971)

Into Unknown England 1866–1913, edited by Peter Keating (Fontana/Collins, 1976)

'The Homeless' from *In Darkest England and the Way Out* (William Booth, 1890)

'On the Verge of the Abyss' from *In Darkest England and the Way Out* (William Booth, 1890)

'The Submerged Tenth' from *In Darkest England and the Way Out* (William Booth, 1890)

'The Bitter Cry of Outcast London', by Andrew Mearns (first published in *The Pall Mall Gazette*, 1883)

'A Night in a Workhouse', by James Greenwood (first published in *The Pall Mall Gazette*, 1866)

Workhouses of the North, by Peter Higginbotham (Tempus Publications, 1999)